CAPITAL and the KINGDOM

CAPITAL and the KINGDOM

Theological Ethics and Economic Order

Timothy J. Gorringe

The Catholic Foreign Mission Society of America (Maryknoll) recruits and trains people for overseas missionary service. Through Orbis Books, Maryknoll aims to foster the international dialogue that is essential to mission. The books published, however, reflect the opinions of their authors and are not meant to represent the official position of the society.

Copyright © 1994 by Timothy J. Gorringe.
Published by Orbis Books, Maryknoll, New York 10545, U.S.A.
First published in Great Britain 1994 by the Society for Promoting Christian Knowledge, Holy Trinity Church, Marylebone Road, London NW1 4DU

Library of Congress Cataloging-in-Publication Data

Gorringe, Timothy.
    Capital and the kingdom : theological ethics and economic order / Timothy J. Gorringe.
        p. cm.
    Includes bibliographical references and index.
    ISBN 0-88344-944-7 (pbk.)
    1. Capitalism—Religious aspects—Christianity. 2. Christian ethics. I. Title.
    BR115.C3G67 1993
    241'.64—dc20
                                                            93-41999
                                                            CIP

British Library Cataloguing-in-Publication Data

A catalogue record for this book is available from the British Library

SPCK/ISBN 0-281-04773-1

Contents

Introduction

Sometime in the 660s or 650s BC, we may imagine, during the tyrannical reign of Manasseh in Judah, a group of people whom E.P. Thompson would describe as "utopian realists," met to analyse the cause of the present troubles and to discuss alternatives. We do not learn a great deal about Manasseh's rule except that he "shed very much innocent blood," and that he revived the practice of human sacrifice, but we can certainly expect that the criticisms of prophets like Isaiah and Micah, who lived a little before his reign, applied *a fortiori*. They attacked the widening gap between rich and poor, the growth of slavery through debt, the way in which land was stolen by the rich, and excessive taxation to keep up a standing army. These practices led to the breakdown of moral consensus so that "everyone did what they felt was right in their own eyes" (Dt 12:8). This breakdown stemmed from the impact of the norms of Canaan, a culture where absolute monarchy, standing armies, slavery, and sacral prostitution were taken for granted, on the formerly tribal society of Israel. The discussion group members therefore placed *idolatry* at the heart of their analysis of what they thought was wrong, by which they meant not so much the use of images as such, but conforming to alien norms, what might be called today *heteronomy*. Images were prohibited because they were visual symbols of an oppressive ideology, and furthermore encouraged all kind of false responses to the problem of creating the society YHWH wanted. It was this which was the real concern of the group—the shape of a future society, when the seemingly endless rule of Manasseh would be over.

Manasseh died in 642. His son Amon, who continued his policies, was overthrown in a palace coup after only two years and the eight year old Josiah was crowned. It was in the middle of his reign (c. 622 BC), whether with his collusion or not we do not know, that this discussion document was "discovered" in the Temple in Jerusalem, and the king attempted to put its provisions into effect. Too little too late, for Judah was already caught in the play of super power politics. Josiah was killed in the struggle between Assyria and Egypt, and within twenty-two years of his death the state of Judah was destroyed. The group which was concerned with reform however did not lose faith in their project. They continued to work on it as the foundation for a new society in a new Judah. According to their analysis society stood before two ways—a way of absolutism, greed, failure to care for the neighbour on the one hand, which they identified with idolatry, and a way of faithfulness to YHWH, egalitarianism, and care for the neighbour on the other. For them the choice between these two ways was a matter of life or death. The document which emerged from all their labours we know as Deuteronomy, the core of which is very probably to be identified with the document found in the Temple during Josiah's reign.

There are so many analogies between the situation of the original Deuteronomists and the present that we could claim that Deuteronomy enjoys a paradigmatic significance for the project of Christian ethics today. The most important analogies are threefold. First, we live like the Deuteronomists in a period when moral discourse has broken down, in a situation which Alasdair MacIntyre has dubbed "after virtue."[1] The reasons for this will be examined in the first chapter, but they are not utterly unlike those which faced Israel in its confrontation with Canaan and the great world empires. Secondly, like those addressed by Deuteronomy we stand very clearly before two ways, a way of life and a way of death. The Report of the World Commission on Environment and Development, published as *Our Common Future*, notes that "hope for the future is conditional on decisive political action now. . . . We are not forecasting a future; we are serving a notice – an urgent notice based on the latest and best scientific evidence – that the time has come to take the decisions needed to secure the resources to sustain this and coming generations."[2] The reason for this is that present ideas of economic growth "draw too heavily, too quickly, on already overdrawn environmental resource accounts to be affordable far into the future without bankrupting those accounts." At the present time thirty million human beings die each year from preventable hunger, resources are transferred systematically from the poor to the rich, and the earth's respiratory system is being destroyed. This is no tragic accident but stems from the way in which the world economy is structured, and the distribution of resources between rich and poor countries.[3] World population is expected to stabilize in the early decades of the next century at a figure two or three times what it is today. This means that rich country consumption patterns cannot be maintained, any more than the gap between the wastefully affluent minority of the world's population and the poor majority can be sustained. The reason these tragically destructive policies are followed suggests a third analogy. Something close to what the Deuteronomists identify as idolatry lies at the root of the problem, an unconditional belief in the generation of wealth as the answer to all problems. It is the underlying assumptions and imperatives of conventional economics which are leading the world to catastrophe. The breakdown of any kind of ethical consensus is one aspect of this catastrophe. As MacIntyre puts it, "the tradition of the virtues is at variance with central features of the modern economic order and more especially its individualism, its acquisitiveness and its elevation of the values of the market to a central social place."[4] We need a new ethic, as a Brazilian witness to the World Commission noted. But such a revisioning of ethics cannot be done abstractly. If the breakdown of moral consensus follows on the disintegration of social life and the systematic malfunctioning of the world economy, then its restoration, likewise, hangs on the construction of a different social and economic order. Such a new order does not drop from the skies. There are aspects which are new, like the possibilities opened up by computer technology, but we cannot begin from the beginning. Morality is, to an important extent, founded on narrative. "I can only answer the question 'What am I to do?' if I can answer the prior question 'Of what story or stories do I find myself a part?' "[5] This is why ancient traditions about human flourishing such as those contained in Deuteronomy (itself cast in the form of narrative), or the gospels, or the letters of Paul, remain relevant to the contemporary task of the recovery of virtue. "When your son asks you in time to come, 'What is the meaning of the testimonies and the statutes and the ordinances?' " said the Deuteronomists, "then you shall say ... 'We were Pharaoh's slaves in Egypt; and the Lord brought us out of Egypt with a mighty hand' " (Dt 6:20-21). The telling of stories has a key part in educating us into the virtues, argues MacIntyre, and the claim of Synagogue and Church is to tell that story which gives us the decisive clue to who we are as humans and therefore what we have to do. It is the story by which we live which makes us accountable and able to call others to account, which gives us an ethic.

The two most profound students of Deuteronomy we know of are Jesus and Paul. Paul's inspired summing up of the vision of human community opened up by the life, death, and resurrection of Jesus of Nazareth — "No Jew no Greek, no slave or free, no male or female" (Gal 3:28) — can be understood as a radicalisation of the Deuteronomic imperatives. For Paul the *ecclesia* which Israel had become was not a new religious grouping gathered around a new cult, but a way of talking about the practical overcoming of humanity's deepest divisions. He saw that what we now call race, class, and patriarchy were the things which destroyed human beings, frustrated their capacity for generous, open, forgiving love. *Ecclesia* was that group where those divisions would be faced in the spirit of open forgiveness, and which would sow the seed of reconciliation throughout the *oikumene*, the whole inhabited earth. The programme of Deuteronomy was deepened and extended to cover all people; it was no longer a programme for Israel, but for all nations. So intense was Paul's vision of what had been accomplished in Christ that he did not stop there but, in a letter to another community, and in a passage of lyrical power, insisted that human salvation was bound up with the salvation of all nonhuman reality: "the creation waits with eager longing for the revealing of the children of God" (Rom 8:19).

Nearly two thousand years after Paul we are still only very stumblingly trying to measure up to this vision. The recovery of virtue, the establishment of a just, sustainable and participatory world order needs to address all four areas Paul outlined. There can be no such order while race and class divisions continue, while patriarchy remains the fundamental social frame-work, and while we refuse to respect the rights of the nonhuman creation. As Maria Mies puts it, "The struggle for the human essence, for human dignity, cannot be divided and cannot be won unless *all* (the) colonising divisions, created by patriarchy and capitalism, are rejected and tran-scended."[6] I write as a Western white male, whose concerns have principally been with class and capitalism. Moreover I believe it is the assumptions behind the world economy, dictated by the economic superpowers, which threaten us all with disaster, rather than patriarchy *per se*. Nevertheless, patriarchy is indubitably part and parcel of these life denying practices. The need to critique present economic assumptions *through* feminist, anti-racist and ecological concerns is fundamental.

What is attempted, then, is a sketch of a new Deuteronomy. Like the first Deuteronomy this can only be a collaborative enterprise. Throughout the world there are thinkers and activists concerned with bringing a new society into being and these are, in effect, the new Deuteronomists. The new order they seek will not emerge solely by the elaboration of theory, but on the other hand, theory and practice hang inextricably together. Ruin-ous practices rest on false theory, what John condemns as "the lie." Ecol-ogists and alternative economists from very divergent backgrounds have recognised the importance of elaborating a new ethic. Thus the Indian environmentalist Rajni Kothari has argued that "the shift to sustainable development is primarily an ethical shift ... a shift in values such that nature is valued in itself"; the North American Henryk Skolimowski like-wise insists that "the resolution of our environmental dilemmas lies in the matrix of our values"; while the World Conservation Strategy begins by demanding a new ethic.[7] In the situation where everyone does what is right in his or her own eyes we need urgently to consider whether there is a common basis for ethical discussion between humans of different creeds and viewpoints. On what grounds do we condemn the gunmen who shoot Brazilian street children as vermin? Or those who, in one way or another, pursue policies of ethnic cleansing? Or who argue that the planet clearly has a "shelf life," and that we are therefore free to pursue environmentally ruinous policies if we wish? The first four chapters address these questions. Though the book is specifically a Christian contribution to a debate which involves people of all beliefs it begins by re-working an ancient Christian tradition which claimed to appeal to all people: that of natural law. The varieties of human love and affection, it is argued, lie at the root of the ethical sense in that they ground the absolute value of life. Ethics are then worked out in the dialectic of wisdom, the practical experience of human communities, and prophecy. The relation of economics and ethics is then taken up, since it is ruling economic assumptions which govern the present practices of death. In the fourth chapter it is argued that an attempt to structure the world economy around equality of outcome is essential to any recovery of virtue.

In the second section of the book I turn to labour and the means of life, examining Christian views of work and leisure, and suggesting critiques of present structures of management, peoples' organisations, and the wage system. Thirdly, I take up the problems associated with managing the commons—what the seventeenth-century Diggers referred to as "a common Treasury for all." I begin with the question of property, and then turn to the question of what the present economic system does to the Third World, and to the environment. The final chapter reviews the argument and considers some of the proposals of the new Deuteronomists.

It will be clear that the book is no abstract treatise on ethics, but neither is it scornful of the need for ethical discussion. The recovery of virtue we so sorely need can only be effected by establishing new forms of social and economic structures but, as the Deuteronomists understood, discussion of what is wrong with the present and sketches of the shape of the future are essential to the emergence of this society. To participate in this Deuteronomic task is the purpose of this book.

Since my concern is with capitalism and its effects it will be unsurprising to some that Karl Marx is a prominent dialogue partner throughout. To others, however, the events of 1989 may seem to make this perverse. Has not the theoretical work of Marx been swept away with the collapse of the Eastern bloc countries? Has not communism been tried and comprehensively found wanting? Does it not lead relentlessly to totalitarianism? My response to these familiar objections has two strands. The first is to insist that socialism as a political project cannot be identified *tout court* with what happened in Russia after 1918. A country with a long tradition of despotism, and none of democracy, was all of a sudden required to work out what communism might mean. That it quickly reverted to another despotism is tragic, but cannot be a matter for surprise. In the same way the repressive regimes in Eastern Europe in the postwar years were shaped by a life and death struggle with Nazism, and then by the political paranoia of the Cold War. This is in no way to excuse or mitigate the repression. It is certainly to say that socialism as a political project cannot be written off by the failure of these regimes. Secondly, and more importantly, E. P. Thompson has taught us to distinguish among Marxisms. There is first Marxism conceived as a self-sufficient body of doctrine, complete, internally consistent, set out in a body of texts. Second is Marxism as a method, as providing tools for historical and economic analysis, but understood within a self-referential system. Third is Marxism as heritage, one of the many items on offer in the cultural super market. Finally, there is Marxism as tradition, by which Thompson means both Marx's work and the discussion it has generated, subjected to free and critical scrutiny.[8] It is in this fourth sense that I appeal to Marx: as one of Ricoeur's "masters of suspicion," as an economic thinker whose work retains great explanatory power, and as (despite himself) someone who stands within the tradition of prophecy as this is set out in the second chapter.

Marx dedicated *Capital* to Wilhelm Wolff, "intrepid, faithful, noble protagonist of the proletariat." This book is dedicated to Bas Wielenga, who, together with his partner Gabriele Dietrich, turned his back on the obvious rewards of a European academic career to throw his weight behind efforts for a new human community in the Third World. The power and imagination of his biblical exegesis, together with an acute and comprehensive grasp of social and political reality, has been an inspiration not only to generations of Seminarians in South India but to Trades Unionists, Women's Groups, Groups working to heal the conflict in Sri Lanka—Hindus, Buddhists and atheists, as well as Christians. In this way he continues the work of Paul, whom he understands so well. As the "onlie begetter" of this book he would have done it far better, had time permitted. Such as it is, it is both a thank you, and a way of putting a shoulder to the same wheel. Thanks too to Rohini Hensman and Nigel Biggar, without whom the book would have even more flaws than it does.

CAPITAL and the KINGDOM

PART ONE

ETHICS, ECONOMICS, AND EQUALITY

1

Choosing Life

*I call heaven and earth to witness against you this day, that I have set before
you life and death, blessing and curse; therefore choose life, that you and
your descendants may live.*

—Deuteronomy 30:19

Ethical discourse is the conversation of the human race about its common project, about where it is going and why it wants to go there. It is
discussion about the *ethos* in which people live, that which shapes peoples'
character, their decision for a particular kind of life.[1] It exists primarily in
the form of myths and stories, drama and, more recently, novels. Works of
moral philosophy and theological ethics constitute a second order discourse
in relation to these. This conversation arises from, and always relates to,
particular social and economic conditions. A slave society gives rise to one
kind of ethical theory, feudal society to another, and industrial or postindustrial society to another. Nevertheless, it is clear that there is no crude
determinism in the relation between mode of production and any kind of
theory. Reflection, in this case the discourse of ethics, follows action and
action reflection in an endless hermeneutic spiral. It follows that there
cannot be two histories, one of political and moral action and one of political and moral theorizing, "because there were not two pasts ... Every
action is the bearer and expression of more or less theory-laden beliefs and
concepts; every piece of theorizing and every expression of belief is a political and moral action."[2] But this one history exists in a conflict of traditions,
not necessarily mutually reconcilable, and it is awareness of this conflict
which most vividly characterises contemporary ethical reflection. This poses
a serious problem for anyone who wishes to critique the global economy.
Economic paradigms and practices are no respecters of cultural boundaries—on the contrary, as we shall see, they are rather their solvents. Ethical
paradigms, on the other hand, evolve only within such boundaries. Is there
any way in which, given the conflict of traditions, a cogent ethical critique
of a global reality can be developed? In the next two chapters I offer the
sketch of a response from within the Christian tradition, which argues that

3

ethics is concerned essentially with the Deuteronomic imperative — Choose life! — and that a way through relativism might be found through an ethics of relationship.

THE END OF ETHICAL CONSENSUS?

Until approximately that era which we call the Enlightenment, thinkers in very diverse cultures assumed that human beings could agree on the nature of the good. Given the caution we have already introduced about the dialectical relation of action and reflection, of ideas and social and economic reality, we can note that this is related to the fact that modes of production in agriculture and industry were widely shared and remained very stable for nearly two millennia. Where the great religions held sway, to be moral was to obey divinely revealed law (even if the way in which revelation was conceived might differ). The breakdown of ethical consensus is to be understood against the background of the great cultural changes which we associate with the seventeenth and eighteenth centuries. It is no accident, for example, that this breakdown is coterminous with ever more efficient printing, with rising literacy, and finally with the communications revolution of our own day. Where formerly people lived in cultures shaped largely by one tradition, they were increasingly deluged by manifestos from every viewpoint. Rival religions and political philosophies now competed in a "free market" for the allegiance of the individual.

A second, and more recent, factor in the breakdown of ethical consensus is the reaction to the collapse of colonial empires. Full of self-confidence, Western conquistadors, merchants, and missionaries went for four centuries to "lesser breeds without the law" bringing enlightenment and expecting "native cultures" to accept their standards. Their successors guiltily realise that these standards have wreaked havoc. Much better, then, in humility to scrutinise afresh the ethics of every several culture, to abstain from judgement. Cultural relativism is in part a fresh expression of the peace formula which followed the end of religious conflict in Europe: *cuis regio, eius religio*. This formula articulates a certain backing off from the claim to absolute truth. The age of Voltaire and Rousseau follows that begotten by Luther and Calvin. Skeptical humanist tolerance succeeds impassioned belief, a modest allowance of differences the self-confident conviction of possession of the truth.

To the extent that current relativism stems from a new found respect for other cultures, this is all to the good. In 1986 the World Wildlife Fund invited five of the world's major religions to Assisi to discuss conservation. They were invited to come "proud of what they had to offer, but humble enough to learn from others," a formula which captures the essence of all forms of interfaith dialogue. This dialogue, as it has developed in the past forty years, can be understood as a kind of principled relativism, which arises from respect for others. It makes the assumption that even where people disagree, it is both possible and necessary to keep talking. When we understand ethics as the *conversation* of the human race about its common project then the same applies. It is important to see that this is not to beg the question of moral relativism any more than interfaith dialogue begs the question of religious difference. In the interfaith dialogue participants do not expect to convert each other in the sense that they believe that at some stage everyone will become Buddhist, or Muslim, or Christian. They recognise that there arc profound differences between their religions which cannot be glossed under the rubric that all religions are essentially the same. At the same time they recognise equally that it is essential to keep the conversation going insofar as all traditions are committed to a search for wisdom and understanding. Keeping talking rules out two opposite positions: on the one hand, no conversation can proceed if one partner insists he or she has all the answers and therefore seeks to drown everything anyone else has to say. This is the position of every form of fundamentalism, religious or political. But neither can it proceed if one partner parries everything the other says with, "Maybe. But this is the way I feel about it and nothing will shift me" — the emotivism critiqued by MacIntyre.[3] Openness to dialogue means readiness for change. Fundamental to the conversation is the recognition that wisdom is not confined to one human tradition.[4] Put in Christian terms, this is the recognition that the Holy Spirit ceaselessly works for life in *all* human traditions, both religious and non-religious.

Enlightenment gains in terms of real tolerance cannot be overestimated, but at the same time current forms of moral relativism cannot be taken at face value. The fact that we can be tolerantly relative on matters of value, but not on matters of "fact" like natural science or economics, puts us on our guard. The suspicion is that moral relativism might be the intellectual response to the hegemony of capitalism, for which the world becomes our supermarket. Philosophies, religions, ethical theories are there along with perfumes, foodstuffs, and curtaining, to be chosen from and consumed as we will, a smorgasbord in which there are no absolute preferences. Ethics becomes a branch of aesthetics, and we cannot dispute about taste.[5] This kind of relativism expresses not a generous tolerance but a weary or cynical giving up on truth. "We have to see that moral relativism represents not a value position but an abdication from holding a value position. You cannot build anything on moral relativism. You cannot establish any programme of conservation on it."[6] Moral relativism provides the wielders of power with a convenient excuse for doing nothing, or rather with continuing with things as they are: "You see, people do not agree!"

The beginnings of this approach to ethics can be found in the eighteenth century. Old forms of community belonging increasingly disappeared before systematic individualism, which itself mirrored the break up of peasant communities and the drift to the anonymity of big cities. The notions of pleasure and happiness, physiologically defined, replaced that of "the good" as that objective in life about which all could agree. In place of a common sense of the good was the commodity, whatever can be marketed to provide us with pleasure, and ethics as a discourse about the good became increasingly problematic, as the course of moral philosophy since the late eighteenth century very clearly shows. But such an imaging of ethical choice does impossible violence to the traditions in which ethical discourse subsists. Traditions cannot be chosen like chocolates from a box, for in them we live and move and have our being. They are not so much supermarket products as vast life support machines. Failure to understand this can lead not to culture shock but to culture death, a future diagnosed for the West with increasing frequency since Spengler. What traditions sustain, as MacIntyre has argued, is a common understanding of the human.[7] The Enlightenment, however, rejected any view of a common human *telos*, of the goal towards which we have to move in order to be fully human, whether stemming from religion or philosophy. The cacophony of contemporary ethics followed.

Even if we understand the importance of cultural traditions, however, a fourth case for moral relativism remains, and arises from the sombre conclusions of Peter Haas in his important study *Morality after Auschwitz*. Haas argues that the twelve years of Nazi rule must be understood as a gigantic experiment in changing the truth conditions by which we live. The Holocaust, he argues, was not the work of a handful of monsters. On the contrary, it occurred over a long period and involved the participation and toleration of hundreds of thousands of people who were not unintelligent, amoral, or insensitive, but who acted consciously, conscientiously, and in good faith in pursuit of what they understood to be the good. The venerable Just War theory was fused with supposedly scientific racial theories to show that the enemy consisted of Jews, gypsies, and homosexuals, who must be eliminated to allow humanity's onward evolution. The major lesson of the Holocaust, according to Haas, is the receptivity of ordinary people to new ethical discourse.[8] The Holocaust represents not so much a breakdown of ethical theory as an attempt to shift the goal posts, to rewrite ethical discourse from the ground up.[9] But if this is possible what becomes of the categorical imperative, of the moral law supposed to dwell within us? The Holocaust breeds a profound skepticism about the human creature as being somehow by nature moral. Perhaps, after all, we are just wax tablets on which any ethical theory whatever can be written. If that is the case it is not just that we live after virtue, but we have to dispense with a normative concept of virtue altogether. Can we avoid this dismal conclusion?

A UNIVERSAL GROUND OF ETHICS

"It is with good reason," wrote Leo XIII, in *Rerum Novarum* in 1891, "that the common opinion of mankind has found no merit in the dissenting opinions of a few. Making a close study of nature, men have found in nature's laws the basis for a distribution of goods and for private ownership and have been fully convinced that these are in the highest degree in conformity with the nature of man and with peace and tranquillity."[10] Faced with the burgeoning confusion of modernity the pope appealed to natural law (without, however, specifying what he meant by it). Although the natural law tradition is very ancient such appeals become increasingly common as a way of dealing with the pluralism of the modern era—they are fundamental, for example, to the legal work of Grotius. The attraction of such theories is obvious, because natural law claims to provide us with an account of morality written into the very structure of how things are, and so culturally invariant. Find out, then, how things truly are, and you can see what it is to be moral.[11] Natural law does not, however, provide us with an automatic answer to relativism in the way Pope Leo thought, for a number of reasons.

In the first place, one source of the natural law tradition is Stoic pantheism, the assumptions of which do not transfer automatically to a theistic system which believes in creation *ex nihilo*.[12] For theism the created order is good and beautiful, but is not in itself divine. There is a fracture, a fall, which makes an immediate move from creation to ethics impossible. Much confusion was caused by Paul's incautious appeal to the Stoic principle at the beginning of Romans (Rom 2:14f). He appeared to endorse the view that we can read God's will, or what is moral, from the created order. Later theologians needed to hedge this assurance with caveats.[13]

The problem with this tradition of natural theology is that, though we can go along with the writer of the nineteenth psalm, and extol the wondrous weave of creation, we also need to remember with Isaiah that there is an aspect of nature (reality) which is "red in tooth and claw." In the Messianic Age, according to the famous vision of Isaiah 11, it is not just human beings who have to learn peace and justice, but only then will the lion lie down with the lamb and predatory relations cease. To the extent that such relations are part of reality in the world we know, corresponding to reality would make Social Darwinism the supreme expression of morality. Nazi paganism extolled a mystical reverence for nature with terrible results. Hayek's account of spontaneous order, which he opposes to any form of made order, is another example.[14] Justice on this account is complete acceptance of the way things are; injustice is to try and change things. Here an appeal to the way things have to be becomes a cynical defence of existing relations of power.

A second account of natural law drew not only on Stoicism but on Aristotle. We find this fusion in Aquinas, according to whom to be moral is to conform to our proper *telos*. Because "the whole community of the universe is governed by Divine Reason," argues Thomas, created reality is, as such, an expression of this divine rationality, the eternal law. It follows from this that creatures have a natural inclination to their proper act and end: "and this participation of the eternal law in the rational creature is called the natural law."[15] The difficulty here is in recognising what the proper act and end actually are. Aquinas thought that homosexuality was clearly contrary to nature, on the grounds that all intercourse must be for procreation, since that was the proper *telos* or end of male semen. A different understanding both of human relations and of nature would call this into question.

Another problem with natural law theory, in other words, is that nature is a social construction. As Mary Mellor notes, "The human race has altered the face of the planet since the first tree was cut down, the first seed planted and the first river dammed."[16] We have to recognise, then, that all conceptions of natural law are to some extent positive at the same time, that is, they arise from specific societies and do in general reflect the interests of dominant groups in those societies. Papal encyclicals such as *Rerum Novarum* are good examples of this, using an appeal to natural law to shortcut arguments about property or the State, largely in the interests of the status quo—something Leo was attacked for from the beginning, despite his liberal intentions. Although this type of confident appeal to natural law continued in papal encyclicals for another seventy years, the anthropological, sociological, and psychological researches of the past century have called it further and further into question. What constitutes what Leo calls "the common opinion of mankind"? Is there genuine community between different religions, between forest dwellers and citizens of Megalopolis? Natural law arguments are no more finished than the cosmological arguments for the existence of God, but neither do they find the kind of consent which could mount a real challenge to moral relativism.[17]

REVELATION AND ONTOLOGY

If traditional natural law arguments will not do to counter relativism, are we left simply to make the best of it? I wish to consider an alternative suggested by the work of the Jewish philosopher Emmanuel Levinas.[18] Natural law begins with ontology and comes to ethics. Levinas believes that this leads to an ontology of power: "To affirm the priority of *Being* over *existents* is to already decide the essence of philosophy; it is to subordinate the relation with *someone*, who is an existent (the ethical relation) to a relation with the *Being of existents*, which, impersonal, permits the apprehension, the domination of existents . . . subordinates justice to freedom."[19] He wishes therefore to invert this process, which he does by establishing a phenomenology of relationship, or as he calls it, "the face." For Levinas the face of the Other is the ground of ethics, and it is ethics which is first philosophy, which plays the foundational role which ontology has in Greek thought. In the state of nature my egoism leads me to put myself first in every situation. The sheer pleasure of life constitutes a first morality which leads me beyond the ego. But it is the face of the Other which really breaks through the totality of the world of which I am the centre. Thus the root of ethics is "Responsibility for the Other, for the naked face of the first individual to come along."[20] Ethics is rooted in the face to face encounter, but it is also in this encounter that God, the Wholly Other (or "otherwise than being," as Levinas puts it) is encountered. "The Other is not the incarnation of God, but precisely by his face, in which he is disincarnate, is the manifestation of the height in which God is revealed. It is our relations with men . . . that give to theological concepts the sole signification they admit of."[21] My question is whether a universal ethic might be grounded in the structure of the face-to-face relationship.

Like natural law, Levinas's account of the face-to-face relation is also positive—arising out of a Western, and specifically Jewish, tradition. It is perfectly clear that we cannot presuppose contemporary Western understandings of relationship for other cultures, whether distant in time or coming from other traditions. What I take from Levinas, however, is the claim that it is through the very structure of human relationships that the ethical sense arises. By way of considering this claim I wish to begin by looking at the oldest human law codes known to us, of which Israel's ten commandments is but the best known.[22] How are we to regard them? They are clearly the result of an immense period of experience and reflection on what destroys and enables human community. Human beings are at the deepest level community beings, both because of the complexity of their needs for survival, and because of the needs which find expression in the high achievements of culture. When community disintegrates life becomes literally impossible.[23] Theft, coveting, adultery, murder—all the things prohibited by the Decalogue—are all things which, in this society, trigger the blood feud and thus the destruction of community. Sometime in the second millennium BC people in these cultures formalised what they saw as the conditions necessary for the continuance of community life, and this is what these ancient law codes represent.

Understanding the commandments thus has a rather Hobbesian ring about it, as if they were early versions of the social contract which prevents mutual destruction. What forbids such a reductionist understanding are the stories which *frame* the law codes, a drama of Abraham and Isaac, Hagar and Ishmael, Jacob and Rachel, people in the face-to-face relation. The law codes are second order discourse: it is the stories of encounter which come first.

For Levinas it is encounter with the stranger which seems to be the normative origin of ethics. Responsibility is awakened simply by the face of the other, especially the other in need. On the other hand, he also offers us a very profound philosophy of erotic experience.[24] In a partial departure from Levinas I wish to focus not only on *eros* and the encounter with the stranger, but on *philia* and *storge* (friendship and parental affection). Experiences of childhood and parenting, and affection and bonding between persons, are universal across cultures. The ability to love (*homo amans*) defines human beings more profoundly than either rationality (*homo sapiens*) or the ability to make and create (*homo faber*). We can concede that patterns of nurture and ways of conceiving relationship vary significantly, but what would remain of the human essence without the capacity to love?[25] Because this account of ethics is, like natural law, situated in a particular cultural and political context, it is open to the question of whether it adequately respects the variety of anthropological data. Yet while the fact that relationships can be construed very differently is indisputable, the claim that the realities of love and affection might be *unrecognisably* different between cultures remains implausible. It is tantamount to the claim that we are dealing with a different species — not human beings at all. In seeking a response to moral relativism, therefore, a recovery of MacIntyre's "human-nature-as-it-could-be-if-it-realized-its-*telos*," may be where we have to look. It is in and through the most fundamental forms of the face-to-face relationship that the moral sense arises. Our *telos* is the fulfillment, enriching, realization of relationship. This is not to define that end in a culture specific way, as in the Thomist account of natural law. It is to recognise that end in the varieties of love and compassion. In the experiences we have of the varieties of love, partial, flawed, and often corrupted as they are, the *depth* and *mystery* of what it is to be human is revealed to us, and it is from this revelation that awareness of the sanctity of *life* springs.[26] Love of life, or awareness of its sanctity, then becomes the basis for all ethical systems.

The claim that ethics is rooted in these relationships makes the ethical sense primordial, for outside of relationship we cannot have humanity at all. If there is a deontological side to ethics, this is it.[27] The ethical sense, that is to say, is rooted to a large extent in relations which are responsible for the continuance of the race: the relations of men and women which make procreation possible, and in parenting. Humans do not mate just because they are obeying instinctive drives, but mating involves depth and affection, and it is this which establishes the sanctity of life. It is to be noted that while it is these relationships which give us the "infinite worth of the individual" so beloved of liberal theorists, in no way is this an individualist ethic. The face-to-face relation both presupposes and calls into being community. Community is not a defence pact, formed because humans prey on each other. On the contrary, it is rooted in the primordial human experience of the varieties of love. In this experience community too is given us primordially.

The face to face also has a theological dimension, as Levinas insists, because the deeper we go into the face-to-face relationship the more we are driven and claimed by a love which knows no limit, or in other words, by an experience of God. We meet God in and through the face of the other in the sense that we encounter here an authority beyond which there is no appeal and which is infinite in its implications.[28]

ETHICS AND THE CHOICE OF LIFE

What we learn in our encounter with the other is the infinite value of life. In tracing the origin of respect for life to our most fundamental relationships we are positioning ourselves against both Albert Schweitzer and Karl Barth. For Schweitzer, ethics is at its heart reverence for life, something he derives from his reformulation of Kant. The will to life takes the place of the categorical imperative, and is understood mystically:

> The elemental fact, present in our consciousness every moment of our existence, is: I am life that wills to live, in the midst of life that wills to live. The mysterious fact of my will to live is that I feel a mandate to behave with sympathetic concern towards all the wills to live which exist side by side with my own.[29]

Reverence for life means being "seized by the unfathomable, forward moving will which is inherent in all Being." Here we find piety "in its most elemental and deepest form." Ethics must become "cosmic and mystical," a manifestation of our inward, spiritual relation to the world.[30] Schweitzer, too, was concerned to go beyond relativism, and thought that with the universal will to life he had found a way of doing so. In contrast to this we have rooted respect for life rather in the structure of human relationships. Barth, on the other hand, though he wished to talk of respect for life, dismissed any attempt to make a principle out of life in itself; he maintained that such respect can only be grounded in the divine command.[31] The problem with this is that it seems to restrict true ethical knowledge to the adherents of one religion. Any command ethic like this has to find a way of communicating with all those philosophies and religions which do not accept the given account of revelation. Faced with this problem at the very beginning of the Christian era, theologians like Justin Martyr (c. 150 CE) appealed to Christ as the Logos, the incarnation of the divine Wisdom which is the source of all that is good, true, and beautiful.[32] In the same way, the bridge between a phenomenology of the face of the Other and Christian theology will be through an account of the face of Christ which, according to the tradition of Christ as cosmic Wisdom, is the ground of all forms of human encounter.[33]

In his second letter to the Christian community in Corinth Paul makes much play with the term *face*. He recalls the story of how, when Moses came down from Sinai, his face shone, literally with reflected glory. Christians are like Moses, Paul wants to say, in that their faces reflect the glory of God, but they do so because they look into the face of Christ. "It is the God who said, 'Let light shine out of darkness' who has shone in our hearts to give the light of the knowledge of the glory of God in the face of Jesus Christ" (2 Cor 4:6). For Paul, the ethical life was not so much an "imitation of Christ," as it came to be called, but more a question of allowing our faces to reflect Christ's glory, or as he puts it in another letter, to have the mind of Christ (Phil 2:5). Following the development of Paul's thought we then have to ask, whose face is it we are reflecting? Not just that of the man of Nazareth, but of the one "in whom all things consist"!

> He is the image of the invisible God, the firstborn of all creation; for
> in him all things in heaven and on earth were created, things visible
> and invisible, whether thrones or dominions or rulers or powers — all
> things have been created through him and for him (Col 1:15).

The face to face, that is to say, understood within a Christian framework,
is wrongly described as anthropocentric — Christianity has always rejected
"Jesus religion." It is Christocentric. The face to face with Christ is the
normative form of that relation, and that is a face to face with one who is
at the heart not just of the human but of all reality.

If, then, for a Christian ethic, the face to face with Christ is fundamental,
it is to the history of Christ we look for the exegesis of what that means.[34]
That history is summed up by John in the words: "I came that they might
have life, and have it in all its fullness" (Jn 10:10). This captures not only
the theme of Deuteronomy (Choose life!), but of the whole of the law and
the prophets. Whatever it is which is seen to enable life, human flourishing
in all its richness, and the flourishing of creation as a whole — as this is
measured and understood through Christ — is the light which guides us. As
Lessing claimed, traditions validate themselves in the proof of Spirit and
of power, which is to say by their explanatory power in the face of the
complexities of real life, and by their power to inform and make fruitful
life giving societies. What is meant by *life* is given us in the biblical narratives
which Jesus presupposed:

> Blessed shall you be in the city, and blessed shall you be in the field.
> Blessed shall be the fruit of your body, and the fruit of your ground,
> and the fruit of your beasts, the increase of your cattle, and the young
> of your flock. Blessed shall be your basket and your kneading trough.
> Blessed shall you be when you come in, and blessed shall you be when
> you go out (Dt 28:3-6).

It is this blessing which makes long life a good to be sought after and
why it is that "all that a person has will they give for their life" (Jb 2:4).
Levinas's description of the love of life stands squarely in this tradition:
"Life is *love of life*, a relation with contents that are not my being but more
dear than my being: thinking, eating, sleeping, reading, working, warming
oneself in the sun."[35] This is the background of Jesus' affirmation that he
has come that people may have life and "life in all its fullness" (Jn 10:10).
For this reason Jesus is concerned to heal people, concerned with their
material well-being. It is true that life as such is not an absolute: "For
whoever would save their life will lose it; and whoever loses their life for
my sake and the gospel's will save it" (Mk 8:35). And yet the gospel of the
kingdom is not otherworldly. Jesus' preaching of the kingdom, like his heal-
ings, picks up the messianic promises of Israel — they are part and parcel
of the same thing (Mt 11:5). In the stories which shaped Jesus' own moral

sense he read that when the Messiah comes "people shall build houses and live to inhabit them, plant vineyards and eat their fruit; they shall not build for others to inhabit nor plant for others to eat" (Is 65:21). When Jesus teaches his disciples to pray "your kingdom come on earth," it is this situation he has in mind. Therefore, as Gutiérrez puts it,

> Although the Kingdom must not be confused with the establishment of a just society, this does not mean that it is indifferent to this society. Nor does it mean that this just society constitutes a "necessary condition" for the arrival of the Kingdom nor that they are closely linked, nor that they converge. More profoundly, the announcement of the Kingdom reveals to society itself the aspiration for a just society and leads it to discover unsuspected dimensions and unexplored paths. The Kingdom is realized in a society of brotherhood and justice; and, in turn, this realization opens up the promise and hope of complete communion of all men with God. The political is grafted on to the eternal.[36]

The preaching of the kingdom is therefore an *ethical* proclamation; it concerns how people ought to live. This means that it is at the same time a political ethic. In his book *Morality and the Market Place* Brian Griffiths argues that while Jesus' teaching on the kingdom is relevant to personal ethics, it "contains little of practical significance for the public policy issues raised by politics and economics."[37] But politics is, as Aristotle argued, the question of how we shape community, and a personal ethic which is not at the same time a community ethic is no ethic at all because ethics is about what we do with our neighbours. We are who we are in relation. Insofar as the gospel affects our approach to life (personal ethics) it affects our stance on politics and economics—on decisions about education, health, employment, the environment, and all the other things which shape a person's life.

Where life is threatened the question of life becomes the question of *justice*—it is the same question from a different perspective. It is because YHWH is a God of life that God is also a God of justice. "Let justice roll down like waters, and righteousness like an everflowing stream," says Amos where the question is ceasing oppression of the poor, making life available for them (Am 5:24). "The Lord of hosts is exalted in righteousness," says Isaiah; therefore, "Cease to do evil, learn to do good; seek justice, correct oppression; defend the fatherless, plead for the widow!" (Is 1:16). Jeremiah says to King Jehoiakim: "Did not your father eat and drink and do justice and righteousness? Then it was well. He judged the cause of the poor and needy ... Is this not to know me says the Lord?" (Jer 22:15-16). What is the content of this justice? According to Deuteronomy just behaviour would always remember its own background in slavery, and would therefore never degrade the neighbour. The result of this would be the nurture of community life.[38] Righteousness (*tsedeq*) is behaviour which honours the claim of a given relationship. Justice in Israel "is not a question of the impartiality with which a formal standard of justice is applied, but of rightly satisfying those claims which are brought forward as a result of particular concrete relationships; justice, *mispat*, is no abstract thing but denotes the rights and duties of each party arising out of the particular relation of fellowship in which they find themselves."[39] Decisive importance could not, therefore, be given to distributive justice in Israel, for justice meant defending the weak and putting an end to violence and oppression (Is 9:7). As this is formulated in the Christian scriptures, for instance in the Magnificat, it entails a *reversal*. The rich are cursed and the poor blessed (Lk 6:24). Lazarus is taken to Abraham's bosom and the rich man is not. The first are last and the last first. God's justice, in other words, consists in refusing the distinctions human beings arrogate to themselves by using their gifts for their own advantage rather than for others, and in acting to change this situation. Another way of putting this is to say that justice is *grace*. The life of grace is the life of following God's own practice of reversal, of putting the last first, and this is justice. This means that justice is not a negative thing — not getting our own back, like Isabella's cry for justice in *Measure for Measure*. On the contrary, justice is wholly positive, the defence and the celebration of life, the divine affirmation of the goodness of creation.

ETHICS AND THE NONHUMAN CREATION

For some time an urgent question will have been intruding itself for many readers. Does not such an ethic, grounded in a human face to face, buy into Buber's flawed distinction between I — Thou and I — It, which seems to denigrate the nonhuman creation? Could we find, in such an ethic, resources which would help us contest the destruction of the planet?

If we were to try and extend our argument, rooted in the experiences of love, an obvious starting point would be the nurturing which is proper to all humans, and in particular to women. Without adopting biologistic conclusions we can agree with Lynne Segal that "mothering is not determined by consciousness, but consciousness by mothering." With her, and against some ecofeminists, we would nevertheless argue that gender is to a large extent a cultural construct, and thus the possibility of nurture extends to men too.[40] The point about this is that if ethics arises from our deepest human experiences, then it seems that the nurturing we learn in them spills over to the nonhuman realm. This is the important truth which ecofeminism has vividly adumbrated. To exclude men from this possibility is, as Segal argues, too Manichaean a view.

We go further by returning to the insight that the face to face with Christ is a face to face with cosmic Wisdom. Christian tradition attempted to formulate this through the doctrine of the incarnation, and it was quickly realised that this involved a theology of matter. Towards the end of the second century we find Irenaeus contending against Gnostics who despised the flesh: "Those who say that our created world was made of 'decay, ignorance and passion' sin against their Father."[41] When people started destroying icons in the eighth century John of Damascus opposed them in the name of a theology of matter, and in doing so defended himself against idolatry, worship of the creation: "I do not worship matter. I worship the God of matter; who became matter for my sake, and deigned to inhabit matter; who worked out my salvation through matter ... Do not vilify matter, for it is not dishonourable. Nothing is dishonourable which God has made. This is the Manichaean notion."[42] It is in this sense that a Christocentric understanding of the face grounds a proper ethics of creation.

Through the centuries this understanding of God's hallowing of the material world, as focused above all in the incarnate Word, has been learned week by week in the best sort of pedagogy—action through involvement—in the eucharist. In the same passage mentioned above we find Irenaeus setting out the implications of the eucharist to those tempted by Gnostic disparagement of creation. First of all the eucharist adumbrates reverence for creation. In passionate indignation Irenaeus challenges his opponents: "How can they consistently suppose that the bread over which thanks have been given is the body of their Lord ... if they allege that he is not the son of the Creator of the World—his Word, through whom the tree bears fruit, the springs flow, and the earth yields 'first the blade, then the ear, then the full corn in the ear.' " This understanding was never quite lost, even in the Western church, and throughout the centuries it has been the celebration of the eucharist which has taught ordinary Christians to reverence matter, to know that God does not despise it, but uses it. But Irenaeus' theology is Trinitarian, and he goes on to speak of the Spirit: "As the bread which comes from the earth receives the invocation (*epiklesis*) of God, and then it is no longer common bread but Eucharist, consisting of two things, an earthly and a heavenly; so our bodies, after partaking of the Eucharist, are no longer corruptible, having the hope of the eternal resurrection." It is the Holy Spirit who is invoked or called down at the heart of the eucharistic prayer, and Christians have therefore learned that the Spirit breathes through, animates, and indwells matter—both the bread and wine and their own *bodies*. Finally, we have the heart of the Christian approach to the nonhuman creation in the very word *eucharist*, namely gratitude. "We are bound to make our oblation to God and thus to show ourselves in all things grateful to him as our Creator ... And it is only the Church which offers a pure oblation to the Creator, presenting an offering from his creation, with thanksgiving." Such gratitude, which is the ground theme of Paul's letters, as of the *Tenakh*, knows about human solidarity with the rest of creation. It is with the trees and animals that human beings rejoice in God (Ps 148), and with the whole of creation that they groan in pain.

The eucharist, then, is on many levels a celebration of the face to face.

It is this in the literal sense in that people come together and exchange the kiss of peace before taking the bread and wine. But in the taking, hallowing, and sharing of bread and wine we are reminded of the indwelling Spirit, of the Word through whom all things were made, and we are brought face to face with the Creator who loves every part of creation, for "behold it was very good." John of Damascus states the Christian approach to creation very precisely: "We do not worship matter; we worship the God who made and became matter." We are not animists, nor, like some deep ecologists, do we refuse a distinction between human and nonhuman reality. But we recognise the God-givenness of all that is good, and with the psalmist, rejoice together with the trees and the animals (Ps 149).

A word by way of conclusion. Ethics has been characterised as the ongoing discussion of the human race about its common project. In this discussion the church is one voice among many, or perhaps better, a collection of related voices. It contributes less in terms of theory than through its account of what it is to be human (which includes an account of the relation to the nonhuman creation). It is a distinctive account of what this means which it brings to the present breakdown of ethical consensus but the recovery of virtue rests on recapturing a *common* vision of the meaning of humanness. The church cannot singlehandedly supply this, but its claim to revelation is the claim that it has something absolutely distinctive and vital to contribute. How this interlocks with other understandings of the human project, as expressed in the variety of ethical theory, is the theme of the following chapter.

2

Prophecy and Wisdom

Then Amos answered Amaziah, "I am no prophet, nor a prophet's son; but I am a herdsman, and a dresser of sycamore trees, and the Lord took me from following the flock, and the Lord said to me, 'Go, prophesy to my people Israel.' "

—Amos 7:14

Bonhoeffer begins his ethics with the combative sentences: "The knowledge of good and evil seems to be the aim of all ethical reflection. The first task of Christian ethics is to invalidate this knowledge."[1] We must remember that Bonhoeffer wrote this in the Nazi period when, as Haas argues, the knowledge of good and evil was being radically redefined. All the same we can ask whether this is simply an irrationalist piece of bravado, a retreat into the ghetto, or whether it represents an essential perception about theological ethics. If it is true, where does it leave non-Christian ethics? To continue our image of ethics as an ongoing conversation, Bonhoeffer seems to be in the position of someone holding up his hand and saying, "Stop! You people have nothing of value to say! Let me instruct you."

Coming from someone who could not wait to go to India this sounds implausible. In trying to tease out his reason for saying it we will first of all look at what Christian ethics share with the ethics of other cultures and religions, and then at what is distinctive. Ethics exists as both discourse and practice, or better, discourse *as* practice. In what follows we will review two possibilities—ethics as the practice of wisdom, and ethics as the practice of prophecy. The former represents the coordination of Christian ethics with all forms of secular ethics, the latter its challenge.

THE PRACTICE OF WISDOM

If we understand ethics (here, the science of moral behaviour) essentially as a set of rules or laws to guide moral behaviour then the problems which arise in the attempts to apply them in concrete cases give us the system of case law, or casuistry. Casuistry is one of the most important ways of trying

17

to understand ethics as *practice*. In a society allergic to the application of rules to personal behaviour it is easy to dismiss casuistry and its variants out of hand, but it is important to realise that this tradition is the direct descendant of the Wisdom tradition of the Hebrew scriptures. In that tradition we find three strata: the international wisdom collected at Solomon's Court and shared with the whole of the rest of the Ancient Near East, which represents widespread perceptions about the nature of the world, the reality to which we have to correspond. Secondly, there is the peasant wisdom of the village elders, which is the fruit of millennia of experience about what enabled human community and what destroyed it. The maxims and aphorisms of Proverbs 10 to 32, for example, do not fall from the skies but represent the chewing over of countless cases, individual stories of characters within village life. Thirdly, in Ben Sirach and Wisdom of Solomon we have a more sophisticated version of this produced by a city intelligentsia in the early centuries before Christ. The importance of these traditions is that they are representative of a genre in all cultures which have a literature. It is the wisdom tradition, above all, which mediates between the particular and the universal.

The casuistry of the medieval church is rooted in all of these forms of wisdom and can properly be described as the attempt to grow in wisdom. Oliver O'Donovan argues that if wisdom is knowledge of the created order, then the moral law is this knowledge formulated so as to evoke action, and casuistry the attempt to apply this law. We need to formulate the moral law in codes, for the purposes of teaching and learning, and the practice of casuistry takes us through the straightforwardness of the moral code to a deeper understanding of the moral law.[2] Put more prosaically we could say that we can, after all, learn both from our own and from other people's mistakes, and that this process of learning is a cumulative process which becomes the wisdom of a particular society. Understood like this the practice of casuistry must seem unexceptionable, something we could not avoid even if we wished to. It gets its bad name partly from the way in which it ignores social context and imagines that practices in one social order can be transferred into another. Thus in the Roman Catholic Church handbooks of casuistry which had been compiled over the previous five centuries were still in use after the Second World War. Only in the sixties were they finally felt to be unusable in a changed world, and so indeed they were. Secondly, it is difficult to deny that casuistry easily breeds a legalist approach to ethics, and Jesus' conflict with the Pharisees and Paul's with the advocates of the law then immediately come to mind.

Seeking to avoid these difficulties, another version of this type of ethical practice prefers to appeal to *principles*, which offer us general guidelines. So-called rule agapaism is an example of this; it maintains that we make ethical decisions by asking, "What rules most fully embody love?" In the area of so-called social ethics a much favoured position from the consultations which led to the Malvern Conference in 1941 was that of middle axioms, which arose from a need to find a middle ground between general statements and detailed policies.[3] Middle axioms are arrived at by bringing alongside one another the total Christian understanding of life on the one side and an analysis of an empirical situation on the other, a procedure which the Wisdom teachers would surely have recognised. They supposedly occupy the middle ground between general statements and detailed policies. An example is that the government has responsibility for maintaining full employment. Another is that private centres of economic power should not be stronger than the government. Their purpose is to help Christians to decide on policies, and avoid the irrelevant extremes of a pietism which is not concerned with the world on the one hand and a perfectionism which can only deal in absolutes and therefore has no relevant word in tangled situations on the other.

We must make no mistake: Wisdom is an indispensable part of the Christian tradition and constitutes a permanently valid contribution to all ethical traditions. The practice of wisdom is the practice of casuistry and we can never escape this. There are, however, very serious problems with taking it as our governing model, which we can summarise in terms of its inherent conservatism on the one hand, and its failure to take adequate account of divine and human freedom on the other. It is for this reason that we find, alongside the practice of wisdom, and governing it, the practice of prophecy.

THE PRACTICE OF PROPHECY

The *ongoing conversation* which comprises ethics is represented paradigmatically by scripture, where we hear many different voices — those of the clan ethic, of the law codes of the Ancient Near East, of Wisdom, of the prophets, of Jesus and of Paul. The Bible however is not a handbook of ethics — we cannot plausibly derive later distinctions between different kinds of ethics from it. It is rather a witness to God's activity in changing situations, in changing the *ethos* by which people live. Christian ethics is, therefore, as Barth described it, a matter of the obedience of the free person to the free God. It was to make this point, which he probably learned from Luther rather than from Barth, that Bonhoeffer spoke of the need to discountenance other forms of ethics. Wisdom we find in all cultures and traditions, but it is difficult for wisdom to honour God's freedom. Barth felt that casuistry replaced the freedom of obedience to which we are called by obedience to a law, a supposedly universal moral truth. But we cannot respond to the living God by following a set of rules set down once and for all. "The foundation of Christian ethics is not a moral code ... but a response to what God has done and is doing for us ... A code is not what is distinctive of Christianity."[4] Discernment of where God is acting now is thus at the heart of Christian ethics, and in this is he in agreement with

Bonhoeffer, for whom truly ethical conduct stems from "unity with the Origin," namely God.

While for Bonhoeffer the attempt to orient ourselves by our knowledge of good and evil is the heart of Pharisaism, for Barth all forms of casuistry represent a domestication of the divine command, "a violation of the divine mystery in the ethical event."[5] The kind of domestication involved is well illustrated by middle axioms which are often so bland as to be almost vacuous, and therefore constitute no kind of challenge to the existing order. Like rules, they fail to penetrate to the "creative heart of the gospel" where neither rule nor purpose will fully serve. The appeal to principles misses the liberation of the acknowledgement of guilt and the forgiveness which meets it. "An ethic of mere principles knows nothing of the ethics of the new man, freed from fear about threats to his being, freed from anxiety about not being accepted by others. Accepted by God, and continually accepting that acceptance, he is freed for existence for others."[6] Christian ethics, as Ellul has impressively insisted, is essentially an ethics of *freedom*.[7] "For freedom Christ has set us free" (Gal 5:1). The categorical imperative of Christian ethics is not that we do our duty, but that we exercise our freedom. This means both a sober recognition of all our manifold determinations, including those of prevailing morality, but also a refusal to be bound by them. The transcendence of prevailing morality means an ethic of service and obedience through which we find our freedom so that, in the fine saying of Luther, "A Christian is a perfectly free lord of all, subject to none. A Christian is a perfectly dutiful servant of all, subject to all." Christian freedom is a matter of living within this dialectic.

How then are we to characterise Christian ethical practice? The shape of the Hebrew bible gives us the clue. Ethics proceeds in a dialectic of *the practise of wisdom* (or casuistry) and *the practise of prophecy*, both of which are rooted in the narrative essential to all ethical discourse, and which is the heart of Torah. Since the Reformation, Torah has been persistently misunderstood as a collection of rules or laws, but of course law codes form only part of it. Fundamentally, it is the story of "man's first disobedience," the establishment of the patriarchs in Canaan, the exodus, and the wilderness wanderings. This narrative provides the framework for the legal and ritual codes which the Torah also contains.

When we turn to the practise of prophecy the first thing we have to say is that, contrary to the impression easily gained from the great prophets, it is *an affair of the community*.

> Behold my servant, whom I uphold,
> my chosen, in whom my soul delights;
> I have put my Spirit upon him,
> he will bring forth justice to the nations . . .
> He will not fail or be discouraged

till he has established justice in the earth;
and the coastlands wait for his law (Is 42:1, 4).

Whether this applied originally to an individual or to Israel is probably unresolvable, but it is not mistaken to apply it to both. The church applied it to Christ but here too the church follows Christ in going to the nations with the gospel of the kingdom.

Because it is a function of the community, prophecy does not come out of thin air but grows from the narrative tradition, from Torah. Barth felt that the church was most faithful to its tradition when, "linked but not tied by its past, it today searches the scriptures and orientates its life by them as though this had to happen today for the first time ... the principle of necessary repetition and renewal, and not the law of stability, is the law of spiritual growth and continuity of our life."[8] What this amounts to is letting ourselves be shaped by the narrative, practising what is today called *intra-textuality*, so that the scriptures provide us with the "spectacles behind the eyes" which enable us to perceive and therefore act rightly in the present. By letting scripture give us our world, the command given to the community then in that specific situation becomes the command given to us now in our very different situation. Things have to be like this because God's will cannot be generalised: the dynamics of God's action in the world exclude both an abstract and a perceptual apprehension of the will of God. To the accusation that this was a kind of ethical occasionalism Barth responded that because God is one and God's will is one, we are always dealing with points on a line, moments in God's history with the world, and it is this which gives unity to the ethical decision. Put concretely, this is a reference to the ongoing conversation of the church which is where the "points on a line" are charted.

Secondly, prophecy can only occur from outside the system of prevailing morality. It begins with Moses, Nathan, or Elijah *outside* the courts of the kings of their day, outside the centres of legal and political power, demanding either that people come out of Egypt (where the prevailing morality reigns) or that they cease to behave as if they were in Egypt, since they are now in the promised land. Likewise the coming of the kingdom is first proclaimed by John the Baptist from the wilderness, and Jesus is born outside of the great centres of power, and is crucified outside of the city by the powers that be. As soon as the church becomes integrated in some kind of Christendom situation, it loses the ability to prophesy. For this reason, during the history of Christendom, there is a continual history of groups which seek marginalisation in order to witness to values and realities beyond the reigning system.

How does prophecy actually bear on events? As we look at the writings of the great prophets we see essentially two activities. First there is *analysis* of what is happening and concrete proposals for ways in which things might be changed. Second there are *messianic* passages, such as Isaiah 9:2-7, 11:1-

9, or 61:1-7. These two genres function in different ways. The function of the messianic passages is brilliantly illuminated by Abensour's work on William Morris. E. P. Thompson summarises the argument thus:

> [Morris's] intention was to embody in the forms of fantasy alternative values sketched in an alternative way of life. And what distinguishes this enterprise is, exactly, its *open*, speculative, quality and its *detachment* of the imagination from the demands of conceptual precision ... Assent may be better than dissent, but more important than either is the challenge to the imagination to become immersed in the same open exploration. And in such an adventure two things happen: our habitual values (the "common sense" of bourgeois society) are thrown into disarray. And we enter into Utopia's proper and new found space: the *education of desire*. This is not the same as "a moral education" towards a given end: it is, rather, to open a way to aspiration, to "teach desire to desire, to desire better, to desire more, and above all to desire in a different way." Morris's Utopianism, when it succeeds, liberates desire to an uninterrupted interrogation of our values and also to its own self-interrogation.[9]

So on the one hand the work of prophecy is the education of desire. But on the other hand it has the same functions as Morris's more prosaic political writings: it constitutes a challenge to the ethical basis of the prevailing system and suggests specific alternatives here and now. Prophecy constitutes a constant pressure on the present of prevailing morality. It should take the form of concrete proposals for the future, just as Deuteronomy outlined a possible constitution for the new post-exilic state of Israel. The social and political proposals of the sixth and fifth century BC, not afraid to discern God's will in the face of the collapse of the state of Judah and in the light of the prophetic critique, have had incalculable results for later ages and continue to do so. The church has no need to be shamefaced in attempting to suggest policies on the basis of its own insights. We need to recognise that the appeal to the expert is part of the ideology of control. Economic and social policy rests on ethics and is not at the mercy of abstract laws which only experts can fathom. In both these ways prophecy is far more than throwing stones from the side line, while the real decisions are made elsewhere. It is a crucial element in that shaping of moral discourse according to which policy decisions are made. Although we do well to be skeptical about the susceptibility of those in power to ethical critique, we have at the same time to recognise the importance of such discussion and the practical policy decisions it generates. MacIntyre tells the story of how Carlyle was once reproached by a business man with the rebuke: "Ideas, Mr Carlyle, ideas, nothing but ideas!," to which he is said to have replied: "There was once a man called Rousseau who wrote a book containing nothing but ideas. The second edition was bound in the skin of those who laughed at the first."[10] The same point was made by Keynes in the closing paragraph of his *General Theory of Employment, Interest and Money* when he argued that "the ideas of economists and political philosophers ... are more powerful than is commonly understood ... Practical men, who believe themselves to be quite exempt from any intellectual influences, are usually the slaves of some defunct economist."[11] If, demonstrably, the ideas of Adam Smith, Marx, and Keynes himself have influenced policy, how much more is this true of the law and the prophets? The shrillness of the reproach from politicians in the face of ethical critique that theologians should mind their own business, and that they lack the economic or political expertise to make an informed comment on affairs, shows that raw nerves have been touched. Every aspect of policy rests on an ethic (or as Dussel would call it, a prevailing morality), and the claim that realities are too complex to allow this to be changed is merely an excuse for preserving things as they are. The church makes its contribution by an uncompromising insistence on its view of the human and on the ethical practice which follows from this. Recognition of the difficulty, or even impossibility (in present circumstances) of its policies being implemented is no reason whatever to modify this ethic, to opt as a piece of realism for the second best.[12] This is a betrayal of the gospel.

The practise of prophecy is marked, once again, by *hope*, vivid in the visions of the new future which characterise every part of the Isaianic tradition, in Ezekiel's vision of the reconstitution of Israel from virtual death, and in Jeremiah's refusal to despair in the face of the endless folly of his fellow citizens. The themes of prophetic hope, remarks Brueggemann, are fairly constant. "There is nothing here that is private, spiritual, romantic, or otherworldly. It is always social, historical, this-worldly, political, economic."[13] The new heaven and the new earth of Third Isaiah are characterized by a new economic order, and the end of infant mortality:

> I will rejoice in Jerusalem, and be glad in my people;
> No more shall there be in it an infant that lives but a few
> days,
> Or an old man who does not fill out his days ...
> They shall build houses and inhabit them;
> they shall plant vineyards and eat their fruit.
> They shall not build and another inhabit;
> they shall not plant and another eat (Is 65:20-22).

Hope is the critical principle of ethics, because it keeps the future open. The enemies of hope, says Brueggemann, are silence, civility and repression; that fulfillment which leads to boredom and cynicism; and the technique which imagines it has all the answers. In the biblical witness it is above all those excluded from the totality, and those who face up to their grief, who are the ones who hope for something better. They are not reduced to silence but voice their hope; they cannot know boredom because they expect God "to do a new thing"; they are not afraid of technique but know that it gives us no insight into the mystery of human being. Living in respect for this mystery and in expectation of newness provide fundamental determinations for the Christian ethic.

MORALITY AND ETHICS: THE CHALLENGE OF REVELATION

If the twin practices of wisdom and prophecy are the two axes on which Christian ethics turns, we need to ask how they are related. The tradition of wisdom, or casuistry, arises from a situation of social consensus where it is assumed that everyone knows his or her place. As representing the shared wisdom of countless centuries it is unavoidably and properly conservative. But

> Remember not the former things,
> nor consider the things of old.
> Behold, I am doing a new thing;
> now it springs forth, do you not perceive it? (Is 43:18-19).

Christian ethical practice is following the living God doing his "new thing" and is therefore unavoidably revolutionary whereas the perceptions of wisdom tend to represent the perceptions of those in power.[14] It is this problem which generates the tension of the Book of Job, where the three friends come to Job as the spokesmen of established wisdom and where Job has to struggle in desperation for the freedom of faith. Building on the work of Levinas, liberation theologian Enrique Dussel discusses the problem in terms of the distinction between morality and ethics. We can approach this by asking what it is exactly that revelation — the knowledge of the living God doing a new thing — contributes to ethical practice.

Anders Nygren's classic study *Agape and Eros*, published in the 1930s, has made the distinction between two types of love, one needy and one disinterested, familiar.[15] It is now more or less universally recognised that he overstated his case in claiming that they were completely antithetical, but the current fashion to identify the two is equally mistaken. Agape is not a matter of doing what comes naturally in the way that loving one's child, or falling in love, or finding a soul mate are. These experiences are perfectly natural and were understood to be so by Greek thought.[16] What is implied by agape, on the other hand, is love for the totally unlike, love for the enemy, turning the other cheek, forgiveness. "If you love those who love you," says Jesus, "what reward have you? Do not even the tax collectors the same?" (Mt 5:46). Levinas finds the demand to love the unlike in the face to face:

> I cannot evade the face of the other, naked and without resources. The nakedness of someone forsaken shows in the cracks in the mask

of the personage, or in his wrinkled skin; his being "without resources" has to be heard like cries not voiced or thematized, already
addressed to God. There the resonance of silence — *Gelaut der Stille* —
certainly sounds.[17]

Revelation comes to us in the face to face, and it goes beyond, challenges, and critiques the relationships of love we know only in eros and
friendship — the love of like for like. This challenge grounds, for Dussel, a
distinction between ethics and morality. For him *ethics* are normative and
show us the goal to which we are moving, while *morality* consists of the
moral codes more or less in place, which always represent compromises
with the status quo. According to Levinas, ethics arises from the duty to
respond to the other and suspends the natural right to self-survival. Ethics
is "against nature," because it forbids the murderousness of our natural
will to put our own existence first. Put theologically, we can say that the
word of God speaks through the glory of the face and calls for an ethical
conversion of our nature.[18] Morality, on the other hand, denotes any system
of the prevailing, established, order. Moral conscience formed by this order
can only tell us if we fail to comply with the laws of the system. The rulers
of Jerusalem who cried "Peace" when there was no peace may have had a
good conscience in terms of prevailing morality, but they did not recognise
that the system itself was wrong. Revelation is what enables this perception;
in this case the revelation constituted by the other (Jeremiah) who is outside the system. *Ethical* conscience, as opposed to moral conscience, begins
with conversion, a breach with the prevailing social relationship; it is part
of the new thing which God is doing which cannot be given by wisdom.
This sets up a tension between prevailing morality and ethics. "Ethical
imperatives are moral 'counterimperatives.' If morality says, 'Respect the
feudal lord,' ethics says, 'Liberate the serf.' "[19] Where moral norms are
what the system proclaims to be good, the ethical is governed by what the
poor require. Where moral systems are relative, ethics are valid in every
situation and age because they are rooted in the other as sacred, as absolute.

Morality and ethics exist, then, dialectically. Morality represents the necessary practical application of the moral code as represented by the wisdom
tradition. Ethics, however, represents revelation's attack on the system. It
is the priority of agape which calls our will to survival and power into
question. It teaches that "whoever shall save their life shall lose it," that
the Lord is the servant and that therefore there must be an ethic of solidarity with slaves. MacIntyre discerns a claim to human equality arising
from the biblical revelation which is not grounded in other ethical systems.[20]
If what Levinas teaches about the face to face is true, however, then we
have to understand revelation as in some sense constituted by that encounter. For him it is precisely the absolute Otherness of God, the fact that
God is "beyond being," which enables such revelation to occur.[21]

We have spoken of ethics as "against nature," but it is important to go on with the Thomist tradition and say that the demands of agape are not "contra natural" in the sense that they demand or imply a twisting or distorting of what it is to be human. Grace—in this case the demands of Christian love—does not destroy but perfects nature, reveals to us the true end of human life and where our deepest fulfillment lies. Our good lies in following the logic of agape through to the end, in realising that the other forms of love are distorted when they are not framed by love of the unlike and of the enemy.

It ought to go without saying that ethics presupposes *community*, though the tenacity of individualist modes of thought should not be underestimated. There is an obvious sense in which an individual ethic, which did not recognise that I was my brother's keeper, would be a contradiction in terms. But where the ethics of the natural human being might simply give us the nuclear family or the clan or the nation, revelation shatters this possibility. The Jew and the Christian are both committed to a community ethic in that the vision towards which they live is defined essentially in terms of universal community. The prophets looked forward to a community of nations in which all people will come to Zion and,

> they shall beat their swords into ploughshares,
> and their spears into pruning hooks;
> nation shall not lift up sword against nation,
> neither shall they learn war any more (Is 2:4).

When Paul said that all had been in Adam but all were now in Christ what he was saying was that this vision of a new order was in some sense realised. "In Christ" the deepest divisions of society are annulled. In the letter to Philemon we see Paul struggling with the question of what happens when both master and slave become Christians. The answer is that they are now brothers and sisters at the deepest level and the old relations of exploitation are no longer conceivable. The problems in Galatia arise from Peter's inability to keep up with Paul in his breathtaking annulment of racial boundaries, while, without any doubt, the problems with "Chloe's people" at Corinth arise from them having taken Paul at his word! If Paul then backtracked on gender, as he may well have done, this still does not call into question the magnitude of the social revolution he proposes. In the *ecclesia* "ought" follows from "is." The situation after the death and resurrection of Christ is no longer the same as it was before. A new *ethos* follows. The church's life is the hermeneutic of the gospel. To be church is to live by that and witness to it, to make real and present here and now Christ's breaking down of all barriers (Eph 3:11f).[22]

As we have seen the principle of new community extends beyond political boundaries to the community of all creation, the vision of that time when "they shall not hurt nor destroy in all my holy mountain" (Is 11:9).

It is this vision which Paul takes up in the hopes he expresses in Romans 8. That "we are all members one of another" applies not simply to the church or to fellow human beings but to the whole created order.

ETHICS AND THE MESSIAH

In the previous chapter we have sought to argue that what enables a response to a global problem, that of the world economy, is the fact that the moral sense arises from the face to face which all humans share. In the present chapter we have asked about the structure of Christian ethics and argued that they can be understood on the pattern of the Bible itself. What is it that this ethic has to contribute to the general ethical discussion today? My belief is that the special contribution is in a challenge to the project of rewriting ethics (in Haas's terms), of establishing an ethic of the strong, which is still very much part of the contemporary Western agenda, as we shall see in later chapters. Torah, the fundamental narrative of biblical theology, is a defence erected against any such attempt. It was fashioned in the midst of a pagan culture which, like all paganisms, privileged the strong, the beautiful, and the capable. From the first, then, it took the side of the slave, the widow, the alien, those who could not fend for themselves. "Look to the rock from which you were hewn, and to the quarry from which you were digged" (Is 51:1). That quarry, said the writers of Israel, was the experience of slavery, oppression, and deliverance, and Isaiah's advice remains indispensable. It is not annulled but deepened by what we can call a *messianic ethic*, the ethic of Messiah Jesus, who took the form of a slave, dying a slave's death. The Christian understanding of this one who insisted that he did not abrogate but fulfilled the law (Mt 5:17-18) is that he is at the same time the fulfillment of wisdom and prophecy (1 Cor 1:24; Jn 6:14). In the messianic writings which constitute the Christian scriptures the concerns of the Hebrew scriptures are not done away with but furthered.[23] A messianic ethic then represents the dialectic of wisdom and prophecy. With the prophets it emphasises the need to follow the command of the living God, but with the Wisdom writers it insists that we need the ongoing discussion of wisdom to help us discern what that is. Above all, the Messiah is the one in whose "face" we encounter God (2 Cor 4:6) and whose "face" we encounter in others (Mt 25:31f). The Messiah is, in Paul's terms, the New Adam, the universal human being, the one in whom the truth of what encounters us in the face of the other is manifest. The universality of the face to face relation, is made known in this particular history. The cosmic Christ, "in whom all things consist" (Col 1:15), is also the Jesus of history, the person who, it is claimed, fulfills the messianic hopes of Israel in these very specific and unexpected ways. When Paul introduces the topic of Christian ethics he does so with the words: "Let the same mind be in you that was in Messiah Jesus" (Phil 2:5). To be Christian is to be disciplined in the face to face we learn from him. The implication of this is that natural

authorities of beauty and might are up-ended. Eros can no longer be simply
love for the beautiful and the like but is transfigured. Not eros *and* agape,
nature *and* grace, but eros understood in a completely new way through
agape, nature seen as it really is, in the resurrection of the crucified, and
not in Dionysian power. Similarly wisdom cannot be unqualified affirmation
of the social status quo but has to learn to see reality from the margins,
from the standpoint of the Wisdom who is crucified "outside the camp"
(Heb 13:12). There cannot be a twofold ethic, one deriving from nature
and one from grace, or one from creation and one from revelation, because
all of these are held together in Christ. There is *one* ethic formed dialectically by the play of revelation—the history of Christ—on created reality.
This is appropriated when we allow scripture to give us our world, enabling
that growth in wisdom which enables us to discern God's will in the present.
Another way of putting this would be to say that it is education in the
discernment of the face-to-face relation, an education which transforms the
concepts with which we operate, and especially the concepts of love and
power. "Do not be conformed to this world but be transformed by the
renewal of your mind," wrote Paul, "that you may prove what is the will
of God, what is good, and acceptable and perfect" (Rom 12:2). The question of both old and new Deuteronomists is—What is the meaning of this
transformation for the economy and for our ordering of society?

3

Ethics and Economics

Can the servant of Mammon say Thou to his money?
— Martin Buber

Economics is conventionally defined as "the study of the production, distribution and consumption of wealth in human society."[1] A refinement of this definition arises from the fact that it has to take account of war economies, and for that matter of famines and other natural disasters, and is not concerned only with the positive aspects of material welfare. This led Lionel Robbins in an influential essay to describe it rather as the study of "the forms assumed by human behaviour in disposing of scarce means."[2] Both of these definitions abstract from the question of power, an abstraction made easier by the abandonment of the old term political economy. But, as Adam Smith recognised, economics is about power because wealth is power. Political economy, therefore, involves the social relationships of power among the members of a community in their attempt to earn a living. This means, as Douglas Meeks has put it, that "the main problem of all economy is domination" — something of which the standard introductions to economics are blissfully ignorant.[3] Referring to the silence of the classical tradition on the question of power J. K. Galbraith remarks that "the pursuit of power and its pecuniary and psychic rewards remains . . . the great black hole of mainstream economics."[4] How is it that this is the case?

Marx found the answer in what he called "mystification." Discussing the transformation of value and price of labour power into wages he commented: "This phenomenal form, which makes the actual relation invisible, and, indeed, shows the direct opposite of that relation, forms the basis of all the juridical notions of both labourer and capitalist, of all the mystifications of the capitalistic mode of production, of all its illusions as to liberty, of all the apologetic shifts of the vulgar economists."[5] Two of the central mystifications by which the centrality of power to economics is disguised are the notion of economics as a pure science and the idea of the free market.

29

ECONOMIC SCIENCE AND THE VIEW OF THE HUMAN

From the moment we find serious reflection on political economy, in the work of Aristotle, a connection between ethics and economics was taken as axiomatic. The art of acquisition, the acquiring of those goods we need to live, forms part of Aristotle's preliminary discussion of the State. A State is made up of households, and household management (*oikonomia*) includes the relation of men and women, parents and children, masters and slaves, and acquisition. As the foundation of political discussion it is automatically part of ethics since ethics itself is a branch of politics. His fundamental assumption is that the good or the good life is what all things, and human society in particular, aim at. He considers the life of the "man of affairs" and the philosopher, and then turns as an aside to the man of business: "As for the life of the business man, it does not give him much freedom of action. Besides, wealth obviously is not the good we seek, for the sole purpose it serves is to provide the means of getting something else. So far as that goes, the ends we have already mentioned (pleasure, virtue and honour) would have a better title to be considered the good, for they are desired on their own account."[6] In the treatise on economy (household management) with which he opens the *Politics* Aristotle takes up the question of how we acquire the goods necessary for life and anticipates the nineteenth-century discussion of exchange and use value. His fundamental ethical appeal at this point is to what is natural and what is not. Hunting and warfare are the primary subdivisions of the art of acquisition, but "the natural form of the art of acquisition is always acquisition from fruits and animals." Exchange can also be said to be natural because it satisfies peoples' natural requirements. The introduction of money as a medium of exchange is, however, unnatural, because, as the Midas story shows, "he who has plenty of coin may often lack necessary food." Those who give priority to money making, as opposed to exchange, mistake living for living *well*. Money in itself cannot be the end of any of the virtues and if courage, for instance, is harnessed primarily to money making it is used unnaturally. Retail trade is "an unnatural procedure whereby men profit at one another's expense." "Usury is detested above all, and for the best of reasons. It makes profit out of money itself, not from money's natural object (that is, exchange of goods), and therefore it is the most unnatural means of acquiring wealth."[7]

These strictures on trade and usury continue through the Christian era to the Reformation. Aquinas repeated Aristotle but added a qualified approbation of trade: "Gain which is the end of trading, though not implying, by its nature, anything virtuous or necessary, does not, in itself, connote anything sinful or contrary to virtue: wherefore nothing prevents gain from being directed to some necessary or even virtuous end, and thus trading becomes lawful." Moderate gain, intended either for the upkeep of the family or for the assistance of the needy or for the public good (for example, to supply a person's country with goods it otherwise lacks), is perfectly in order.[8] The principle of moderate gain was enshrined in the doctrine of the just price, which lingered on into the sixteenth century. Justice was defined in terms of the maintenance of status. Commutative justice, as it was called, was socially determined. This principle was augmented by distributive justice, which required that every household should receive the minimum necessary for the pursuit of the good life. Usury was thought to be contrary to both forms of justice. Tawney summed up the teaching of the medieval church as follows:

> To take usury is contrary to Scripture; it is contrary to Aristotle; it is contrary to nature, for it is to live without labour; it is to sell time, which belongs to God, for the advantage of wicked men; it is to rob those who use the money lent, and to whom, since they make it profitable, the profits should belong; it is unjust in itself, for the benefit of the loan to the borrower cannot exceed the value of the principal sum lent him; it is in defiance of sound juristic principles.[9]

This tradition continued to the Reformation. In his 1524 *Treatise on Trade and Usury* we find Luther condemning the practice of credit ("grossly contrary to God's Word, contrary to reason and every sense of justice"), the law of supply and demand, and the growth of monopoly. He too appealed to a just price based on something like the labour theory of value:

> In determining how much profit you ought to take on your business and your labour, there is no better way to reckon it than by computing the amount of time and labour you have put into it, and comparing that with the effort of a day labourer who works at some other occupation and seeing how much he earns in a day. On that basis figure how many days you have spent in getting your wares and bringing them to your place of business, and how much labour and risk was involved.[10]

The story of how this ethical consensus evolved into something quite different, whereby trade became an exercise of godly vocation, has been classically told by Weber and Tawney.[11] Tawney noted that in the growth of capitalism there had been a revolution of thought which "set a naturalistic political arithmetic in the place of theology, substituted the categories of mechanism for those of theology and turned religion itself from the master interest of mankind into one department of life." Where economic thought had been understood as part of a hierarchy of values embracing all human interests and activities, of which the apex was religion, it was now increasingly separated from ethics as part of a far-reaching dualism which separated body and mind, fact and value, the humanities and the sciences, and the personal and the religious from the political.[12] Partly in response to the growing market economy Hobbes reformulated both ideas of human nature and of economic justice. Hobbes had no time for theories of the just price because "the value of all things contracted for, is measured by the Appetite of the Contractors: and therefore the just value, is that which they be contented to give." This applied also to human labour: "The value or worth of a man, is as of all other things, his Price; that is to say, so much as would be given for the use of his Power."[13] In assuming that the market price was the just price he was followed by Locke, a move which Macpherson calls "the death of the concept of economic justice."[14] This development was taken for granted by the founding father of contemporary economics, Adam Smith, ironically a professor of moral philosophy.[15]

Reinforcing the abstraction from ethics was the increasing appeal to economics as a pure science. As early as 1836 the once and former professor of political economy at Oxford, Nassau Senior, could be found disavowing any connection between ethics and economics. Astronomers do not offer advice on navigating a ship, he said; nor can the science of political economy have anything to do with practical or moral issues.[16] In 1871 W. S. Jevons argued that "economics, if it is to be a science at all, must be a mathematical science," and moral values have nothing to do with this.[17] This attitude has been dominant for most of the present century. In *An Essay on the Nature and Significance of Economic Science*, first published in 1932, Lionel Robbins brought together the scientific positivism of the previous century and an unqualified enthusiasm for Weber's notion of "value free" science. The fusion of these two currents brought Robbins to a complete disjunction of ethics and economics. "Economics deals with ascertainable facts," he wrote, "ethics with valuations and obligations. The two fields of enquiry are not on the same plane of discourse. Between the generalisations of positive and normative studies there is a logical gulf fixed which no ingenuity can disguise and no juxtaposition in space or time bridge over."[18] All that economics does is to inform our preferences. It makes clear to us the implications of the different ends we may choose; it is not itself in any sense about ends. Economics was a deductive science and chief among its postulates was the theory of value, the fact that individuals can and do rank their preferences in an order. This might suggest to most people an automatic connection with ethics, through the question of how we arrive at these preferences, but Robbins believed that preferences cannot in fact be compared. He could admit no way of measuring different satisfactions. Lecturing to the College de France thirty years later he still insisted that economists "have nothing to say on the true ends of life." He recognised the impact of economic ideas on political policy but remained unable to see that politics (and therefore ethics, if we follow Aristotle) likewise determined economic thinking.[19]

Appeals like these lie behind the distinction between positive and normative economics still current in the literature, and the assumption that such a distinction makes sense. Positive economics are supposedly descriptive and verified by observation of events in the "real world"; normative economics are prescriptive and often identified with "welfare economics," the study of the social desirability of different economic arrangements. The distinction is part and parcel of the profoundly flawed distinction between fact and value. The facts appealed to are, as is now generally recognised, interpreted data, and into the business of interpretation come values. In the history of the great scientific controversies, remarked Polanyi, investigators of the same phenomena did not recognise the same facts as facts, or evidence as evidence. "Almost every major systematic error which has deluded men for thousands of years relied on practical experience."[20] Objectivity of the kind Weber aspired to is simply not available; norms are built into the axioms which generate positive science. Writing at much the same time as Robbins, Popper had argued that all facts are theory laden. There is no objective haven where we can escape normative reflection.[21] All economic controversy, writes Peter Donaldson, concerns issues of both fact and value. On the *fact* side the data economists deal with are generally outdated, incomplete, or unreliable. Having analysed it they then have to decide what to *do* with it, and this is the question of *value*. Should we make cuts on public housing or defence? Is it more important to reduce inflation or unemployment? Such decisions rests on values.[22] Marx treated ideology as a form of thought which masked reality, and the appeal to science is part of the ideology of political economy. The concealed bias in this sort of appeal was brought out by the Brazilian sociologist Rubem Alves at a W.C.C. Conference entitled "Faith and Science in an Unjust World" in 1979. Alves responded to a Western presentation of the objectivity of science with the parable of the wolf and the lamb:

Once upon a time a lamb, with a love for objective knowledge, decided to find out the truth about wolves. He had heard so many nasty stories about them. Were they true? He decided to get a first hand report on the matter. So he wrote a letter to a philosopher-wolf with a simple and direct question: What are wolves? The philosopher-wolf wrote a letter back explaining what wolves were: shape, sizes, colours, social habits, thought, etc. He thought, however, that it was irrelevant to speak about the wolves' eating habits since these habits, according to his own philosophy, did not belong to the *essence* of wolves. Well, the lamb was so delighted with the letter that he decided to pay a visit to his new friend, the wolf. And only then he learned that wolves are very fond of barbecued lamb.

From this parable Alves drew a number of lessons. Knowledge, he said, is always a function of practical interests, and any attempt to deny this is disingenuous. Rather, we should follow Max Scheler and recognise that scientific methods are a specific form of the will to power. The notion that science is disinterested pursuit of truth for truth's sake is an ideology which allows researchers to avoid possible embarrassing questions about the bad consequences of their work. This ideology draws on the myth of the "expert" and Alves remarks that experts never give advice to the poor and oppressed but rather to those who pay the bills. Again, the ideology of science contrasts itself with superstition, but if we look at the military, political, and economic practices of our scientific civilization then "no superstitious culture has exceeded us in insanity." Science, we have to recognise "is nothing less than the total amount of its social relations and results."[23] All these remarks apply *a fortiori* to economics where the appeal to endless laws (sometimes called "iron laws" for good measure) such as the law of supply and demand makes the point that we cannot change economic conditions. If there are laws of the market as there are laws of gravity or relativity, then all we can do is accept them. "The laws of commerce are the laws of Nature, and therefore the laws of God," wrote Burke, making the theological implications plain.[24] But economy is not fate and is not divinely sanctioned. "In principle everything about economy can be rethought and changed."[25] This is particularly the case since the so-called pure science invoked by Robbins turns out to rest on presuppositions of the crudest kind.

UTILITARIANISM AND ECONOMIC THEORY

The famous passage in the *Wealth of Nations* where Smith maintains that self-interest produces the common good has been invoked countless times in the intervening two hundred years, and has almost the status of a metaphysical principle. Where Aristotle moved from the fact that only human beings have speech to the fact that they are political animals, Smith moves from the same fact to our existence as *commercial* animals. More cautiously, he notes the undeniable fact that we need the help of others and maintains that we cannot rely on their benevolence. A person "will be more likely to prevail if he can interest their self-love in his favour, and show them that it is for their advantage to do for him what he requires of them ... It is not from the benevolence of the butcher, the brewer, or the baker that we expect our dinner, but from their regard to their own interest. We address ourselves, not to their humanity but to their self-love, and never talk to them of our own necessities but of their advantages." Later, discussing protectionism, Smith notes that although the capitalist acts only for personal gain "he is ... led by an invisible hand to promote an end which was no part of his intention ... By pursuing his own interest he frequently promotes that of society more effectually than when he really intends to promote it."[26] Writing in 1987 Sen comments that "it is fair to say ... the assumption of purely self-interested behaviour remains the standard one in economics, providing the behavioural foundation of standard economic theory and policy analysis."[27] Sen attempts to defend Smith by going back to his earlier *Theory of Moral Sentiments*, which presupposed Stoic notions of the common good according to which we have to be prepared to sacrifice our interest for others. Moreover, Smith underlined the contemporary nature of his concerns, and the defence of self-interested behaviour was "particularly related to various contemporary bureaucratic barriers and other restrictions to economic transactions which made trade difficult and hampered production."[28] Nevertheless, the assumption that self-interest is what really motivates human beings made possible the appearance of "economic man" in J. S. Mill's *Essays on Some Unsettled Questions of Political Economy* written in 1829, and this creature still stalks the pages of books on economics. In a lecture entitled "Economics or Ethics?" in 1981 George Stigler maintained that where there is a conflict between self-interest and ethical values which are widely subscribed to, self-interest will always win.[29] This crude and reductionist view of human nature is bound up with the utilitarianism which has underlain economic theory since Bentham and Mill.

Bentham was in effect responding to the collapse of moral discourse visible in Hobbes's making the market the standard of value. For the rationalist eighteenth-century philosopher, appeal to the notion of Deity is superstitious, so where do we turn for notions of value? In a version of the natural law argument he proposed to derive morality from psychology. Humans are driven by two sensations, pleasure and pain. To act morally is to strive to increase the amount of pleasure, or happiness. Applied economically, this becomes a demand for the maximization of the production of goods. While these proposals had a profoundly liberal inspiration, their effect was the opposite for it meant that no matter how acute the suffering of the lesser number, it must be accepted as a price for the greater good. This can be seen in the famous Pareto Principle, which underlies welfare economics, and which is the purest statement of utilitarianism. Put positively, it states that social welfare increases if the welfare of at least one other individual increases without decreasing the welfare of any other individual. As Sen remarks, Pareto optimality can come "hot from hell" because a state can be Pareto optimal with some people in extreme misery and others in misery so long as the miserable cannot be made better off without cutting in to the luxury of the rich.[30]

Among moral philosophers utilitarianism has attracted a great deal of criticism and in no sense constitutes the mainstream of contemporary moral philosophy. It rests on a primitive psychology long forgotten, and the attempt to provide a calculus for pleasure or pain proved from the first impossible. Is happiness (identified with pleasure) wine, sexual pleasure, and song, or reading the *Critique of Pure Reason*? The injunction to pursue happiness is simply an injunction to pursue what we desire, but there is no way of discerning between different objects of desire.[31] Mill introduced the criterion of utility, but even here rival choices present themselves. Bentham and Mill both presuppose societies which rest on nonutilitarian norms of decent behaviour, but, as Haas has shown in his study of the Nazi ethic, this cannot be taken for granted. "Utilitarianism which appears under the pretext of offering a criterion, among other things, for distinguishing good and evil, is in fact offering us a revision of those concepts, such that if we accepted it, we could allow that no action, however vile, was evil in itself or prohibited as such. For all actions are to be assessed in terms of their consequences, and if the consequences of an action are going to be productive of the general happiness, then that action, whether it is the execution of the innocent or the murder or rape of children, would be justified."[32] For the Nazis, public happiness, or utility, was in fact promoted by the mass murder of Jews. The widespread acceptance of this theory by economists can only be explained by what Sen speaks of as the lack of interest economists have displayed in any kind of complex ethical theory.[33] Along with utilitarianism has gone, as we have seen, assumptions about the primacy of self-interest in human behaviour. It is therefore not surprising, though nonetheless disturbing, to find the crudest kind of Social Darwinist arguments about the survival of the fittest in contemporary economic theory.[34] Utilitarianism on the one hand, and the assumption that human beings are motivated principally by self-interest on the other, have provided the norms for the development of economic science since Adam Smith. If a science is only as good as its assumptions, the Babel of present-day economics should not surprise us. The fundamental flaw in both sets of assumptions is the view of the human. In the first place, it is avowedly and methodologically individualist, as, for instance, in the enunciation of the Pareto Principle. For Aristotle there was an automatic connection between economics and ethics because he understood humans as essentially social, and therefore as necessarily concerned with questions about the common good. Contemporary economic theory is concerned, however, with what Marx called derisively, "Robinson Crusoe on his island." Such an individual is not only an empty abstraction but an ideological rationalization for giving priority to the strong. It ignores the interdependence of human beings and has difficulty in coming to terms with the need to care for the handicapped, the aged, and other "nonproductive" members of society.

Secondly, it has an intolerably impoverished view of human motivation. Sen points out that it ignores the role of commitment in human decision-making, but this is only the tip of the iceberg. Far from being creatures motivated chiefly by self-interest we are motivated by love, hatred, beliefs, and convictions. We can be rationally and nonrationally persuaded about things. Letwin, adducing the usual arguments for economics as a non-evaluative science, says that economics recognises this but seeks to explain that part of human behaviour which is rational and self-seeking (euphemistically called maximizing behaviour). "For an economist to assume maximizing behaviour is like for a physicist to assume the law of gravity: in doing so the physicist neither lauds nor blames gravity, nor does he make the silly mistake of saying that because gravity is the dominant cause of *some* motions (such as free fall) it must be the sole cause of *all* motion."[35] But apart from the infelicity of the analogy (human behaviour cannot be subsumed under laws like that of gravity) human action cannot be parcelled out into economic (and strictly rational) portions and others which are emotional and evaluative. Letwin illustrates once again either the naivete or the duplicity of economic assumptions about human nature and therefore underlines the point that the debate about economics is also the debate about what counts as human. If we accept a different account of what it is to be human, as, for instance, Aristotle or Marx did, then we have to revise our economic theory.[36] MacIntyre points out that it was only in the seventeenth and eighteenth centuries that morality came to be understood as offering a solution to the problem posed by egoism. If, instead of an individualist anthropology, we are educated in the virtues then "my good as a man is one and the same as the good of those others with whom I am bound up in human community."[37] Quite apart from this, the contention that defence of market capitalism does not involve sanctifying greed is highly questionable. As Marx noted, "At the historical dawn of capitalist production — and every capitalist upstart has personally to go through this historical stage — avarice, and desire to get rich are ruling passions ... Accumulate, accumulate! That is Moses and the prophets!"[38]

THE MARKET AND MYSTIFICATION

If the appeal to pure science is one of the major mystifications in economic theory, the other is the concealment of the question of power under the rhetoric of the market. The mystification of power and of the market belong together.

Taking their lead from Adam Smith, Milton and Rose Friedman extol the market as a kind of benign and impartial providence, a theme which was a major part of evangelical Christianity in the early days of the Industrial Revolution.[39] The key insight of *The Wealth of Nations* for the Friedmans is that a voluntary exchange between two parties will not take place unless it is beneficial to both. The prices which emerge from voluntary transactions between buyers and sellers coordinate the activity of millions of people, all seeking their own interest, in such a way as to make everyone better off. Prices transmit information — indicating where there is demand, and for what products; they provide an incentive to adopt the least costly modes of production; and they determine the distribution of income. The market economy grows like language, culture, or science "through voluntary exchange, spontaneous cooperation, the evolution of a complex structure through trial and error, acceptance and rejection."[40] The market system requires only Smith's "natural liberty," a concept which looks back to Locke's idea of every person equal in the state of nature. Smith wrote: "Every man, as long as he does not violate the laws of justice, is left perfectly free to pursue his own interest his own way, and to bring both his industry and capital into competition with those of any other man, or order of men."[41] Marx was highly ironical about this paradise of what he called the "bourgeois economists." Their world, he remarks, is "a very Eden of the innate rights of man."

> There alone rule Freedom, Equality, and Bentham. Freedom, because both buyer and seller of a commodity, say of labour power, are constrained only by their own free will . . . Equality, because each enters into relation with the other, as with a simple owner of commodities, and they exchange equivalent for equivalent. Property, because each disposes only of what is his own. And Bentham, because each looks only to himself . . . Each looks to himself only, and no one troubles himself about the rest, and just because they do so, do they all, in accordance with the pre-established harmony of things, or under the auspices of an all-shrewd providence, work together to their mutual advantage, for the common weal and in the interest of all.[42]

The perfect freedom the Friedmans eulogise is a perfect fiction. Peter Donaldson illustrates this by drawing an analogy between the market and an election, where votes count for spending, and candidates for goods and services. This enables us to see that the market is a highly undemocratic way of deciding what should be produced, because the number of votes varies so widely. "Spending by consumers on low incomes (with few votes) may reflect basic needs; votes cast by those with high incomes may be the expression of trivial wants or whims. The market does not distinguish between them." For instance, the "right" to spend money sending children to expensive private schools is only meaningful for a few with high incomes who can therefore purchase a privileged opportunity for their children.[43] Tax benefits for the wealthy drain resources from the public to the private sector and the provision of superior health or education facilities for those who can pay means deteriorating standards for those who cannot. The market economy leads us to believe that "we can 'afford' oversize private cars, thousands of brands of patent medicines, and billion dollar industries devoted to pet foods and cosmetics, while we cannot 'afford' nurses, teachers, police, fire and sanitation services."[44] Policies which favour a free market thus favour the rich since the market responds to those who have the ability to pay. Greater freedom of choice for those who can pay may be won at the expense of reduced freedom for those who cannot. This operates far more seriously in terms of the global economy. The World Commission notes that "among the many causes of the African crisis, the workings of the international economy stand out." The market, too, privileges men's work over women's. "Male definition of what type of work is to be valued, and therefore waged, means that women who do unpaid domestic work have no independent right to resources except through a male wage or a welfare system . . . Most of women's work is unpaid because it is never bought or sold as a commodity on the market."[45] Defenders of the market system, like Friedman and Griffiths, trade in abstractions about human nature, as if the starting position of people in the race were equal. But behind capital stands what Marx called "primitive accumulation," which "plays in Political Economy about the same part as original sin in theology." This is explained to us (till today!) in terms of a contrast between two sorts of people, the diligent and the idle. In fact, "it is notorious that conquest, enslavement, robbery, murder, briefly force, play the great part." "And from this original sin dates the poverty of the great majority that, despite all its labour, has up to now nothing to sell but itself, and the wealth of the few that increases constantly although they have long ceased to work."[46]

Smith allowed only three duties to the Sovereign, or commonwealth: that of protecting society from external enemies; that of protecting every member of society from the injustice or oppression of other members; and that of undertaking public works and institutions which cannot be beneficial to individuals. The first two tasks, the Friedmans claim, are clear and straightforward: "Unless there is such protection, we are not really free to choose. The armed robber's 'Your money or your life' offers me a choice, but no one would describe it as a free choice or the subsequent exchange as voluntary." They do not see that the market confronts the poor with exactly this demand. The idea of voluntary cooperation among free individuals has always been a fiction, for the strong have the weak at their mercy. Marx's *Capital* is to a large extent an account of what market capitalism does to the lives of people, based on the reports of Factory Inspectors and the Blue Books. Brian Griffiths, in his condemnation of Marxism, rightly draws our attention to the murderousness and inhumanity of Stalinist regimes.[47] He glosses over the fact that all newly industrialising countries, from eighteenth-century Britain, to Malaysia and the Philippines today, have been no less inhumane, and we have only a faint idea of the number of casualties. Marx comments on the "fanatical opposition" of mill owners to clauses of the Factory Act which sought to impose necessary safeguards on machinery, "an opposition that throws a fresh and glaring light on the Free-trade dogma, according to which, in a society with conflicting interests, each individual necessarily furthers the common weal by seeking nothing but his own personal advantage!"[48] These casualties are now known in the Third World, where market economies are defended by daily disappearances, torture, mass murder, and by industrial accidents like Bhopal, which happen on a smaller scale daily.[49] If these economies are threatened the need to intervene suddenly becomes miraculously clear.[50] On a less dramatic but still vital level Jeremy Seabrook draws attention to the ways in which the market economy leads to an endless series of food scares, spawns so-called mindless violence, and disintegrates our fragile solidarities. "Mass markets are capitalism's degraded version of solidarities it has broken, of human belonging it has brought to ruin."[51]

The notion that no one controls the market, that, as Adam Smith put it, "so long as cooperation is strictly voluntary, no exchange will take place unless both parties do benefit," also overlooks the fact that desire for profit is at the heart of this system. The money markets are not operated with a view to producing an efficient and fair system for the benefit of all, but simply to make profit by people who neither know nor care about the lives of the people ultimately affected by their deals. Thus, in the opinion of one who worked at the centre of banking for many years, "the financial system that exists today is systemically corrupt."[52] Ninety-five percent of transactions today are about making money out of money. The mystification of this process is essential to its continuance. Peter Drucker now takes this to new limits, explaining it in terms of chaos theory. "Economic policy," he writes, "requires that lay people such as politicians understand the key concepts of economic theory. But economic reality is much too complex for that. It is already difficult, if not impossible, to give answers understandable to a lay person to the simplest economic problem."[53] In fact, there *are* no answers: Chaos theory shows "with rigorous, mathematical proof" that complex systems do not allow prediction. Like the weather, economics is not predictable and totally unstable. We must abandon the search for a unifying principle and be content only with theorems. The lay person, who cannot possibly understand such complex theorems, must be content with his or her fate.

Baffled by the complexities of so arcane a science, the hapless citizen in Birmingham, Bombay, or Buenos Aires must put up with so-called externalities, another economic euphemism to refer to the fact that in order to maximize profits firms will not spend unnecessary money on safe disposal of waste. The acid rain which British power stations drop on Scandinavia is an externality, as is the death of fish in the Rhine due to the effluent of factories in Basle. "Uneconomic" railway lines are closed and railway subsidies withdrawn forcing more traffic onto the roads and increasing the pollution of towns and cities and helping to destroy the ozone layer. A member of the Canadian Parliament asked pertinently:

> How long can we go on and safely pretend that the environment is not the economy ... We are now just beginning to realize that we must find an alternative to our ingrained behaviour of burdening future generations resulting from our misplaced belief that there is a choice between economy and the environment. That choice, in the long term, turns out to be an illusion with awesome consequences for humanity.[54]

Global economy and global ecology are linked together in a seamless net of causes and effects. The ruin of the ecosphere will destroy all economies, but who cares, while profits are good.

In all these ways there is in fact a concealed exercise of *power* within the market. "To accumulate is to conquer the world of social wealth, to increase the mass of human beings exploited by him, and thus to extend both the direct and the indirect sway of the capitalist."[55] According to Luther the usurer "wants to be God over all men." Pius XI—not the most noted radical of the twentieth century—felt that avarice had been supplanted by the lust for power in the economic developments of the first thirty years of this century:

> The ultimate consequences of the individualist spirit in economic life are these: free competition has destroyed itself; economic dictatorship has supplanted the free market; unbridled ambition for power has likewise succeeded greed for gain, economic life has become tragically hard, inexorable and cruel.[56]

The market leaves us free to choose, but at the same time market forces are irresistible and those responsible for externalities take refuge behind the impersonality of the market. Masked behind this impersonality and supposed inevitability is the domination which Dussel defines as the essence of sin. It is the destruction of the face-to-face relationship, which is infinite respect for another's otherness and thus the destruction of morality.

Ethics are concerned with life—the enhancement of life, life in all its fullness. What is ethical is what enhances life, and what is unethical is what denies it. The claim of capitalist economies is that they enhance life by producing wealth. The claim of their critics is that they do so only at the expense of some members of the system, not accidentally but necessarily. These claims are susceptible of exactly the kind of empirical analysis which Marx attempted in *Capital*. Defenders of capitalism can point to the extraordinary growth in technology in the past three hundred years and to the rise in the standard of living for most members of Western societies. How far this is a product of the uninterrupted working of entrepreneurial enterprise remains a question. Furthermore, capitalism seems to assume a necessary inequality of reward between persons—it is incompatible with equality of outcome.[57] The human cost of this development, conveniently forgotten by its defenders, has been devastatingly high. If money comes into the world "with a congenital blood stain on one cheek," said Marx, "capital comes dripping from head to foot, from every pore, with blood and dirt."[58] Such a cost has been justified in terms of the necessities of human nature and of market laws. Against this we have to insist that the shape of an economy is not the product of any kind of mysterious laws; we are, in a very different sense to what the Friedmans intend, free to choose. This is all the more the case if we recognise that ruling ideas of democracy emerged in the seventeenth and eighteenth centuries under very different conditions of production. Different facts call for different values, and we cannot continue to presuppose, as both Locke and Smith did, the inferiority of the labouring class. As we move away from the old dualisms in so many areas we need once again to reintegrate ethics and economics, to recover the notion of distributive justice, and beyond that of the justice which is grace, which opposes every form of meritocracy. Economics then needs to be both understood and structured as the science of the allocation of scarce resources to the whole human household. No one laments the collapse of the destructive and antediluvian command economies of Eastern Europe, and their trail of environmental destruction. But equally the market economics of the present Western world have to be recognised as a heathen atavism, as irrelevant today as the Deist theologies which are their theological counterparts. Atavisms are ways of death. We cannot afford them.

4

On Human Equality

Things cannot go well in England, nor ever shall until all things are in common and there is neither villein nor noble but all of us are of one condition.

—John Ball, 1381

To choose life is the fundamental ethical imperative; it arises from the gospels. This is the criterion by which the social and economic formations of our society must be measured. The concern of the legal provisions of the *Tenakh* was, as we have argued, the preservation of community, for it is the disintegration of community above all else which makes life impossible. The three anti-life forces Paul considered *ecclesia* had to overcome were, as we now call them, race, class, and patriarchy. These are the forces which destroy what Jeremy Seabrook speaks of as our "fragile solidarities." In different ways, but together, all of them deny the equal value of human beings. Analysts vary as to which of the three is most fundamental, but the truth is that they cannot be separated. If life is a seamless web, then the same applies to anti-life forces. In what follows, class provides the framework of discussion, but this is emphatically not intended to prioritise class issues. Just as we need a Marxist conceptualisation of the women's question, as Gabriele Dietrich has argued, so we need a feminist conceptualisation of class and, as bell hooks and other Black feminists have insisted, a race analysis of class and patriarchy. We have to learn from that socialist feminism which "emerged as a distinct tendency precisely because it has refused [the] kind of simplistic analysis which concentrates exclusively on finding 'root' causes, whether of class, gender or patriarchy."[1] As a way in, we begin with a look at the two classical theorists of social stratification, Marx and Weber.

KARL MARX ON CLASS

"No credit is due to me," wrote Marx to Weydemeyer in 1852, "for discovering the existence of classes in modern society nor yet the struggle

43

between them."[2] Raymond Williams has charted the slow growth of the vocabulary of class in relation to the language of estate, rank, and order from the seventeenth century onwards. Cobbett and J. S. Mill had both used the word in its contemporary sense to refer to economic groupings, and it was common in journalistic discussions of economic questions in the early nineteenth century.[3] The language of class is nevertheless indelibly associated with Marx, somewhat ironically as he died just as he began to address himself to a properly worked out account of what he meant by the term. This has therefore to be inferred from scattered references throughout his writings. A basic marker is the *Communist Manifesto* of 1848, an early work in which Marx indulges his very considerable rhetorical skills to the full. All hitherto existing society is the history of class struggles, the *Manifesto* proclaims, which, under the conditions of industrial capitalism, are reduced to the struggle between two classes: the bourgeoisie who own the means of production, and the proletariat who live by selling their labour. Marx predicts the eventual downfall of capitalist economy because of its internal contradictions, the victory of the proletariat, and the arrival of a classless society. To this day sociologists write as if this dichotomous account of society were Marx's last word on the subject, and it is therefore maintained that Marxism as an explanatory theory cannot cope with the rise of the middle class.[4] In fact, discussion of the role of the middle class predated Marx, and he was well aware of it. As a prelude to his full discussion of class Marx noted that "intermediate and transitional strata obscure class boundaries," and he agreed with Malthus that it was the tendency of bourgeois society that the middle class would increase as the proletariat diminished.[5] What, then, did Marx understand by class?

Class cannot be understood apart from the *division of labour*, the earliest form of which is that between men and women in the family. Engels commented on this: "The first class antagonism that appears in history coincides with the development of the antagonism between man and woman in monogamous marriage, and the first class oppression coincides with that of the female sex by the male."[6] The latent slavery in the family is the first form of property because property is, as the bourgeois economists defined it, "the power of disposing over the labour power of others."[7] From the very beginning the relationship between classes is always exploitative. Social structure in tribal society is an extension of the family: patriarchal chieftains, members of the tribe, and slaves. Society and economy developed together, for the mode of life of a society arises from its mode of production. Beyond tribal society there is communal and state property, feudal or estate property, and finally, with the growth of towns and trade, the beginning of capitalism. Each of these modes of organisation is exploitative in a different way. Ancient society rests on slavery; in feudalism serfs have to give so much labour to the lord; in capitalism profit arises from the surplus value of industrial labour. We can distinguish, with Raymond Williams, between class as an economic category, and class as formation (following Weber's "class in itself" and "for itself"). As an economic category, class refers to where people stand in relation to the means of production. As we have seen, in the *Manifesto* Marx distinguished between those who owned the means of production, and those who had nothing but their labour to sell, thus yielding a broadly two-class structure in which the classes are set in irreconcilable opposition. Such an analysis in no way implies that this way of understanding class is not capable of illuminating a society with a burgeoning middle class. Intermediate strata may either be understood as disappearing (like the peasant class, for example), or as standing in intimate dependence on one or other class, as some managers do on the owners of property, or as forming an underclass.[8] Giddens draws on Marx in defining class as "a large-scale grouping of people who share common economic resources, which strongly influences the types of life style they are able to lead."[9] To talk of class in an economic sense refers to objectively structured economic inequalities in society and to "objective conditions which allow some to have greater access to material rewards than others."[10]

The word *class*, however, is commonly used to refer to class *consciousness*. Discussing the position of the peasants in the French coup d'etat of 1851 Marx wrote:

Insofar as millions of families live under economic conditions of existence that separate their mode of life, their interests and their culture from those of other classes, and put them in hostile opposition to the latter, they form a class. Insofar as there is merely a local interconnection among these small-holding peasants, and the identity of their interests begets no community, no national bond and no political organization among them, they do not form a class. They are consequently incapable of enforcing their class interests in their own name, whether through a parliament or through a convention.[11]

Class in this sense implies class consciousness, and right-wing apologists who dismiss the importance of class categories dismiss the importance of the concept by pointing to the widespread lack of such consciousness on the part of the working classes.[12] Once again, however, Marx was well apprised of this problem and discussed it in terms of ideology or false consciousness. From his critique of the left-wing Hegelians, who thought they could change the world by improving their philosophy, Marx moved on to the mystification involved in capital, the concealment of the exploitation which makes profit possible, according to which the market economy is, as we have seen, "a very Eden of the innate rights of man," where "under the auspices of an all-shrewd providence" all things work together for good.[13]

In addition to the objections that Marx's analysis of class cannot cope with the rise of the middle class, and that it rests on a mistaken view of working-class consciousness, it can also be argued that not all societies are class societies.[14] Feudal Europe and present-day India are adduced as examples. But in the case of medieval Europe it is not the case that high birth was prior to economic ownership; on the contrary, it was by and large conquest which led to that distribution of land which established the power of the aristocracy. In the case of India such a conclusion ignores the intense debate as to how far the caste system is to be understood in terms of class. The position of Brahmins (who may be, but usually are not, very poor) can easily be accommodated within Marx's account of transitional classes.

Marx and Engels were among the first to address themselves seriously to the subordination of women, and understood that subordination as an aspect of the class struggle, as it stemmed from the division of labour. More than a century later we are clearer on the way in which patriarchal assumptions systematically oppress women within class structures. Women bear the major burden for less reward, and do so against a background of constant sexual exploitation and harassment. Marx seems to have romanticised the proletariat to some extent. At the very least his project of a classless society underestimated the power of patriarchy in all socialist movements, and especially trade unions.

Writing within a European perspective, Marx attacked imperialism but did not address racial problems as such. Racism, in Alan Boesak's definition, "is an ideology of racial domination that incorporates beliefs in a particular race's cultural and/or inherent biological inferiority."[15] This domination is cultural, political, and psychological, but also economic. In all racial systems ownership of the means of production tends to be concentrated in the hands of the dominant racial group. If, as in pre-Fascist Germany, a group like the Jews, who are not identified with the ruling race, come to exercise significant economic power, then steps must be taken to remove that power. As Helmut Gollwitzer insisted, racism must be understood against the rise of capitalism.[16] Marx's class analysis is therefore not irrelevant to understanding it, though, equally, racism cannot be understood as a *function* of class and capital. Like patriarchy, it intensifies oppression within a class system.

WEBER ON CLASS AND STATUS

Weber's concern with class arises from a wider interest in power structures in society, and the way in which these are validated. His categories of class, status, and party can therefore all be understood as ways of understanding power and domination within society.

Like Marx, Weber defined class in broadly economic terms. We can speak of a class when what determines a number of peoples' life chances "is represented exclusively by economic interests in the possession of goods and opportunities for income and this is represented under the conditions of the commodity or labour markets."[17] Classes therefore presuppose a market in which people bid for goods and, allowing for the view that property includes labour, property and its lack are the basic categories of all class situations. Class situations may be differentiated according to property and services but "always this is the generic connotation of the concept of class: that the kind of chance in the *market* is the decisive moment which presents a common condition for the individual's fate."

> "Class situation" is, in this sense, ultimately "market situation." The effect of naked possession per se, which among cattle breeders gives the non-owning slave or serf into the power of the cattle owner, is only a forerunner of real "class" formation ... The creditor-debtor relation becomes the basis of "class situations" only in those cities where a "credit market," however primitive, with rates of interest increasing according to the extent of dearth and a factual monopolization of credits, is developed by a plutocracy. Therewith "class struggles" begin.[18]

Class then is a way of talking about power in relation to the market. Those have power who control what others need. Those who share the same class situation vis à vis labour on the market form a class. Those without property are differentiated by the services they offer, and those who own property by what they own and how they use it. Among those with property Weber distinguished between ownership classes and commercial classes, between which stood the middle classes who owned small properties or worked in administration in government or industry. Simplifying Weber's detailed analysis Giddens describes the social class composition of capitalism in terms of four classes: the manual working class; the petty bourgeoisie; propertyless white-collar workers, technicians, and intelligentsia; and dominant entrepreneurial and propertied groups.[19]

Weber was critical of the thesis of historical materialism that modes of production determined consciousness. An essentially economic factor, such as class, could not therefore account for the ways in which people valued each other, status. Status expresses the power implicit in "a specific, positive or negative, social estimation of honour." The category of status has an obvious ability to illuminate discussions of both patriarchy and racism. In patriarchal society women frequently have a very low "estimate of honour," a fact which appears with crystal clarity already in Aristotle. According to Weber, status groups, unlike classes, are normally communities marked by a specific style of life and codes of behaviour. Ethnic segregation and caste are both examples of status groups. Status is different from class but overlaps with it in various ways. Status groups can influence the market and, while status does not automatically follow from ownership of property, the two are usually intimately related.

Classes and status groups influence the legal order. Besides these there are "parties," which "live in the house of power," that is, political power. A party is an interest group which aims to acquire social power and thus to influence communal action. Party actions are always directed towards a goal which is striven for in a planned manner. They vary according to the class or status group they seek to influence but above all else in the structure of domination within the community. All three forms of social structure presuppose comprehensive societalization and a political framework of communal action.

Weber's classifications provide a more discriminating apparatus for assessing social power than Marx's category of class. Nevertheless, when we seek to analyse the effect of social stratification on peoples' life chances it is clear that economic factors, determined as they are by both patriarchy and racism, are the primary consideration.[20] A stable disparity between economic returns accruing to the major classes is generic to capitalism, according to Giddens. Taxation schemes aimed at redistribution of wealth have effected only marginal changes in relative differentials.[21] Some progress has been made by the women's movement in terms of equal opportunities and equal pay, but globally this is still at the very beginning. Domestic labour, "the production of labour," is still unrecognised as work, and equal pay legislation ignores the fact that most women do part-time work, and work which is in any case classified as low grade. The studies of Maria Mies in India indicate that the increasing dominance of capitalism there has led to a worsening of the situation for women. "Capitalist penetration, far from bringing about more equality between men and women ... has, in fact, introduced new elements of patriarchalism and sexism."[22]

The result of racism, meanwhile, is that ethnic minorities always head the numbers of unemployed, and always qualify for the most menial work. This can be summed up by saying that *capitalism is predicated on human inequality.* "The structure of power and the profit orientation of economic enterprise make for strong resistance to any policies of even modest positive redistribution beyond mitigation of poverty. Moreover, inequality breeds further inequality, and cumulatively strengthens the public ideology which takes inequality for granted."[23] Inequality is perpetuated by inheritance, which breaches any pretension to equality of opportunity. The right of privilege to breed privilege is thus enshrined in law. Does this matter? The answer to this question hangs upon the effects of those forces which divide us.[24]

LIFE CHANCES

Class, patriarchy, and racism all mean inequality, an inequality which refuses to disappear under the influence of the trickle down of affluence. In class societies "the deepest division of all is the inequality in the ownership of wealth ... Wealth begets income and opportunity, status and power; and from each of these springs wealth. The inequalities are circular and self-perpetuating."[25] Where "money breeds money" through the stock market the vast majority of shares are owned by the super rich and the corporations.[26] Monetarist policies, advocated with religious zeal by the IMF from Chile to Asia, and pursued in both the United States and Britain, have produced a massive increase in inequality generally within society, so that the gap within each 10 percent of the population at the bottom is getting wider.[27]

Apart from wealth we also get fundamental markers of inequality by looking at education and health. Reviewing the statistics for 1985, Reid comments on the first that "contrary to much popular belief that educational achievement is solely or mainly dependent on individual ability, there are extremely important social aspects. Educational experience and achievement are clearly related to each form of social stratification."[28] Inequality of opportunity is therefore built into class division, and this is all the more serious as it prejudices equality before the law. Needless to say, women and the ethnically disadvantaged come at the very bottom.

When it comes to health many reports have shown that "all the major killer diseases affect the poor more than the rich." At every level and in every area the lower classes die younger and have worse health. "Lower occupational groups . . . experience more illness which is both chronic and incapacitating . . . Other direct measures of affluence and poverty, such as housing tenure and employment status, also highlight inequalities in health. Owner occupiers continue to have lower rates of illness and death than private tenants . . . It is now beyond question that unemployment *causes* a deterioration in mental health and there is increasing evidence that the same is true of physical health."[29] Anthony Giddens sums up this picture, noting that physical differences are correlated with class membership: "Working-class people have on average lower birth-weight and higher rates of infant mortality, are smaller at maturity, less healthy, and die at a younger age, than those in higher class categories. Major types of mental disorder and physical illness including heart disease, cancer, diabetes, pneumonia and bronchitis are all more common at lower levels of class structure than towards the top."[30]

Inequalities such as these are defended on a number of grounds. In *The Constitution of Liberty* Hayek argues that attempts to establish equality of opportunity or outcome undermine legal equality. Policies of positive discrimination amount to decisions to treat people in different ways, in principle no different from South African apartheid laws. Secondly, capitalism is a dynamic system fired by competition. The benefits capitalism produces are won at the cost of inequality, and the benefits are worth it. In a famous image he pictures society as a moving column. There is a big distance between those at the head and those at the rear of the column, but those at the rear are moving. Hayek also believes that vesting all economic control in government is a sure recipe for totalitarianism. "If we face a monopolist we are at his mercy. And an authority directing the whole economic system would be the most powerful monopolist conceivable."[31] The way out of this dilemma is the anarchy of the price system, which is not the conscious will of anybody. But Hayek presupposes a situation where there is vigorous competition between small producers. He does not envisage the situation where the whole economic system is effectively in the hands of a few companies who exploit it for their own end and operate a system which can bring a democratically elected government to its knees, as Peter Drucker boasts of President Mitterand's failed socialist experiment.[32] According to Hayek, competition is "the only method by which our activities can be adjusted to each other without coercive or arbitrary intervention of authority."[33] But, in the first place, planned economies of the Stalinist type are not the only alternative to free competition, and secondly, where the "free" market operates totalitarian regimes have often been needed to keep them operating. More fundamentally, Hayek's view of society amounts to Social Darwinism in its crudest form, the denial of cooperation and compassion on the grounds of an idea of nature which is constructed in the image of the worst forms of aggressive capitalism.

Nozick defends capitalism differently in terms of legitimate ownership. According to him, justice relates to the means through which things are acquired. As long as we have acquired any form of property justly we should be able to keep it. Since things are often acquired unjustly he adds a principle of rectification of injustice but, as Saunders points out, if this principle is taken seriously, "it effectively undermines the whole basis of modern-day property ownership in a country like Britain. At the very least it would seem to justify ... the immediate expropriation of all land held by such as the Duke of Westminster and the house of Windsor, and in all probability it would also justify the public ownership of all land given the impossibility of sorting out which individuals were entitled to which plots."[34] Imagine, too, its impact in countries like the United States, Australia, or Latin America, where land was taken from indigenous populations. But what this demonstrates is the arbitrariness of the principle of just acquisition in the first place. Nozick implies a social *tabula rasa* of the type beloved of eighteenth-century political theorists quite as much as Rawls, whom he criticises for his postulated "veil of ignorance." Nevertheless, Saunders believes that, since inequality may be the price we pay for progress, "we should be wary of assuming that inequality is necessarily immoral or socially damaging."

It is clear that the defence of equality cannot, as the authors of the American constitution imagined, appeal to truths held to be self-evident. For Leo XIII it was the very opposite that we are taught by nature: "Men must put up with the human predicament: in civil society it is not possible for those at the bottom to be equal with those at the top ... The differences which exist naturally between men are great and many. There is no equality in talent, or skill, or health, or strength, and these unavoidable differences lead of themselves to inequalities of fortune. This is clearly of advantage both to individuals and to society."[35] The philosopher Brian Magee maintains that history has passed by the great defenders of the idea of equality, such as R. H. Tawney. Only middle-class socialists, fired by guilt and perhaps by envy, are any longer concerned with the notion. Magee's experience in East London taught him that provided people had enough they were indifferent to disparities of wealth, and even enjoyed stories about colourful tycoons. The argument for equality was based on the premise that poverty was a result of poor distribution, and that equal rights involve equal access to public services and equality before the law. These ends, he believes, are being reached by other means than by achieving more equal distribution. What originally was a proposed means got muddle-headedly turned into an end in itself, and then further elevated to the status of a moral principle. This is an illusion which needs to be disposed of, the more so as the absence of envy or covetousness is "morally impressive."[36]

Magee seems to be naive in his views both on the elimination of poverty and on the degree to which equality before the law and equality of opportunity have been realised, if the evidence marshalled above is anything to go by. Moreover, references to "guilt ridden intellectuals" are danger signs of extremely insidious arguments. Guilt is a proper part of being human; the sense of guilt registers failures in compassion or justice, notifies us that we have failed the fullness of our humanity, and demands a fresh start — in theological terms, repentance and conversion. Kenneth Minogue, of the London School of Economics, believes that the repudiation of collective guilt marks a historic cultural turning. If there is indeed such a repudiation then there is indeed such a turning, but on a road which leads directly to the gas chambers. Anthony Sampson comments:

> To equate compassion with irrational and undesirable guilt, as the new right does, is to turn back the whole process of civilisation, which has been built over the centuries on gradually accepting the need for fairer societies. And to repudiate collective guilt is to deny the ability of nations to develop any social conscience.[37]

If we cannot appeal to "self-evident truths" in the defence of equality, to what should we appeal? R. H. Tawney, the target of Magee's argument, advanced three main reasons for considering policies which promoted inequality wrong. First, there was a purely *practical* argument. Inequality, he argued, meant a perpetual misdirection of resources to the production of costly futilities, the systematic under-development of the majority of the population, the creation of a jungle of vested interests, and a perpetual class struggle fatal to the cooperative effort on which society rests.[38] Inequality therefore does not make *economic* sense. As in every sphere this has now to be understood globally. The World Commission report notes that inequality between rich and poor nations "is the planet's main 'environmental problem.' "

> The sustainability of ecosystems on which the global economy depends must be guaranteed. And the economic partners must be satisfied

that the basis of exchange is equitable; relationships that are unequal and based on dominance of one kind or another are not a sound and durable basis for interdependence.[39]

Secondly, Tawney appealed to *moral* arguments. Gross contrasts of wealth and economic power involved, he maintained, "moral humiliation" which affected both rich and poor. It was "absurd and degrading" for people to make much of their intellectual and moral superiority to each other, and still more of their superiority in the arts which bring wealth and power because, judged by their place in any universal scheme, they are all infinitely great or infinitely small.[40] Furthermore, such gross inequalities always involved the corruptions which attend privilege and tyranny.

In this moral argument Tawney has Aristotle on his side. Aristotle discerned a profound connection between justice and equality.[41] Distributive justice, which is concerned with the distribution of honour or money in the community, is a matter of "equality of ratios." "When quarrels and complaints arise, it is when people who are equal have not got equal shares." Political justice is manifested between those who share a common way of life "in which they will have all that they need for an independent existence as free and equal members of society." He then goes on: "Between persons who do not enjoy such freedom and equality there can be no political justice but only a simulacrum of it." Aristotle, of course, has in mind the distinction between those who are citizens, and therefore under the law, and those who are not. He also accepted a hierarchical view of society which meant that "do as you would be done by," which he calls "simple reciprocity," cannot be justice. But if we reject hierarchy and accept the fundamental equality (equality before God) of all people then his argument still holds: where there is no equality, there is no justice, and this is the end of all moral possibility, the end of ethics.

Finally, Tawney turned the classic liberal appeal to liberty on its head. Liberal thought has always maintained that there is a fundamental conflict between the liberty and equality. Lecky declared they were "irreconcilable enemies" long before Hayek. According to Hayek, in an argument widely repeated, equality before the law is incompatible with any policy aiming at a substantive ideal of distributive justice.[42] But the question is, whose freedom is in view, for, as Tawney remarked, freedom for the pike is death for the minnows. Freedom means "the ability to do, or refrain from doing, definite things, at a definite moment, in definite circumstances, or it means nothing at all." In a class society what is lauded as freedom, said Tawney, is the ability of a minority to do much of what they please and of the majority to do little of what they ought. A society where some are servants and others masters excludes freedom. In that situation liberty is the privilege of a class and not the possession of a nation.[43] Furthermore, in urban communities with dense populations someone must make policies and see that they are carried out. "If public power does not make them, the effect is not that every individual is free to make them for himself ... they are made by private power. The result is in either case a dictatorship, which is not less obnoxious because largely unconscious."[44] The economic system is a power system, and those who exercise the power have an effect on countless people's lives. Such power is too great to be entrusted to people whose primary motive is profit maximization. In restricting this exercise of power there is, Tawney points out, both loss and gain. Loss for those who enjoy power; gain for those who do not.

When apologists for market freedom complain that measures taken in the name of equality restrict individual liberty they do not say *whose* liberty they are talking about. It is probable that they are not thinking of the liberty of shanty-town dwellers. Equality, then, is to be contrasted not with liberty but with a particular interpretation of it. If liberty is construed as meaning that the economically weak are not at the mercy of the economically strong then equality, far from being inimical to liberty, is essential to it. Therefore, "there is only one solution of the problem of liberty, and it lies in equality." There was a time, Tawney remarks, when the refusal to allow the strong to do what they want with their physical strength would seem an outrageous interference with personal liberty. But this is the sum of the liberty defended by Griffiths and Hayek. "The liberty of the weak depends upon the restraint of the strong, that of the poor upon the restraint of the rich, and that of the simpler minded upon the restraint of the sharper. Every man should have this liberty and no more, to do unto others as he would they should do unto him; upon that common foundation rests liberty, equality and morality."[45]

Alasdair MacIntyre has attacked Tawney's writings for their "cliche-ridden high-mindedness." The moral values of fraternity and equality which he adumbrated were, according to him, too vague and general for political guidance. Tawney's essays are a monument to the impotence of ideals.[46] But MacIntyre himself has indicated the important place ideas have in shaping political realities, and Tawney's work represents that education of desire, which is one of the key functions of prophecy. He opposes, and enables others to oppose, the enemies of hope: silence, submission, and fatalism. MacIntyre's finding that equality is something which properly follows from Christian revelation is much more to the point. This makes the argument of Brian Griffiths all the more astonishing. According to him,

> The idea that the value and merit of individuals should be related to their income or wealth is wholly repugnant to a Christian view of the world. As a result, it is impossible to derive egalitarianism in the Marxist sense from a Biblical foundation. Equality before the law it is certainly possible to deduce: equality of opportunity it may be possible to deduce; but an egalitarianism implying equality of material reward is both logically and exegetically impossible to deduce.[47]

What Miranda calls the "abyss of immorality" in this passage is truly appalling. If our belief that someone is equal to us has *no* practical effect, which is to say no effect on another's life chances, the gospel is indeed turned into an opiate to give the rich a quiet conscience and to keep the poor in their place. This is very comprehensively to make the gospel of no effect. In fact, there are four decisive reasons for Christian commitment to equality of outcome.

Griffiths appeals to a creation theology which leads him to acknowledge that all are in the image of God. He could have added (since he does not want to exclude the Christian scriptures) that if the Word became flesh then we are all brothers and sisters of Christ. What can this possibly mean if, within one family, life chances are vastly different for one member than for another? "If any one has the world's goods and sees his brother in need, yet closes his heart against him, how does God's love abide in him?" (1 Jn 3:17). This cannot mean *charity*, the rich giving to the poor, the haves to the have-nots because, *post Christum*, there is one human family. Idealistic nonsense? This is to condemn the entire incarnational theology of the early church as unreality. Or is Griffiths covertly smuggling in an appeal to the orders of creation, which justify the oppression of Jews in Nazi Germany, or of black Africans in South Africa?

Secondly, Griffiths has, of course, reminded us that the kingdom has nothing to do with this world (whereas John meant that it did not operate by this world's standards, the standards of Wall Street and the Stock Exchange). If he was alive to the gospel of the kingdom he might remember the Song of Mary, such a prominent part of the church's liturgy:

> He has put down the mighty from their thrones,
> and exalted those of low degree;
> he has filled the hungry with good things, and the rich he
>   has sent empty away (Lk 1:52-53).

This reversal does not belong to "never never land" but has implications for the present. If the gospel is *exclusively* to do with the next world, and if its key announcements have *nothing* to do with this, what is God supposed to be doing? Clearly God cannot be saving souls because human beings are a body-soul unity, and what is done to the one is done to the other (which is why torture and promiscuity are wrong).

Thirdly, Christian egalitarianism has always appealed to the decisive image of the *body*. The church, we have seen, is not some self-contained institution but was from the first understood by Paul as the firstfruits of the new humanity. There is not one rule for the church and another for the world. Rather, to the extent that the church is obedient she structures her life in conformity to reality, which is to say to the revelation of the heart of creation in Christ, and therefore it is in this respect a model for all humanity. To explain the way this new society worked Paul had recourse to a well worn metaphor, that of the body, but he completely reversed its classical use. Where Marcus Agrippa had used it to quell a plebeian rebellion, and to explain why the plebs must remain plebs and the patricians patricians, Paul uses it to explain that greater honour must be given to the inferior part (1 Cor 12:24). The inversion of this world's values seen in the crucifixion of Jesus applies equally to the new society. There is *one* Spirit and therefore there is *one* body: "To each is given the manifestation of the Spirit for the common good" (1 Cor 12:7). For Leo XIII it was precisely this which justified inequality: "A community needs to have within it different capacities for action and a variety of services at its disposal; *and men are most impelled to supply these by the differences of their condition.*"[48] In other words, the class system is a providential dispensation for the well ordering of society! But this misses both the sense in which revelation confutes "the wisdom of this world," and the fact that human society is not static but constantly in progress. It is yet another instance of the dangers of the classical natural law tradition. The rejection of the whole notion of deserts arising from natural talents (and therefore of meritocracy) is one of the most crucial aspects of revelation's contra-natural ethic. "What is there that you have not received?" (1 Cor 4:7). The gift which is ourself is given not for private gain, but for the good of all. To use this principle to justify acceptance of inequality, and all that goes with it, is, however, to sin against the light.

Finally we return to the point from which we began: that the fundamental ethical imperative is to choose life. But life is not abstract, nor is it mere life, keeping body and soul together, but it is life in all its fullness. This is why the gospel is incompatible with a classist, patriarchal, and racist society because these divisions are not, as Magee seems to think, about harmless social status but about both quality of life and life itself.

MacIntyre's criticisms of Tawney are reminiscent of Marx's contempt for the Christian Socialists. His dislike of pious moralising sprang from his perception that sentiment is no substitute for analysis. Nevertheless, as Steven Lukes points out, "from his earliest writings, expressing his hatred of servility through the discussions of alienation ... to the excoriating attacks on factory conditions and inequalities in *Capital*, it is plain that Marx was fired by outrage, indignation, and the burning desire for a better world."[49] Marx spent his days and nights studying the origin and effects of capital not out of curiosity or to better his academic position (he had none) but because of his concern for the realisation of the human. His concern, like that of the biblical authors, was life, and life in all its fullness. It is this passion which accounts for the continuing power of his work. *Class, patriarchy, and racism are of ethical concern because they destroy people.* They are fetishes which diminish and devour life. The graphs to measure what we mean by *life* are not complex: they measure things like infant mortality, average age of death, chances of self-fulfillment as given by education, or the chance of having a job, and beyond that a satisfying job. These things are not everything, but without them there is nothing. If it be objected that this is materialist then it must be replied that there is nothing so material as the Word taking flesh. Christian ethics is the continual re-taking of flesh: "By this you know the Spirit of God: every spirit which confesses that Jesus Christ has come in the flesh is of God" (1 Jn 4:2). It follows from this that equality — equality of outcome and not some phantasmal equality which is merely an apology for oppression — is fundamental to ethics. "No justice without equality," said Aristotle — and this is to say that there is no ethics without equality either. Back in 1381 the priest John Ball, one of the leaders of the abortive Peasants Revolt, saw that without equality there was no gospel either. The recovery of virtue will be effected by the construction of a society in which human equality is taken with proper (that is to say practical) seriousness. All compromises with this principle undermine such a recovery at its root.

Apologists for capitalism argue that it is getting us there in the end, and that the cost of the journey is worth it. To this we have to reply, with Ellul, that Christian ethics is an ethics of *means*. We cannot arrive at a truly human situation by treading on the generations on the way. In attempting to do this revolutionary terrorism and Hayekian capitalism are identical. That this is no exaggeration is made only too plain, as we shall see, by the cost of the free market for the poor, for the Third World, and for the environment.

PART TWO

LABOUR AND THE MEANS OF LIFE

5

Work, Leisure, and Human Fulfillment

This then is the claim: It is right and necessary that all should have work to do which shall be worth doing, and be of itself pleasant to do; and which should be done under such conditions as would make it neither overwearisome nor over-anxious . . . if Society would or could admit it, the face of the world would be changed.

—William Morris

Humans are distinguished from other animals not only by the possession of a much larger brain relative to body weight but also by the seemingly negative attribute of being much less well adapted to survival. What marks them out, therefore, is not only speech, and the use and enjoyment of other signs, but also the employment of complex activities—making weapons, making fire, cooking, all the activities involved in making clothing—activities necessary to survival. Work has its origin here, in what this creature must do to survive. But from the very beginning it goes beyond this, in the urge to decorate, to celebrate through artifacts, perhaps to make magic—one thinks of the cave paintings of southern France, or the Bushmen paintings of the Kalahari—which go beyond mere survival. As is frequently pointed out the word *poetry* is derived from the Greek *poieo*, "to make"; work and art are bound together from the beginning. From the beginning, that is, there is involved in work something we can call exteriority, self-realisation. It is self-realisation above all which marks humans off from animals, manifesting itself in language, sign, and artifact. And from the beginning, if the reflections we have in Genesis and the Greek philosophers are any guide, it is the possibility or otherwise of self-realisation which has marked off toil and drudgery, on the one hand, from "proper work," in which there is the possibility of fulfillment, on the other. The distinction is fluid; all work involves drudgery, and there is drudgery which gives over into creativity and depth. But a distinction there certainly is. In all societies we find reflection on what William Morris spoke of as useful work and useless toil. What is it that marks the distinction? It is impossible to give an abstract answer for a number of reasons. Firstly, reflection on work is bound up with the mode of production of a particular era. The answers from preindustrial, industrial, and postindustrial eras differ in very important respects, as do the answers from town and country and between different groups in society. Even more important, most studies of work have been written exclusively with male work in view.[1] Both "women's work," that is, all the activities involved in caring for communities, and the work women do over and above that, are often ignored. One suspects that the famous statistic of the United Nations Report in 1980, that women do two-thirds of the world's work for next to nothing by way of reward, has been true throughout history.

In what follows accounts of work and leisure relate mostly to the industrialised West, and particularly to Christian attitudes to them. Work has always been a key area for ideologists, and theology has had a great deal to say. Different accounts could, of course, be written from different cultural standpoints. We find significantly variant attitudes to work even across cultures which share a common ideology.[2] I am nevertheless assuming, perhaps rashly, strong analogies between pastoral, peasant, industrial, and postindustrial societies throughout the world.

WORK AND LEISURE IN PREINDUSTRIAL SOCIETIES

The wearisomeness of toil impressed itself vividly on early human culture. We find at least three ways of reflecting on this. One way is to identify work and toil and understand it as human fate or destiny. Thus we find in the Atraharsis epic a picture of the gods labouring and becoming exhausted. Accordingly they create the Igigu, the lower gods—a short-lived solution since they go on strike and picket the place of the high gods. After lengthy negotiations it is decided that the great mother goddess will create human beings:

> Create man, that he be the bearer of the yoke ... let him bear the toil of the gods![3]

On the one hand, then, toil is something written in to specifically *human* destiny, but on the other hand these texts already came from a society where some ruled while others toiled. The human order reflected the divine order: the king ruled and others laboured for him. In many societies this was institutionalised in slavery.

Slavery

We find a secularised reflection on this situation in Aristotle. Leisure is needed for the growth of virtue and for the fulfillment of political duties, he says, but a state obviously cannot consist only of philosophers engaged in reflection. Aristotle posed the question, whether all should take part in all occupations, and answered with a decided negative.[4] There must, of course, be mechanics, traders, and farmers, but below them, guaranteeing the truly human life, are slaves. A slave, for Aristotle, is a human tool, "an animated instrument," one who belongs to another, an article of property. Might slavery be a violation of nature? No, answers Aristotle, for in reason and plain fact it is clear that "some are marked out from birth for subjection, others are born to rule."[5] This convenient doctrine reserves toil for one class and liberates the aristocracy for fulfilling tasks like philosophy and military service. Aristotle speculates that in a fully automated society "no builder would need assistants and no master slaves," but given that Daedalus has not managed to provide these he presses natural law into the service of the vindication of slavery.[6]

At this stage wealth is not valued for its own sake. The enquiry is rather as to which kind of property creates the best citizens. Commerce and manufacture are regarded by the ruling class with suspicion. Mossé has remarked that the significance of work is in inverse proportion to the significance of slavery:

> It is significant that the glorification of labour and laws against idleness ... only occurred either at a time when slavery was still in its very first stages, or when it was declining, when the scarcity of labour of any kind and the rise in prices put a premium on free and individual labour, thereby creating suitable conditions for an anti-slavery ideology to develop and for a partial rehabilitation of the idea of work.[7]

The eighteenth-century campaign against the slave trade was so potent ideologically that it convinced successive generations in the West that slavery was abolished once and for all. It needs to be noted then that, whether in the form of bonded labour or enforced prostitution, there are an estimated two hundred million slaves in the world today, many of them women and children, and many working in the big cities of the Western world.[8]

Work and Toil in Ancient Israel

If Mossé is correct then the fact that Israel was a society hostile to the idea of slavery is doubtless responsible for its very different reflections on work, toil, and leisure. Here all knew about work and all knew about toil. On the one hand Genesis offers us a sober account of drudgery, which is put down to alienation from God. Because man (the sexual division of labour is presupposed) has disobeyed the command he is told:

> Cursed is the ground because of you,
> > In toil shall you eat of it all the days of your life;
> > thorns and thistles it shall bring forth to you ...

In the sweat of your face you shall eat bread,
till you return to the ground (Gn 3:17-19).

On the other hand, the impact of this toil is limited in three ways. First, everyone shares it. Israel was profoundly suspicious of the royal ideology which fundamentally elevated one above another. It was not divinity which hedged a king, for the Deuteronomists, but rather a set of provisions to make sure that he remained "one from among his brethren" (Dt 17:15f). Further, we do not find the same distinction between intellectual work and other forms of work which we find, for example, in Aristotle. The Rabbinic tradition of combining study of Torah and Talmud with quite humble occupations is firmly rooted in scripture, and we find it prefigured in Paul. This was because, secondly, work, as opposed to toil, was understood both as exercising dominion (Gn 1:28, the Priestly source) and stewardship (Gn 2:15, the Yahwist source). It was, as Pope John Paul has described it in *Laborem Exercens*, a form of "co-creation."[9] Tilling and keeping the ground was not simply toil but was also sharing in God's care for creation. The God of the Bible is also a worker who labours for Israel, and human beings enter into this labour. As labourers they are in the image of God. Paul's admonitions to his congregations sum up a long Jewish discussion. The Christians in Thessalonica are told to "work with their hands" (1 Thes 4:11) and "labour in quietness and eat their bread" (2 Thes 3:10f). In Ephesians we are told, "Let the one that stole steal no more: but rather let them labour, working with their hands the thing that is good, that they may give to those who need" (Eph 4:28). Paul distinguishes between *ergazesthai*, which is laid on all ("If he will not work, neither let him eat" — 2 Thes 3:10) and *periergazesthai*, "superfluous busyness," work for work's sake, manic working. Making an idol of work was ruled out and the *Tenakh* promised that one day useless toil would cease. In the Messianic Age people will no longer labour in vain (Is 65:23). The story of the miraculous catch of fish is perhaps an echo of this messianic promise. The disciples complain to Jesus that "we toiled all night and took nothing." In the Messianic Age which Jesus inaugurates, however, there is more than enough for the taking, bread and fish to share so that all are filled. The concrete sign of this was the sabbath. God not only labours but also rests, and people are called also to enter into this rest. The sabbath made relative the significance of work: "Six days you shall do your work, but on the seventh day you shall rest; that your ox and your ass may have rest; and the son of your bondmaid, and the alien may be refreshed (Ex 23:12). The Deuteronomists grounded this in the liberation from Egypt. The sabbath was a sign that as God had liberated Israel so there could be no permanent servitude in Israel (Dt 5:13-15). How unusual this institution was is shown by Tacitus's complaint that it constitutes a weekly strike. Moreover, B. Wielenga has shown that it had revolutionary significance in a slave-owning society. The sabbath meant that once a week the slave was free, and therefore not by nature meant for toil. "Throughout the centuries this celebration has been a quiet, joyous protest against the takers of time, the exploiters."[10]

Women in Preindustrial Society

Aristotle was as clear on the sexual division of labour as he was on slavery. Though he believed that man and wife should be friends (the highest form of human relationship), this was a friendship with a difference because the woman's function is to obey. He discerns in nature a wise dispensation for the continuance of the race:

> For nature has made the one sex stronger, the other weaker, that the latter through fear may be the more cautious, while the former by its courage is better able to ward off attacks; and that the one may acquire possessions outside the house, the other preserve those within. In the performance of work, she made one sex able to lead a sedentary life and not strong enough to endure exposure, the other less adapted for quiet pursuits but well constituted for outdoor activities; and in relation to offspring she has made both share in the procreation, but each render its peculiar service towards them, the woman by nurturing, the man by educating them.[11]

This is surely the classic statement of "complementarity" patriarchy, though what we find in Aristotle is doubtless "what oft was said but ne'er so well expressed." Even in present discussion this description of the ancient division of labour is repeated as fact almost word for word, though without attribution.[12] It is important to note that like many recent feminists Aristotle's analysis is rooted in claims about biology. Most damagingly, this great thinker, who exercised an immense influence on both Christianity and Islam, established for succeeding ages the identification of men with rational pursuits and women with nurture.

Marx and Engels traced the division of labour to the different roles of the sexes in procreation. From there further division "develops spontaneously or 'naturally' by virtue of natural predisposition (for example, natural strength), needs, accidents etc. Division of labour only becomes truly such from the moment when a division of material and mental labour appears."[13] They characterise the role of women and children in the family as domestic slavery, and the reservation of intellectual work to men and material labour to women followed from this. So imbued are we with the idea that it is men who do manual labour that this comes as a surprise to many. Yet the comment of a seventeenth-century traveller among the Huron in Canada speaks precisely for the position of women in many third-world countries. He found

> powerful women of extraordinary stature; for they till the soil, sow the corn, fetch the wood for winter, strip the hemp, and spin it, and

with the threads make fishing nets . . . They have the labour of harvesting the corn, sorting it, preparing it and attending to the house
and besides are required to follow their husbands from place to place,
in the fields, where they serve as *mules* to carry the baggage.[14]

In rice-growing countries women undertake much of the immensely
arduous task of planting and harvesting rice, while before mechanisation
their job in the northern hemisphere was the back-breaking task of pulling
root crops.[15] Today it is calculated that women are responsible for from 40
percent to 80 percent of agricultural production, and it seems likely that
this represents historical reality in all preindustrial societies. As for what
is described as women's work, we can take as typical the work of Tendai,
a young girl in Lowveld, Zimbabwe, "who starts her day at 4 A.M. by walking
twenty two kilometres to collect water. From 9 A.M. until lunch time she
collects firewood. She then cleans the breakfast utensils and prepares lunch.
All afternoon she collects wild vegetables and then cooks supper. After
supper she does another round trip to the borehole to fill a thirty litre can
with water. Childcare and agricultural work are additions to this punishing
schedule."[16] The description of such a life as domestic slavery is only too
apt.

Work Ideology in Preindustrial Societies

One of the richest sources for ideology of work through the Christian
centuries has been the wisdom literature, especially Proverbs and Ecclesiastes. Proverbs such as these have been repeatedly cited since the rise of
the work ethic:

> Go to the ant, O sluggard;
> consider her ways, and be wise . . .
> A little sleep, a little slumber,
> a little folding of the hands to rest,
> and poverty will come upon you like a vagabond,
> and want like an armed man (Prv 6:6, 11).

> He who tills his land will have plenty of bread,
> but he who follows worthless pursuits will have plenty of
>   poverty (Prv 28:19).

In the course of time, and especially after the seventeenth century, these
proverbs came to be treated as abstract, timeless truths. In fact, they come
from the small peasant society of Israel where it was perfectly true that the
farmer who refused to toil would end up serving his neighbour. They also
became moral prescriptions, where in Israel they simply record the fruit of
long observation. They state what is actually the case: "If, in this kind of

society someone behaves like this, then . . ." Most important, all of these proverbs are put into the context of the fear of the Lord. It is the fear of the Lord which is the beginning of wisdom, which is to say the observation of the law and the prophets. When proverbs like these are detached from their theological and social context, harnessed to an exaltation of work *as such*, treated as abstract moral prescriptions, and applied in the completely different setting of the factory system, then they are totally distorted. This is a prime case of the ideological use of scripture or, in Shakespeare's phrase, the devil citing scripture for his purpose. The same is true of the use of Ecclesiastes to endorse a godly hedonism.[17] This book comes from the upper class of Jerusalem under Seleucid rule, and its announcement that "all is vanity" ultimately constitutes bad news for the poor. The leisure and happiness which are certainly intended for human beings are not grounded in the vanity of human purposes for the good, but much rather, as the prophets saw, in attempts to show that all is not vanity.

The heyday of the feudal system in Europe was to a large extent both nonmercantile and nonindustrial, and the theology of the time reflects this. The different orders did very different kinds of work, and this could be validated, by Anselm for example, by appeal to a kind of natural law argument. Clergy and the military were supported by serfs who worked partly for themselves and partly for their lords. The absence of a market economy doubtless discouraged working for a surplus since there would be nowhere to dispose of it. An echo of the Greek ambivalence towards manual work is found in the theology of the period. On the one hand we find vigorous affirmation of the importance of manual work in Augustine, in the Benedictine rule, and to a lesser extent in Aquinas. Manual work is a command, said Aquinas, and is therefore laid on most people. It not only provides us with the means of life but is useful to remove idleness, a source of many evils, to curb concupiscence, because it afflicts the body, and to provide means for almsgiving.[18] On the other hand the counsels of perfection emphasised that prayer, study, and contemplation were a "more perfect work." Work therefore is commanded, and useful, but in no way glorified. There is no hint of the later doctrine of self-realisation through work.

WORK AND LEISURE IN A MARKET ECONOMY

Conditions of production remained preindustrial in many ways well into the eighteenth century, but a decisive change is marked throughout Europe from the twelfth century onwards, with the growth of markets and of wage labour, the latter of which was greatly increased by the impact of the Black Death (1348). Under these conditions the rigid social order of feudalism began to disintegrate. Guilds were formed in the towns and the status of merchants and craftsmen rose. While usury continued to be condemned well into the eighteenth century it also found its defenders. Because ideologies cannot survive new worlds, theologies too began to change. The two tier, sacred and secular, division of work was one of the first casualties. The Reformation established that people could properly serve God in any honest occupation. Thus Luther remarks that household work "has no appearance of sanctity; and yet these very works in connection with the household are more desirable than all the works of all the monks and nuns . . . Seemingly secular works are a worship of God and an obedience well pleasing to God."[19] He could speak beautifully and amusingly of the need of men to be able to change nappies and cradle babies, though of course he was quite clear on the subordinate position of women.[20] Calvin too taught that "no work will be so mean and sordid as not to have a splendour and value in the eye of God."[21] These remarks already imply what went with this: a new valuation of work in itself. For Luther the necessity of work stands in some tension with justification by faith alone. We must work, but we must ascribe the rewards of work to God alone.[22] For Calvin, on the other hand, the vocation which every person has is God's answer to "the boiling restlessness of the human mind."[23] Weber maintained that the doctrine of calling, developed by Luther and canonised by Calvin, was one of the crucial aspects of the development of capitalism. Life is given to be lived to the glory of God, but this can only be done in terms of one's calling. To work hard was the surest antidote to vice and was, as the fulfillment of one's calling, itself a sign of being elect. The cycle of sin, repentance, atonement was not available to the Calvinist, whose God demanded not single good works, but a life of good works combined into a unified system.[24] A side product of this doctrine was an ideology of oppression. "A truly Godly servant," wrote Richard Baxter, "will do all your service in obedience to God, as if God himself had bid him do it."[25] Such a doctrine could later be pressed into service for factory hands, as it was, for instance by Andrew Ure.

These changes likewise meant important changes for the understanding and availability of leisure. There is an increased stress on the vice of idleness, which applies to leisure time as well. "It is swinish and sinful not to labour," wrote Richard Baxter; "Certainly God curses idleness and loafing," said Calvin.[26] Pastimes were timewasting according to Baxter who wrote,

> Keep up a high esteem of time and be every day more careful that you lose none of your time . . . And if vain recreation, dressings, feastings, idle talk, unprofitable company, or sleep be any of them temptations to rob you of any of your time, accordingly heighten your watchfulness.[27]

In Protestant countries many of the holy days of medieval Catholicism were abolished.[28] There was a return to earlier church discipline on recreation; games of chance, gambling, bear baiting, and horse racing were all condemned. On the other hand, John Milton was not atypical in writing that people "have need of some delightful intermissions, wherein the enlarged soul ... may keep her holidays to joy and harmless pastime."[29] The sabbath was enforced, not in a joyless sense but in recognition of the necessity to protect the rights of workers who, as Baxter said, "would be left remediless under such masters as would both oppress them with labour and restrain them from God's service."[30] Similarly, the 1647 Parliament in England made every second Tuesday of the month a holiday for the recreation of workers. Nevertheless, the Puritan balance sheet is more in debit than credit. There was, as Ryken puts it, both a legalistic and a utilitarian approach to leisure. Baxter has eighteen qualifications which govern a Christian's choice of leisure and the Puritan condemnation of the theatre was extremely unconvincing. Worse, leisure was understood as essentially refreshment to enable work. "Recreation," said William Burkitt in *The Poor Man's Help*, "serveth only to make us more able to continue in labour."[31]

Despite this Protestant ideology, in which leisure is understood through the work ethic, work and leisure remained closely integrated before the advent of industrial capitalism. Agricultural work was seasonal, and where cottage industry was the rule, time was more freely structured. Times of intense activity were followed by more leisurely periods. The agricultural year had great common celebrations at sheep shearing and harvest home, and there were the traditional holidays of Christmas, Easter, and May Day. Local wakes and fairs all gave opportunity for recreation.

> The fluidity of the boundaries between work and leisure was apparent in the street culture of village and town. Workshop and tavern opened side by side on to the street. Drinking, producing, bargaining, passing the time of day, all contributed to a common flow, eddying around street traders, itinerant salesmen, balladeers. Here work and leisure intermingled, both aspects of a life which was, above all, *public* in its orientation and presence.[32]

Such a pattern characterises all free peasant cultures, and serves to soften both the toil of agricultural labour and the oppression of local landlords and grandees.[33] On the other hand we have the testimony of Leonard Thompson, one of the farm labourers recorded in Ronald Blythe's *Akenfield*, to the cruelty of much agricultural work. "I want to say this simply as a fact," said Thompson, speaking of the early years of the present century, "that village people in Suffolk in my day were worked to death. It literally happened. It is not a figure of speech. I was worked mercilessly. I am not complaining about it. It is what happened to me."[34] Thompson, who became a lifelong unionist, here speaks for women and men throughout the world.

WORK AND LEISURE IN INDUSTRIAL SOCIETY

Appendages to the Machine

The market economy of the thirteenth to the seventeenth centuries was based on the labour of peasants, artisans, and guilds, small producers working for local markets. The origins of capitalism, according to Marx, are to be found in the break up of this artisan system, partly under pressures of an expanding market. Land was enclosed for different and more efficient kinds of production, and the producer was separated from the means of production. This created a large pool of people available for wage labour, the proletariat, those who exist by selling their labour. At the same time the expanding market created the demand for large-scale production which made capitalism possible. A person with sufficient capital could now dispense with inefficient piece work and gather workers together under one roof to do all the tasks necessary for making particular products. The full potential of the division of labour was really discovered, as eulogised in Adam Smith's famous pin factory. The need for greater amounts of capital for reinvestment led, for the first eighty years of this system, to an extraordinary lengthening of the working day—time which was only clawed back with great difficulty through a series of factory acts in the nineteenth century. The division of labour also grew more intricate. Cumulatively these developments produced what Marx spoke of as alienation. Labour now becomes the major form of property, and there are those who buy and those who sell it. This brings about the situation remarked in the famous peroration in *Capital*:

Within the capitalist system all methods for raising the social productiveness of labour are brought about at the cost of the individual labourer; all means for the development of production transform themselves into means of domination over, and exploitation of, the producers; they mutilate the labourer into a fragment of a man, degrade him to the level of an appendage of a machine, destroy every remnant of charm in his work and turn it into a hated toil; they estrange from him the intellectual potentialities of the labour process in the same proportion as science is incorporated in it as an independent power; they distort the conditions under which he works, subject him during the labour process to a despotism the more hateful for its meanness; they transform his life-time into working time, and drag his wife and child beneath the Juggernaut of Capital.[35]

This process was intensified by the management strategy known as Taylorism, and even today it is estimated that many factory operatives use more skill driving to work than they do actually in their work.[36]

Women in Industrial Society

Marx writes of the labour of men. But he knew very well, as the footnotes in *Capital* record, that the Industrial Revolution had, and has had in every country where it has happened, tremendous impact on the lives of women, an impact which has been double edged. On the one hand, the involvement of women in traditionally male tasks, especially in the factories during the two world wars of this century, proved a decisive factor in women attaining a limited degree of political power and domestic autonomy. On the other hand, women were, from the start, understood as a source of cheap labour and trade unionism often endorsed this rather than opposing it. Women were (and are) valued for their docility and nimble fingers, the fact that they were more adept at many tasks than men. For the agricultural tasks which women did alongside housework in preindustrial society was substituted gruelling work in mine and factory. The worst excesses of the early days of the Industrial Revolution in Europe are now repeated in the Third World: a sixteen-hour day, dangerous working conditions, sexual harassment, and gross underpayment.[37] At the same time the traditional sphere of women's work, in food production, health care, child rearing, "the entire range of so-called basic needs" remains "vital to the survival and ongoing reproduction of human beings in all societies."[38] What has resulted is what Mies calls "super exploitation," the coexistence of necessary work with underpaid labour.[39]

The Ideology of Industrialisation

As industrialisation proceeded a new utilitarian ethic arose to meet its needs. For Benjamin Franklin and Samuel Smiles work and utility become the supreme virtue, and idleness the supreme vice. Franklin's aphorisms, written at the very beginning of this period, are a bizarre parody of the biblical proverbs:

> Remember, that *time* is money. He that can earn ten shillings a day by his labour, and goes abroad, or sits idle, one half of that day, though he spends but sixpence during his diversion or idleness, ought not to reckon *that* the only expense; he has really spent, or rather thrown away, five shillings besides.
>
> The sound of your hammer at five in the morning, or eight at night, heard by a creditor, makes him easy six months longer; but if he sees you at a billiard table, or hears your voice at a tavern, when you should be at work, he sends for his money the next day.
>
> He that idly loses five shillings' worth of time, loses five shillings, and might as prudently throw five shillings into the sea.
>
> He that loses five shillings, not only loses that sum, but all the advantage that might be made by turning it in dealing, which by the time that a young man becomes old, will amount to a considerable sum of money.[40]

No one can doubt that Mammon has comprehensively displaced the fear of the Lord here. It is essentially the same note sounded one hundred years later by Samuel Smiles, whose *Self help* was published in 1859. "Steady application to work is the healthiest training for every individual. Honourable industry travels the same road with duty; and Providence has closely linked both with happiness ... Labour is not only a necessity and a duty, but a blessing: only the idler feels it to be a curse."[41] Providence here is the law of capital.

More odious still was the explicitly religious appeal of Andrew Ure. Opposing the Factory Act of 1833, which sought to limit the work of children under eleven to nine hours per day, he eulogised the activity of the "lively elves" in the factories where they frequently choked to death. He recognised however that economic incentives were not enough to keep them at work and saw the necessity of Christianity to keep people at work. It taught them that their chief happiness lay in another world, and that we must learn to live by self-immolation for the good of others. "Where then shall mankind find this transforming power? — in the cross of Christ ... it atones for disobedience; it excites to obedience; it makes obedience practicable; it makes it acceptable; it makes it in a manner unavoidable, for it constrains to it; it is, finally, not only the motive force to obedience, but the pattern of it."[42] E. P. Thompson proposed, in a famous thesis, that Methodism as a whole acted in the first half of the nineteenth century to prepare people to accept the rigours of industrial capitalism. Even those who were sympathetic to the plight of the labourer, like Carlyle or Ruskin, often romanticised work. "Even in the meanest sorts of Labour," said Carlyle, "the whole soul of man is composed into a kind of real harmony ... All true work is religion ... in all true work, were it but true hand labour, there is something of divineness."[43]

Leisure in Industrial Society

The new pattern of work meant changes in both the nature and the attitude to leisure. Holidays were a threat to profit. By 1834 the number of bank holidays had been reduced from seventeen to four. A sustained attack on popular culture harried itinerant entertainers as vagabonds, drove games such as football off the streets, and restricted hunting of animals to the upper classes. And where work is indistinguishable from toil leisure becomes simple compensation. "The antithesis of work and leisure ... is not a given social fact, but an historical creation. That people may gain in leisure satisfactions they do not derive from work is not a psychological but an historical phenomenon."[44] Deprived of many traditional pastimes the public house increasingly became a centre of leisure. From the entertainments provided here the music hall developed.[45] The mass commercialisation of leisure developed apace from the 1850s onwards, leading to the resort culture of the late nineteenth century and the cinema culture of the 1920s. At its best, as Ewan MacColl put it in his song *The Manchester Rambler*, the wage slave of Monday becomes a free man on Sunday, an exact echo of the Deuteronomic view of the sabbath. At worst the alienation

known in work is reflected in leisure, a possibility reflected in the speci-
alisation and institutionalisation of leisure from the 1880s onwards, and in
the segregation of class and gender involved.[46] Such alienation has become
immeasurably deepened by the advent of the television culture, disturbingly
analysed by Neil Postman in his book *Amusing Ourselves to Death*. Drawing
on a mass of different studies Postman shows that television, which accounts
for 47 percent of most people's leisure time in Western societies, encour-
ages passivity, lack of ability to conduct sustained thinking on a subject,
lack of deliberation, and triviality. "It floods us with information with which
we are expected to do nothing. What we get from television lacks action
value and therefore produces a sense of impotency. As a medium, moreover, television has produced a world of broken time and broken attention."[47] When this is the case possibilities for Huxleyan manipulation are
obvious. The danger does not come from Big Brother but from our own
distraction by trivia, from the situation where cultural life is redefined in
terms of entertainment, serious public conversation becomes a form of baby
talk. In this situation culture death is a clear possibility.[48] According to this
view the leisure which was originally claimed under the impact of industrialisation in order to humanise the impact of meaningless toil becomes
the ultimate instrument in our dehumanisation.

Work and Leisure in a Postindustrial Age

From all sides, left as well as right, we now have predictions of an entirely
different pattern of work and leisure in the microchip age.[49] It is not clear
how accurate these forecasts are, though they are now more plausible than
they were when made in the early days of the Industrial Revolution, or
indeed by J. M. Keynes in 1930.[50] The predictions amount to this: the
sophistication of new technology means that full employment as it was
conceived during the ascendancy of Keynesian economics, is now gone for
good. Very soon 10 percent of the work force will be able to do all the
labour which is needed for the means of life.[51] What happens in this situation? We can imagine, says the French Marxist André Gorz, an "exit left"
and an "exit right." One version of the right exit envisages an intensified
hierarchy with those who control information at the top and the "hewers
of wood and drawers of water" at the bottom, degenerating into outright
social conflict.[52] A second version is the increasing use of computers to
privatise things like education and health, which the state can increasingly
control. People will be paid to use these facilities as a way of preserving
the semblance of the wage and market structure. In fact what is at stake
is domination, a totalitarian society run by a technocracy.[53] The alternative
is a reduction of the number of hours expected in a lifetime's employment
to fifty thousand hours and a form of job sharing so that we all have job
portfolios consisting of our regular job plus various kinds of marginal and
gift work. Where the regular job could provide money but no status, the

gift work could give us status in the community. "We could be street clean-
ers for (part of) the night, writers by day." This vision of Charles Handy's
is close to Marx's famous utopian vision in the *German Ideology* where
"nobody has one exclusive sphere of activity but each can become accomplished in any branch he wishes" so that it is possible "to do one thing
today and another tomorrow, to hunt in the morning, fish in the afternoon,
rear cattle in the evening, criticise after dinner, just as I have a mind,
without ever becoming hunter, fisherman, shepherd or critic."[54] In other
words, work and leisure could be reintegrated, both understood as forms
of self-realisation. Gorz calls for the decentralisation of production since
economies of scale no longer apply for most consumer goods, but above all
for a break with the ideology of privilege. This ideology feeds the "necessity" for growth in capitalism; as soon as everybody has a product something
better must be produced for those at the top. Handy too endorses the theme
that enough is enough: "Longer lives and shorter jobs will tend to mean
lower incomes . . . Sacrifice, therefore is inevitable."[55]

There are a number of questions about this vision. All the writers cited
come from the so-called First World, a tiny fragment of existing humankind.
The majority of human beings are still peasants, using technology little
changed for the past two thousand years. True, these people are caught in
the grip of what the First World is doing, since this controls global economies, but it is not clear how or how quickly the new technology, and its
answers to the problems of employment or underemployment, can be
applied to these societies. A second, and even more serious question, which
we come up against again and again, is whether those who enjoy affluence
and power will be prepared for the inevitable sacrifices Handy refers to.[56]

"The right to ownership must belong to a man in his capacity of head
of a family . . . A most sacred law of nature ordains the head of a family
should provide for the necessities and comforts of the children he has
begotten."[57] This text of 1891 invokes the authority of natural law to guarantee patriarchy. A century later, as we move into a postindustrial era, it
is at last becoming clear that the division of society into a female part,
involving nurture and the family, and a male, involving politics and "high
culture," distorts reality for both sexes and is responsible for present patterns of aggressive male-oriented dominance. A century after Leo XIII's
pronouncement an Indian feminist notes that "we have reached a point in
history where a drastic rethinking and restructuring of human civilisation
as a whole is needed," which will seek to unravel the double exploitation
of women imposed by patriarchy.[58] If work is re-envisaged to comprehend
both the public and the private sphere, both the personal and the political,
then it has to be recognised that men and women need to be involved
equally on both sides. What we need, argues the Green economist James
Robertson, is a situation where *everyone* has a work profile similar to those
of many women at present: part domestic, part away from home, part voluntary, part paid.[59] Any escape from patterns of work which are dehuman-

ising for both women and men must rest both on the recognition that domestic work, hitherto "women's work," is of equal importance to paid work, that this production of life needs to be shared equally by both sexes, and that other forms of work require equal remuneration. "The first condition for the liberation of women," wrote Marx and Engels, "is to bring the whole female sex back into public industry." They believed this meant the end of the monogamous family, but there is no reason to think that this follows automatically.[60] The strain experienced by many families where both partners work follows partly from the fact that society is still fundamentally geared to old patterns.

Mary Mellor criticises Robertson's view as retaining "male orientated individualist overtones."[61] To assess whether this is the case we turn, finally, to an attempt to pull the threads of this brief historical sketch of the work of women and men together.

CHRISTIAN APPROACHES TO WORK AND LEISURE

Traditionally work has been identified with one's means of earning a living, and leisure with its opposite (cf. the Latin *neg-otium*, "work"). In the case of housework this was often only marginally recognised in saying that the woman set the man free to do his work. If we follow Gorz and Handy, however, then we will need to define work more widely. Since work and leisure have been defined in a complementary way we can begin with definitions of leisure and arrive at an understanding of work in that way.

Work and the Purpose of Life

A minimum definition of leisure is in terms of residual time, time not spent working, eating, or sleeping, but considerations of quality supervene on this. Max Kaplan suggests that the main elements of leisure are an antithesis to work as an economic function; a minimum of involuntary social role obligations; a psychological perception of freedom; and activities often characterised by play.[62] If we use this to define work then this would give us economic activity in the context of necessity—what we have to do to earn our bread—but this will not entirely do. We need to distinguish, in the first instance, as we have seen throughout, between work and toil, or work and labour, in Hannah Arendt's terms. When P. D. Anthony talks of work as something "we would all avoid if we were not compelled to it," it is toil he is talking about. The same goes for Studs Terkel's equation of work and violence and the conclusion that "work, for most people, has always been ugly, crippling, and dangerous."[63] Both capitalism and Stalinist communism developed ideologies designed to persuade the worker that work in this sense was noble.[64] We have to beware both of middle-class romanticisation of labour of the type we have seen in Carlyle and of a pseudo Marxist glorification of labour as such. This by no means implies that we should minimise the importance of work. Rather, we have to *redefine* it, and a story of Charles Handy's helps us to do this. He tells of the girl who, in reply to the question, "What do you do?" said that she wrote plays. None of them was actually published, and she earned her living by packing eggs, but the one was work and the other a distraction. This suggests a common understanding of work as that activity in which I find meaning and purpose in my life, quite apart from the expectations of the work ethic. It is not simply that people have been conditioned to find purpose in work, but rather that humans live by purpose; it is the framework of their lives. Thus work is not a moral duty and idleness a shirking of that duty. This is a serious distortion. The law is the form of the gospel: *the life-giving side of work is that it structures meaning and purpose for us*. Absence of purpose is anomie and nihilism, and is not ultimately sustainable. The middle-class dream of back-breaking work down at the farm is, says Anthony, "a search for purpose, to recreate meaning in life by repairing the link between work, use and survival, work and life."[65]

It was in this sense that Marx spoke of labour as "the very touchstone for man's self-realization, the medium of creating the world of his desire." In Hegelian terms he saw work as "objectification of the subject," a liberating activity which potentially gave us real freedom.[66] This is partly because human beings are *homo faber*, makers. Toil is not absent from work, but it is redeemed by hope, as William Morris said. But again, *making* must be defined rather widely. There is an important distinction between pleasure and satisfaction, and purpose finds its fulfillment in both. Anthony instances people who find pride and satisfaction in cleaning boilers or working as waiters. Moreover, the arduousness of toil can sometimes add to the sense that a job is worthwhile.[67] The question of what we do with our *time* is fundamental to this, as the Puritan divines rightly saw. *Our project, what we do in our allotted span to make sense of our lives, is our work.* Implicit in this definition is a distinction between autonomous work, which we do under our own volition, and heteronomous work, imposed on us from above. We can only give shape to our life project *in freedom*. In this respect work dictated by need, as for instance in a subsistence economy, is very different from work over which we have no control.[68]

Thus understood, work provides us with the sense of purpose without which there can be no ethics. Just as the alienation of work has played a large part in the disintegration of any ethical sense, so a new understanding of work, as whatever it is we do in which we find meaning and purpose, is essential to the recapturing of virtue.[69] In relation to the work of women it is significant that a recent study found that two-thirds of the women interviewed found meaning and purpose in motherhood.[70] The percentage might have been even higher had parenting been something that both partners shared equally.

Purpose is fundamental, and yet play also involves purpose, often of a very serious order, as children's play reveals. If we think of Marx's list of activities, fishing can be either work or play. The difference between the two is not so much economic as the willed suspension of normality in play. In play we will to enter another world; we willingly suspend not disbelief but belief for a time.

If these considerations are anywhere near correct, we can understand why unemployment is so difficult for people to cope with. It is not just that people are deprived of a living wage or of status in a work-oriented society. Rather, they are robbed of a sense of *purpose*, and welfare measures which pay benefits "until you find a job" underline this. Having work (a project) and doing a job must not be identified as they are in some doctrines of vocation. The doctrine that it is through our work that we serve God, or that God provides for our needs through our calling, lays burdens which cannot be borne on the unemployed. If full employment in the sense of a paid job has gone forever, then the need to understand work in terms of our life project is stronger still.

True Work

We have seen that necessity is part of work (Gorz calls it the "heteronomous" aspect of work) and this is perfectly clear in relation, say, to housework or agriculture. If we are to include it in a definition of work, however, we need to broaden our understanding of it. True, Mozart had to write symphonies to live, but even had he had the best pension in Europe he could not have done otherwise than write music. Work may often express inner rather than external necessities, the drive of the imagination. It is this, according to Marx, which distinguishes human from animal labour. "What distinguishes the worst architect from the best of bees is this, that the architect raises its structure in imagination before he erects it in reality. At the end of every labour process, we get a result that already existed in the imagination of the labourer at its commencement."[71]

In an attempt at a theology of work Barth proposed four fundamental criteria. Work had to be *true work*, done to the best of our ability, and doing justice to the task in hand. It had to be *honest work*, a criterion which looked back to the discipline of the early church which forbade a whole variety of trades, including military service and teaching in school. These two criteria resemble those of the work ethic, and yet it would be odd to think of not doing our project to the best of our ability.[72] Again, there are obvious questions about work in armaments factories or in military research establishments, as well as many kinds of research directed not to enhancing life but destroying it. In addition there is the *periergazesthai* of Paul, work which is not criminal but intrinsically superfluous or useless. Third, a criterion which Marx also insisted on, human work ought to be *cooperative work*, serving the whole community. Again we have to be careful in the way this is stated. "The practice of service is the heart of Christian morality," writes Ryken. But such appeals have been pressed into the creation of dutiful servants or factory hands. Rather, Christianity understands society as a body in which there is profound mutual responsibility and where honour is given to the most despised part. In terms of our ethical framework, true work is done face to face. Finally, recalling the role of imagination in work, work must be *reflective*. If people are to work aright, they must "primarily work within and on themselves, in order that on this basis they may meaningfully approach the intellectual and material things of the external world." It is this criterion which enables us to make sense of the work of the sick and disabled. "Sickness, and in many cases age, do not mean dismissal or banishment from the field of work, but transfer to its other side, where it is no longer possible to work externally apart from dallying over trifles, but instead the inward work of reflection can be pursued the more intensively."[73]

Perhaps these criteria enable us to respond to Mary Mellor's doubts about James Roberton's SHE (sane, humane, ecological) society. She distinguishes between a ME world and a WE world, the former a male self-seeking world, the latter a feminine cooperative one. The idea of a *freely chosen* sharing of work buys in to the paradigms of the former. On the other hand, other feminists consistently note a need for space and autonomy, classically expressed by Virginia Woolf in *A Room of One's Own*. The question is whether we can have true cooperation *without* a measure of autonomy. Is this not about the possibility of creativity and reflection, rather than *necessarily* about aggressive individualism?

True Leisure

The Christian tradition has always contained a certain suspicion of leisure, and we find admonitions against idleness throughout Christian history. Tertullian's main reason for condemning pagan shows was on the grounds that they were bound up with idolatry, but a certain measure of suspicion of pleasure in itself creeps in. Pleasure, he thinks, is a kind of lust which provokes rivalry; and where you have rivalry "you have rage, bitterness, wrath and grief, with all bad things which flow from them, the whole out of keeping with the religion of Christ."[74] He could be talking about football or any other contemporary spectator sport.[75]

Just as there can be true work so can there be true leisure. Clarke and Critcher have demonstrated the way in which capitalism has taken over the leisure industry and through advertising is able to mould people's expectations of what they really want.[76] They are critical of middle-class definitions of worthwhile leisure, and yet leisure, like work, must deal with humanisation. True and honest leisure serves my and my neighbours' humanity, and it can only do this by putting me in touch with the depth of myself. There is accordingly a difference between three hours on a "one-armed bandit" and three hours practising the recorder, three hours at the races and three hours playing football, three hours reading and three hours simply acquiring a suntan. These distinctions do not arise solely from middle-class prejudice. It is not a question of denying cakes and ale in the name of virtue but of recognising that we cannot take our humanity for granted and that there are things we can do which will damage it. True leisure is a form of play, as Huizinga understands it. Play, according to Huizinga is voluntary, an exercise of freedom, disinterested in the sense that it is satisfying in itself, and includes fun and the use of the imagination though not to the exclusion of seriousness.[77] True leisure is not utilitarian. Understood, as some of the Puritan divines understood it, as the necessary means of recharging our batteries to get back to work, as Sunday worship is sometimes understood, it ceases to be leisure. It is true that work without the context of leisure loses creativity. Nevertheless, leisure is not *for* this, any more than human love is *for* our health and well being. It is an end in itself, an indispensable part of the self-realization of the human project (which includes the corporate realization of culture). Thus the question whether we work in order to play or vice versa is irrelevant. At the great Jewish festivals one of the *megilloth* or small books was always read as well as texts from the Torah. At the Passover the book which was read was the Song of Songs. The purpose of revolution, of the exodus from bondage, is the celebration of love for which we need leisure. All of this is subverted, however, if, as Postman has argued, our leisure simply increases our bondage. Like Huxley he sees Western civilization caught in a race between education and disaster. What afflicts people in the "brave new world" of instant communications is not that they are laughing instead of thinking, but that they do not know what they are laughing about and why they have stopped thinking.

Both work and leisure, properly understood, are about human realisation. It is doubtless true, as Gorz argues, that there will always be intrinsically alienating work to do, but the possibility of both minimising and sharing this is now really on the horizon. At this point, therefore, as both Gorz and Handy emphasize, from very different points of the political spectrum, two ways are set before us. In the Western world, at least, great reductions in the working week could be effected and people could be freed for all sorts of humanising activity.[78] This would be the choice of life. Instead, the number of workers in employment are cut, and the numbers of unemployed rise. Numerous studies have established the connections between unemployment and deteriorating physical and mental health, showing therefore that unemployment is a structure of death. Gorz finds the reason for this choice in the fact that the freeing of time constitutes a threat to the established order. If the ethic of performance collapses, then the values and imperatives of management are challenged. Wage earners would then have to be treated as autonomous individuals, their cooperation requested rather than obedience demanded.[79] Clarke and Critcher likewise take a pessimistic view of the future, envisaging the creation of permanent structural unemployment. "For visions of the future we should look not to dual career families, communes of craft workers, or the autonomous leisure seeking professional, but to the streets of the inner cities and the picket lines of our major industrial conflicts."[80] What determine these decisions are not any iron laws of economics but the desire of those who have power and affluence to hang on to it at all costs. This will become clearer in the examination of ideology in the next chapter.

6

Ideology and Alienation

And the young men who had grown up with him said to him, "Thus shall you speak to this people . . . My father chastised you with whips, but I will chastise you with scorpions."

— 1 Kings 12

The word *manage* comes into English from the Italian *maneggiare*, to handle or train horses, to cause them to do the exercises of the *manege*.[1] It was first extended to operations of war where it had the sense of taking control, taking charge, and directing. This sense is continued in contemporary views of management. Management is about control, getting things done through people. Reviewing the principal twentieth-century views of management Michael Fores ingenuously remarks that management was known well before the Industrial Revolution: "It is inconceivable that the slave labour and the devices used for obtaining and moving huge masses of rock in the construction of pyramids were not 'controlled' in some way that is akin to the way that that topic is covered in current management text books."[2] It is scarcely surprising that a system of control produces ethical problems.

If we wanted evidence for Alasdair MacIntyre's thesis that we now live "after virtue," in a state where there are no longer any cogent moral appeals, we need go no further than Antony Jay's immensely successful *Management and Machiavelli*. It is difficult to know whether to be shocked at the cheerful amoralism of the argument or glad that a minor priest of Mammon should, without any inhibitions, blab out the secret of the inner sanctuary. What we find there, as we might expect, is an image of power.

Jay's argument, compelling to management trainees throughout the world, rests on an analogy between the State and the corporation. The science of management is a continuation of the art of government. "Corporations and states are essentially the same organism" and both need to be studied through political history. The true predecessors of modern managers are the kings and princes of medieval Europe. Top managers seek power both for the exhilaration of it and because it gives them freedom to

79

control their environment which, since giant corporations have bigger annual revenues than many governments, may well be a world environment.[3] The conflict of corporations, like that between States, is impelled by greed, fear, and pride, self-interest, opportunism, and a desire for security. The creative manager is marked by egotism, vanity, selfishness, desire for recognition, and speed at taking offence. Machiavelli's *The Prince* is recommended as a work of extreme realism which may be confidently studied by those interested in management. It is essentially about leadership and the only legitimate criterion by which to assess this is success. We must turn away from the fruitless quest to discern whether the ultimate purpose and effects of management are moral. "The only helpful way to examine organisations and their management is as something neither moral nor immoral, but simply a phenomenon; not to look for proof that industry is honourable or dishonourable, but only for patterns of success and failure, growth and decay, strife and harmony, and for the forces which produce them."[4] Jay's theology is interesting; it is polytheistic. The creative leader is cut out for the role of supreme being, but since we do not yet have one world corporation there must presumably be several of these beings. "Some corporations are too vast: but there is no reason why the head of Cadillac should not be put over to the Cadillac division as their divinity, rather than the President of General Motors. The priests of Apollo do not deny the divinity of Zeus."[5] The conversation of the board of directors is appropriately compared to Milton's account of the meeting of devils, with "Satan himself an example to all Chairmen." "The interplay between groups of Gods and tracts of the firmament is the essence of theology."[6] Never mind, behind these deities, as Brahman stands behind the Hindu pantheon, stands the high god, Growth, worshipped by all Western nations. The bantering tone of the book should not deceive us: what is revealed here is a counter ethic, a non-ethic, as serious in its own way as the counter ethic of Nazism. If the argument of the first chapter is correct then what Jay is commending is the way of death.

MANAGEMENT AND ALIENATION

As we would expect, an apologist for entrepreneurial management such as Jay pays no attention whatever to the effects of managerial policies. Nevertheless, modern management's agenda has significantly been determined by the problem which Marx discussed, in his early writings, as alienation, a phenomenon which Braverman has argued is actually bound up with the growth of management science. Though the word later tended to drop out of Marx's vocabulary, perhaps owing to his controversy with thinkers he felt worked on too abstract a level, the reality he spoke of is vividly impressed on the pages of *Capital*. He discerned three aspects of alienation. First, the worker is alienated from the *product* of his or her labour. In the old craft system workers made something and sold it as their work. Now the product, which expresses the workers' life, is not theirs. They make it but have no control over it — it is strange to them. It is sold on the market and, as this happens, so capital increases and gains a greater hold over their lives. It is of the first importance to understand this analysis of the surplus value theory of labour as a *moral* one. Marx is talking about life: the time, energy, and imagination of the workers are reified in the product, but it is no longer theirs. Moreover, it is used to oppress and control them. This is the first level of alienation.

Second, the worker is alienated from the *act of production*. Again, under the craft system, or where peasants work for themselves, work is part of a person's life project. No longer. Now labour is a commodity bought and sold on the market. Where peasants or craftsmen are free to take breaks when they want, or to continue in the evening for as long as they want, now comes the factory day. In the section "The Working Day" in *Capital* Marx cites many stories from Factory Inspectors Reports and the Childrens Employment Commission.

> J. Lightbourne: "Am 13 ... We worked last winter till 9 (evening) and the winter before till 10. I used to cry with sore feet every night last winter." G. Apsden: "That boy of mine ... when he was 7 years old I used to carry him on my back to and fro through the snow, and he used to have 16 hours a day ... I have often knelt down to feed him as he stood by the machine, for he could not leave it or stop."

This is not a thing of the past. Compare this plea from women in the Free Trade Zone in Sri Lanka:

> We are being made to work both day and night ... Not a single moment of the day is there for rest, both the machines and the workers.

In other Free Trade zones women work forty-eight hours at a stretch and are fed stimulants to keep them awake.[7] We can see, therefore, why Marx concluded that "the labourer is nothing else, his whole life through, than labour power ... Time for education, for intellectual development, for the fulfilling of social functions, and for social intercourse, for the free play of his bodily or mental activity, even the rest time of Sunday ... moonshine!"[8]

Thirdly, Marx saw from reports like this that the worker was alienated from his or her fellow human beings. Industrial capitalism destroyed communities, turned people into stations on a conveyor belt, a simple appendage of a machine, and made them competitors for scarce jobs.

At the heart of this diagnosis are the problems of the division of labour and of the *subordination which goes with it*. It was the division of labour which Smith eulogised as responsible for the "great increase in the quantity of work." He instanced a pin factory:

> One man draws out the wire, another straightens it, a third cuts it, a fourth points it, a fifth grinds it at the top for receiving the head ... the important business of making a pin is, in this manner, divided into about eighteen distinct operations.[9]

Intent only on production Smith failed to observe what this did to the worker, as Ruskin pointed out:

> We have much studied and perfected of late, the great civilised invention of the division of labour; only we give it a false name. It is not, truly speaking, the labour that is divided; but the men: divided into mere segments of men—broken into small fragments and crumbs of life; so that all the little piece of intelligence that is left in a man is not enough to make a pin, or a nail, but exhausts itself in making the point of a pin or the head of a nail. Now it is a good and desirable thing, truly, to make many pins in a day; but if we could only see with what crystal sand their points were polished—sand of human soul, much to be magnified before it can be discerned for what it is—we should think there might be some loss in it also. And the great cry that rises from all our manufacturing cities, louder than the furnace blast, is all in very deed for this—that we manufacture everything there except men.[10]

Braverman's study of "the degradation of work in the twentieth century" centres on the fact that the division of labour has divorced mental from physical work, has turned the worker into Aristotle's "animated instrument." Taylor's *Principles of Scientific Management*, the first management textbook, published in 1911, was designed precisely to do this. As the title indicates, the book was an attempt to apply the methods of science to the problem of the control of labour. Managers were conceived as specialists who were needed to analyse operations. The duty of the manager is to develop a science for each person's work which would replace the old rule of thumb method. It is the manager's job to hire the right person for each job and ensure adequate training. If this is done the enterprise will run smoothly. To ensure this Taylor enunciated three principles. The first was that managers should gather all the traditional knowledge of workmen and reduce it to rules, laws, and formulae. Second, "all possible brain work should be removed from the shop and centred in the planning or laying-out department." The third principle was to replace the skill of a trade with a task specified by management. "Perhaps the most prominent single element in modern scientific management is the task idea. The work of every workman is fully planned out by the management at least one day in advance, and each man receives in most cases complete written instructions, describing in detail the task which he is to accomplish, as well as the means to be used in doing the work ... The task specifies not only what is to be done, but how it is to be done and the exact time allowed for doing it."[11]

Braverman's comment on this system echoes Ruskin's:

> Thus, after a million years of labour, during which humans created not only a complex social culture but in a very real sense created themselves as well, the very cultural-biological trait upon which this entire evolution is founded has been brought, within the last two hundred years, to a crisis, a crisis which Marcuse aptly calls the threat of a "catastrophe of the human essence." The unity of thought and action, conception and execution, hand and mind, which capitalism threatened from its beginnings, is now attacked by a systematic dissolution employing all the resources of science and the various engineering disciplines based upon it. The subjective factor of the labour process is removed to a place among its inanimate objective factors. To the materials and instruments of production are added a "labour force," another "factor of production," and the process is henceforth carried on by management as the sole subjective element.[12]

Management science did not stop with Taylor. Five years after Taylor the French engineer Fayol published his *General and Industrial Management*. For him there are five elements of management, all of which have discernible military overtones: organization, command, coordination, control, and planning. Military analogies continue to be important, although not all management analysts agree with Fayol's type of analysis. The elements he draws attention to, it is pointed out, can be found in all human activity, and, further, the scheme ignores the unpredictability of human response. An article in *Management Today* argued that rather than trying to reduce uncertainty, management should tolerate it. "Management is improvisation, not application of tried and trusted methods."[13] Nevertheless, Braverman judges that "Taylorism dominates the world of production; the practitioners of 'human relations' and 'industrial psychology' are the maintenance crew for the human machinery. If Taylorism does not exist as a separate school today, that is because, apart from the bad odour of the name, it is no longer the property of a faction, since its fundamental teachings have become the bedrock of all work design."[14]

Correlative to this is the problem of subordination. In alienated labour a person "creates the domination of the man who does not produce over the production and the product. As he alienates his activity from himself so he hands over to an alien person an activity that does not belong to him."[15] Taylor was absolutely clear about this. He tells the story of how he increased production at a steel factory by exploiting a labourer of low intelligence. Recalling their conversation he comments: "This seems to be rather rough talk. And indeed it would be if applied to an educated mechanic, or even an intelligent labourer. With a man of the mentally sluggish type of Schmidt it is appropriate and not unkind, since it is effective in fixing his attention on the high wages which he wants and away from what, if it were called to his attention, he probably would consider impossibly hard work."[16] Braverman cites a study entitled "Industrialism and Industrial Man" which claims that in any industrial society "one of the central traits is the inevitable and eternal separation of industrial men into managers and the managed." Thus the antagonistic relations of present modes of production are sanctified in quasi religious language.[17] Dealing with these antagonisms is the central problem of *management*.

A third aspect which gives rise to alienation is rationalisation. The rationalistic approach to management was most fully theoretised by Weber who was, of course, clear that power was the issue. He distinguished between traditional, charismatic, and rational legal authority. While early industrialists like Watt and Arkwright exercised charismatic authority, management is chiefly concerned with the rational legal type.[18] The distinctive mark of capitalism for Weber is not wage labour but the introduction of modern methods of bookkeeping. Essential marks of capitalism are "the rational permanent enterprise, rational accounting, rational technology and rational law ... Necessary complementary factors were the rational spirit, the rationalization of the conduct of life in general, and a rationalistic economic ethic."[19] Weber saw that this development meant the end of ethics. "The more the world of the modern capitalist economy follows its own immanent laws," he wrote, "the less accessible it is to any imaginable relationship with a religious ethic of brotherliness. The more rational, and thus impersonal, capitalism becomes, the more is this the case. In the past it was possible to regulate ethically the personal relations between master and slave precisely because they were personal relations. But it is not possible to regulate ... the relations between the shifting holders of mortgages and the shifting debtors of the banks that issue these mortgages: for in this case, no personal bonds of any sort exist."[20] He also understood this kind of authority as a structure of domination. In *The Managerial Revolution* Burnham used Weber's theories to understand management. The main defining features of bureaucracy are explicit goals, a hierarchical authority structure, and substitutability of personnel. These emphasize clear specifications of tasks and of positions in the hierarchy, unified control, and disciplinary procedures, and also the possession of formal qualifications, formal career and salary structure, and promotion on the basis of merit or seniority. The management theory which derives from this "rational" enterprise is that of analysing all possible problems, costing out each possible alternative, and making decisions accordingly. There are many difficulties with this approach. Transnational corporations work across many different cultures, but cultures differ widely in their views of rationality. Work and management patterns are significantly culture relative. Secondly, while rationality is certainly to be valued, rational*ism* led, in Weber's terms, to disenchantment and lovelessness (or, in Marx's term, alienation). As the basis of a theory of management Fores points out that it is flawed because it rests on an impossible assimilation of people to machines. So R. G. Collingwood commented that "the extent to which people act with a clear idea of their ends, knowing what effects they are aiming at, is easily exaggerated. Most human action is tentative, experimental, directed not by a knowledge of what it will lead to but rather a desire to know what will come of it."[21] Moreover, Anthony finds management ideology to be characterised by its refusal to discuss ends: these are taken for granted. Only methods can be discussed. This means, again, that the fundamental ethical questions are forespoken.

Alasdair MacIntyre has also understood managerial ideology to be near the centre of the present collapse in ethical discourse. Because it entails the obliteration of any distinction between manipulative and nonmanipulative social relations managerialism is bound to emotivism, the doctrine that moral judgements are nothing but expressions of preference or feeling. Weber, says MacIntyre, is an emotivist, for he believes that conflict between rival values cannot be rationally settled. The only type of authority that can justify itself is bureaucratic authority which appeals to effectiveness. The character of the manager, who embodies this authority, MacIntyre finds to be one of the central moral representatives of twentieth-century Western society. Along with the rich aesthete and the therapist, the managerial character is a social role which provides Western culture with its moral definitions. All share the emotivist view of the distinction between rational and nonrational discourse. The emotivist makes a key distinction between fact and value. In the latter there are no rational ways of settling disagreements. This gives us a society where bureaucracy and individualism are partners, the individual's sovereignty limited only by bureaucracy. In fact, MacIntyre argues, effectiveness is not a morally neutral value. It is inseparable from a mode of human existence in which the contrivance of means is the manipulation of people into compliant patterns of behaviour. The existence of managerial expertise he considers to be a moral fiction because there are in fact no law-like generalizations available for the social sciences, and managerial science therefore has no real predictive power. To the extent that morality is identified with effectiveness, that morality is a theatre of illusions. MacIntyre concludes, "the social world of everyday hard-headed practical pragmatic no-nonsense realism which is the environment of management is one which depends for its sustained existence on the systematic perpetuation of misunderstanding and of belief in fictions. The fetishism of commodities has been supplemented by another just as important fetishism, that of bureaucratic skills."[22] The myth of managerial expertise and the findings of experts simply disguises the tyranny of arbitrary private preference.

MANAGEMENT AND IDEOLOGY

The problems addressed by managers are part and parcel of any industrial society. Large-scale industry needs labour power — it has to persuade people to do intrinsically alienating work willingly. The first way of doing this is obviously financial incentive, but this is often insufficient to encourage work of sufficient energy and intensity. In the nineteenth century the appeal was above all to religion, and the sense of duty to firm and country, and these appeals are by no means dead. Potentially successful strikes are always met with complaints that they are unpatriotic. The Protestant work ethic may have died of cynicism, but it has been replaced by Jay-type polytheism. A study of thirty-seven successful companies found that management promoted clearly articulated values "with an almost religious zeal." Jay notes the resemblances between successful corporations and religious sects. "Some corporations are extremely religious. They hold regular revivalist meetings at which rousing hymns are sung to the glory of the corporation and its products, and salesmen are encouraged to stand up and give passionate personal testimony about why they believe ... Corporations which would never go to the extremes of hymnsinging and emotional personal testimony may yet contain much stronger religious feelings and observances than is apparent from outside."[23] Capitalism can use coercion through the law by political lobbying, as it did in Britain in relation to the Factory Acts in the nineteenth century, and more recently in imposing restrictive legislation on Trades Unions. Jon Clarke notes that employers receive strong backing from the law in the area of job content and work organization. In Britain judge-made common law of contract "obliges employees, among other things, 'to be ready and willing to work', 'to obey orders,' and 'to observe fidelity towards the employer's interests.' " The individual contract of employment is, in the words of a leading labour lawyer, "a command under the guise of an agreement."[24] Another sanction is the pressure of scarce jobs created by the "industrial reserve army" of the unemployed newly resurrected by monetarist policies. None of these policies is fully adequate, however, and this failure gives rise to management ideology. Nevertheless, this too has been found to fail, and so the psychologists and social scientists have been wheeled in. Two strategies are advanced: psychological strategies directed at re-educating individuals so that they get the satisfaction out of work they are supposed to, and sociological strategies which understand the balance of power in industry differently. As examples of the psychological approach we may look at the work of Argyris and of Blake and Mouton. Argyris argued that conflict in industry continued because the worker did not receive enough psychological success and self-esteem from the job.[25] His favoured way of achieving this is through mutually shared control, though the procedure for firing someone sounds like something out of *Animal Farm*.[26] Altogether more sinister is the "education" of employees proposed by Blake and Mouton, in which the exercise of group dynamics help people adjust to their situation and think through the concept of profit, whose legitimacy is not otherwise obvious.[27] These authors regret that "the integration of people into the organization through more effective supervision has not as yet been as fully realized as it might have been." While this is the case, in their view, we have reluctantly to concede the existence of unions, even though this is only one better than sabotage. Similarly bemoaning the inadequacy of prediction and control of human behaviour, McGregor lists social problems resulting from it such as "juvenile delinquency, crime, the high traffic fatality rate, management labour conflict, the cold war"(!)[28]

Management theories characteristically appeal to different understandings of human nature, giving rise to confrontational or consensual management patterns.[29] In the article just cited D. McGregor distinguishes two views of human nature which he calls Theory X and Theory Y. Under Theory X managers assumed that:

1. Employees inherently dislike work and, whenever possible, will avoid it.
2. Since this is the case they must be coerced, controlled, or threatened with punishment to achieve management's goals.
3. Employees will shirk responsibilities and seek formal direction wherever possible.
4. Most workers place job security above all other factors associated with work, and will display little ambition.

Reviewing industrial conflict in America in the early 1950s Harbison confirmed this picture. He noted that "the industrial worker for the most part works harder than he likes at tasks which are frequently arduous, usually monotonous, and sometimes dangerous. On the job he is nearly always subject to the direction of higher authority. His income is seldom sufficient to cover what he thinks his needs demand. The natural state of the worker is therefore one of discontent."[30] This reflects the understanding of work as toil, the idea that people do not really *live* while at work, which we saw earlier. Some sociologists, whose work has been taken over by management theorists, suggest that conflict is not a bad thing, and that it simply needs to be channeled. Dahrendorff argued that conflict contributes to stability and can be institutionalized so that it acts as a social dynamic.[31] What Dahrendorf is concerned to see ended is "guerilla warfare." He does not recognise that this may be the only form of warfare possible for some groups.

The alternative theory assumes that

1. Employees can view work as being as natural as rest and play (cf. Andrew Ure's "lively elves").
2. People will exercise self-direction and self-control if they are committed

to the objectives laid down for the company (employee participation in decision-making will lead to commitment to decisions).
3. The average person can learn to accept, even to seek, responsibility.
4. Creativity in decision-making is dispersed throughout the population and is not necessarily the sole possession of those in management positions.

Studies of Japanese management have shown that their good results resulted from adopting the second theory, and from the fact that social snobbery scarcely existed in their society. There are no separate canteens for staff and management, and the distinction between office and shop floor is not observed. In the Japanese Trust Circle the managers, dressed like workers, sit with workers for a certain period each week to discuss work and objectives and to take suggestions. This is the principle McGregor takes from Theory Y: "The creation of conditions such that the members of the organisation can achieve their own goals best by directing their efforts towards the success of the enterprise."[32] There is a distinction, however, between psychological and objective participation. The former is the extent of influence persons think they have on a decision; the latter is what they actually have. This may be achieved by a distinction between ends and means, so that, to take Anthony's example, a typist can decide on her carpet but not on the intensity of effort required of her. Of the many disagreeable aspects of this whole process identified by Anthony one of the worst is the way in which norms are identified with management objectives so that even the individual's definition of sanity is defined by "positive" attitudes to work and the organization.

Part of the function of consensus theories of management is to provide a more legitimate basis for authority in industry. The old appeal was to ownership, but this cannot automatically be assumed where the bosses are managers. Burnham argued that managers are the directors and coordinators of the process of production, distinct from owners, and that they are the ones who effectively control society.[33] Wright Mills replied, however, that in contemporary business there is no real separation of control and ownership. Managers are usually large shareholders, they are recruited predominantly from the upper strata of society, and they form a single social group with the owners of property. In this sense they are part of the ruling class.[34] Even if the managers continue to be owners, however, it can still be seen to be an advantage that the employer has gone. If Western business management is to succeed, says Anthony, first, the boss must be buried, but second the consent of the subordinate must be obtained by claiming the establishment of industrial democracy. It can then be maintained that the old picture of two completely opposed sides, one exploiting and the other exploited, is over. After the managerial revolution "we are all workers now." This legitimates an appeal to common interest: we sink or swim together. A final appeal is to management expertise, which the workers lack. The speciousness of these appeals can be seen in the evolution of the role of personnel management. Personnel managers began as welfare officers but were forced by the logic of the need for efficiency and profit to become control engineers. The personnel manager's role is now defined as discovering how people's efforts can be organised and developed to attain the highest levels of efficiency, adaptability, and productivity drawing on the techniques of psychological manipulation we have already reviewed.

These are all ways of integrating the alienated worker within the assumptions of liberal democracy. The question of how to achieve effective industrial output is also addressed in different ways by Democratic Socialism, Fascism, and Communism. Fascism solved the problem by a reversion to slave labour, but both Socialism and Communism reverted to managerialism. In the United States and in Europe a hierarchical and managerial model was adopted. Stalinism, on the other hand, was bureaucratic managerialism at its worst. Because the State is involved in the management process the problem of legitimating managerial authority is easier but the same mix of coercion, incentive, and moral exhortation is needed as in the West. The incentive was less, propaganda less subtle, and coercion far worse, but in terms of a truly different vision of organising labour nothing was really on offer. The critique of managerialism is not, therefore, a playing off of one system against another (which can be said to have failed). *Mutatis mutandis* the same questions arise for both.

The two fundamental ethical questions about this process both relate to the question of power in society and highlight the ethical significance of human equality. It should be no surprise that firms incorporating egalitarian principles often work better than ones that do not. A comparative study of British and Japanese factories found the egalitarian ethos of the latter to be a major component of their success.[35] Mintzberg characterised one type of organization as "adhocracy." Firms like this do not make sharp distinctions between line and staff, there are few formal procedures, and there is little emphasis on planning and control. Decisions are decentralized and made in a democratic atmosphere.[36] Given that leadership is necessary, it can be shared between tasks, and can be supportive or participative rather than directive. In the face of this evidence it is clear that the rejection of joint decision-making is about hanging on to power.[37] The question here, then, is about what kind of society we are ultimately committed to, and this reflects our fundamental beliefs about the human. Once again, policies which realise equality prove essential to the recovery of virtue.

Another set of questions arise with respect to the relation of big business to the State. Rather than the State controlling big business, the prospect is now rather of big business controlling the State. Multinational companies increasingly dictate the economic, and therefore the political, agenda. They do this partly by acting as political lobby groups; they have specialized government relations department whose function is to maintain regular contacts with politicians and civil servants.[38] The debate about sovereignty in the E.E.C. is a good example of the way in which national boundaries need to be dismantled to make way for market development. As long ago as 1941 Burnham prophesied that the big corporation threatened democracy, and the conclusion that their claim for loyalty transcends that of the national state is made explicit by Jay. Citing the head of a U.S. chemical corporation, who thinks of the corporation essentially internationally, he comments that the divergence between corporation and government is likely to grow ever wider and the government cannot go on winning the loyalty tug of war forever. "One day soon what's good for General Motors may be great for West Germany and South Africa but lousy for America."[39] This has been the experience of many third-world countries for many decades. Policy is put into the hands of non-elected power groups whose only responsibility is to produce profits for shareholders. The prospect of growing internationalism could be encouraging, but the question is, what values underlie it. Both State and politics, Anthony argues, come to be invested by managerial assumptions and values, and government is measured by managerial criteria rather than by criteria of justice. Managerial ideology aims at achieving large-scale changes in society in order to facilitate business objectives. "Managers . . . are encouraged to treat society by reference to managerial concepts which may be quite inadequate for promoting social changes which the application of those very concepts demand."[40] Business leaders become dominant models in our society, and their achievements and values become a type of the excellent. Managerial aims of economic rationality, economic growth, and technological progress are the only "values" on offer.[41] The ideology of management, therefore, plays a central part both in the subversion of democracy and in the present collapse of ethical discourse. Those engaged in that education of desire whose goal is the recovery of virtue have at this point an urgent task of demythologisation ahead of them.

Is there truly no alternative to a society of managers and the managed? Braverman notes that people accuse him of being nostalgic for an age that cannot be recaptured. Rather, he says, "my views about work are governed by nostalgia for an age that has not yet come into being, in which, for the worker, the craft satisfaction that arises from conscious and purposeful mastery of the labour process will be combined with the marvels of science and the ingenuity of engineering, an age in which everyone will be able to benefit, in some degree, from this combination."[42] Since he wrote, we have more reason to be skeptical about some of these marvels and some of this ingenuity, but it is a society where staff and line are things of the past, and all of the Lord's people are prophets, including women, which has the potential to be truly life-giving. There is no more need to take current management ideology for granted than there is to accept the iron laws of economics: both are creations of men, which is to say male creations, to justify power. The recovery of moral discourse which is part and parcel of the creation of a new human community must also involve this restructuring of the process of work. For this to happen an alternative vision needs to be kindled, for "where there is no vision the people perish" (Prv 29:18). It is this which is the concern of the new Deuteronomists.

7

Solidarity and Resistance

If the sum of improvements should become vast and deep reaching enough to give to the useful or working classes intelligence enough to conceive of a life of equality and cooperation; courage enough to accept it and to bring the necessary skill to bear on working it; and power enough to force its acceptance on the stupid and the interested, the war of classes would speedily end in the victory of the useful class, which would then become the new society of Equality.

— William Morris

One of the key discoveries which made the Industrial Revolution possible was that work was done much more efficiently if people were gathered together from the cottages in which they lived and set to work together under one roof. This was the origin of the factory system, and we have seen in the discussions of work and management accounts of the exploitation to which it gave rise. From the very first it generated collective action on the part of employees. Trade unions were born in a fight for survival. As early as 1718 in the first industrialising country, Britain, a Royal Proclamation was issued against

> lawless clubs and societies which had illegally presumed to use a common seal, and to act as Bodies Corporate, by making and unlawfully conspiring to execute certain By-laws or Orders, whereby they pretend to determine who had right to the Trade, what and how many Apprentices and Journeyman each man should keep at once, together with the prices of all their manufactures, and the manner and materials of which they should be wrought.[1]

In the course of the next two hundred years these combinations won very significant improvements in conditions for working people, in the teeth of ferocious resistance from government, industry, and the judiciary. The history of how, from the 1940s on, in both Europe and the United States, this movement was in many ways tamed and domesticated, has been told

91

with exemplary power and clarity by Kim Moody, writing of the United States, and by Ken Coates, Richard Hyman, and others in Britain.[2] The original purposes and ideals of unions have not been entirely lost, however. In some cases, as Moody argues for the United States, ideals have been re-found through the bitter struggles of the past decade, but more important is the emergence, throughout the world, of a plethora of people's organi-sations, women's groups, action groups, slum dwellers groups, civil liberty groups, which carry the torch lit by those early pioneers of eighteenth-century Britain. Formally organised trade unions remain an important part of such people's groups, but it is doubtful whether they constitute more than a tiny part of it world wide. As examples I take thumbnail sketches of five such movements from different parts of the world, engaged in dif-ferent kinds of struggle.

There is little doubt that the greatest force for change in the past twenty years has been the women's movement. Within unions and all the other groups mentioned it is women who have developed the most radical per-spectives on change. We can begin with women in one of the Free Trade Zones already mentioned, in Sri Lanka. Here independence found trade unions already established, but sectionally organised and male dominated. The result was that "after nearly 50 years of working long hours and car-rying the triple burden of being a woman, worker, and Indian Tamil, a plantation female labourer earns less than her male companion who works fewer hours in less arduous forms of work." In this situation women, often from church groups, are organising women workers to meet, discuss, and plan action. Organisers are subject to constant police harassment, ques-tioning, false rumours, and intimidation, but "the future prospects are not bleak. We realise there are women who are willing to take risks—even at the expense of their jobs. And this gives us courage to go on. The number of women participating in different ways increases daily, and this is very positive."[3]

In Guatemala, scene of a particularly repressive civil war waged by the rich against the poor, and especially indigenous peoples, more than one hundred union, peasant, and other organisations linked together to form the National Committee of Trade Union Community. This supports labour groups undergoing police repression, and also embraces women's groups struggling for women's rights as well as human and civil rights. Here armed struggle has been an option. The participation of Indian women in partic-ular has been less in terms of mass organisation and more through armed opposition.[4]

In Zambia, 1980 saw the creation of the Village Development Founda-tion. Operating in the north of the country, in an area the government has neglected, it aims to promote small-scale cottage industries, to dissuade young people from emigrating, to provide adult education, and to train locals in more efficient food production techniques. It operates among seven villages, total population 12,500, just over half of whom are women.

So far projects have enjoyed a high level of success because people have been involved at every stage and discussed each move together. Where previously initiatives were resisted because they were imposed from above, now they are taken up with enthusiasm.[5]

In Thailand where integration into the world economy has led to large-scale prostitution, action groups have been mobilising to raise public awareness about this trade. They provide shelter, legal aid, and financial assistance to women who want to return home. These groups, run by women, have a very different agenda from government rehabilitation schemes, which function to punish the women who come to them. Ultimately they are concerned with changing attitudes with regard to sexuality based on patriarchal ideology.[6]

Finally we can take the famous Chipko movement from Uttar Pradesh in India. Though there is a long history of women taking action for forests in India, the present phase began in 1972 when people were urged to "embrace" (*chipko*) the trees to save them from being felled. Vandana Shiva tells how determined plans to fell the trees have been thwarted by even greater determination of local villagers, led by women.[7] This movement was not to protect trees as trees, but was a movement by tribal people for control over their local resources.

Anyone who has been involved in these groups knows that success is only gained at the cost of many defeats. The power of organised capital is genuinely awesome. Rape, torture, and murder are common. Stress and bitter ideological division breaks up relationships even within the movements themselves; as with every other part of life different kinds of corruption can destroy initiatives. All this has to be said if we are to avoid a cheap and facile optimism. And yet, there are hundreds of thousands of such groups throughout the world; pressure groups and lobby groups in the North play their part. Through them resistance to the forces of death is carried on. One movement may be concerned with trees, another with water, another with health, another with prostitution, another engaged in armed struggle. In each the experience of collective struggle against the powers that be breeds new perceptions which go far beyond original limited objectives. Sooner or later all the dimensions of race, class, and patriarchal oppression heave into view.

PEOPLE'S MOVEMENTS – DEFENCE OR HARBINGERS OF A NEW WORLD?

In their pioneering *History of Trade Unionism*, written in 1894, Beatrice and Sidney Webb defined a trade union as "a continuous association of wage earners for the purpose of maintaining or improving the conditions of their employment." The definition makes clear the limitations of much union thinking, which was essentially *defensive*. Many unionists insisted that they had no political agenda. Here are the London Compositors writing to their masters in 1786:

> As we disclaim all proceedings militating against justice, or that are subversive of decent and respectful behaviour, we presume that any communication, which the present situation of the business renders necessary to be opened with our employers, will be received in a manner suitable to its importance, and with candour coinciding with its equity.[8]

When in 1925, again in Britain, Churchill raised the spectre of political strikes the leader of the General and Municipal Workers Union replied that their struggle was "wholly and solely . . . in defence of wage standards, indicating a deep sense of responsibility." Similar affirmations were made during the bitter miner's strike of 1984-85.[9] In the United States the period after the Second World War saw the emergence of business unionism, given classic expression in Richard Lester's book *As Unions Mature.* His thesis was that once the giddy days of youth are past we enter adult responsibility marked by recognition of the problems of management. The emphasis in unions switches to administration, negotiation, and contract enforcement. Moody comments,

> Business unionism . . . leaves unquestioned capital's dominance, both on the job and in society as a whole. Instead, it seeks only to negotiate the price of this domination. This it does through the businesslike negotiation of a contractual relationship with a limited sector of capital and for a limited portion of the working class.[10]

The various ways of understanding the purposes of people's organisations reflect different ways of understanding society, described by Jon Clarke in terms of unitary, pluralist, and radical frames of reference, and we shall look at them in turn.[11]

Society as a Unity

Both the oldest and newest way of understanding society is paternalistic and thinks of it as bound together by a common purpose with one focus of allegiance. According to this scheme employees have a duty of loyalty to the firm and the firm has a duty to care for employees. The rhetoric of patriotism can and frequently does apply the same scheme of thinking nationally. Governments appeal to the national interest in their efforts to oppose trade unionism when this is supposed to be inimical to the interests of the majority of the nation's inhabitants. Even so sympathetic a scholar as Phelps Brown, looking back over the 1960s and 1970s, believes that "the exertion of trade union power had been most conspicuous where it was least in the national interest."[12] But what if the national interest is the further aggrandisement of the rich and powerful? And where does the power of transnational corporations fit into this picture?

The unitary scheme is that advocated by Leo XIII in the encyclical we have already had occasion to refer to a number of times, *Rerum Novarum*. On the one hand, he recognised that the "wretched workers" must be saved from the brutality of those "who make use of human beings as mere instruments for the unrestrained acquisition of wealth." On the other hand, the right to strike was not really endorsed. Preferably, "the law should intervene in good time." The church's role is to remind both parties of the duties they owe each other:

> Among the obligations of justice which bind the unpropertied worker are: to fulfil faithfully and completely whatever contract of employment he has freely and justly made; to do no damage to the property nor harm to the persons of his employers; to refrain from the use of force in defence of his interests ... For his part, the rich employer must not treat his workers as though they were his slaves, but must reverence them as men who are his equals in personal dignity.[13]

This unitary or paternalistic scheme has been revived in recent management thinking through the Japanese trust circle or the team approach. Moody describes its effects:

> The "team concept" provides a permanent, institutional change in day-to-day company operations and labour relations ... Its focus is not on wages or benefits per se, but on productivity, the exploitation of the workers' understanding of the production process, and above all the consciousness of the worker.[14]

The goal is to get workers to identify with company goals. Unions in North America, Australia, and Canada are particularly vulnerable to this because it is part of the mythology of their culture that, as opposed to the "old" cultures of Europe, these are classless societies, fully open to opportunity for anyone with the ability. On the other hand, black people within these cultures know the myth to be false. Where alternative groups spring up they do so principally because the claim that society is a unity is seen to be hollow.

Society as Necessarily Conflictual

The second view, represented by Dharendorf and Galbraith, thinks of society as a coalition of different groups with divergent interests who work together through compromise and accommodation. Dahrendorf believes societies which recognise conflict are more stable than those which do not because conflict helps to release tensions and can result in a deeper unity. Trade unions are an important interest group which may promote conflict but, providing such conflict is kept within bounds, may contribute to the common good. He was anticipated by Galbraith's notion of "countervailing power." Under American capitalism, Galbraith argued, unions were one among a number of interest groups. They were legitimate as long as they concentrated on pay and conditions, illegitimate if they went beyond these limits.[15] Such views presupposed the classic division of labour of industrial capitalism between command and file, and implicitly between intellectual and manual skills. Management's job is to plan the production and distribution of goods or supply of services and the role of labour is to watch out for its own interests in terms of work place safety and wage levels.[16] Moody points out that the concept of capitalist class was replaced by that of management in the work of people like Drucker, implying a new world of classless pluralism. The dominance of capital over labour is taken for granted.

Phelps Brown gives expression to this point of view when he writes that peace cannot be the object of industrial relations policy:

> What is to be aimed at is evidently the efficient working of industrial relations as a system with a social function to perform, and this function is to enable parties who in the nature of things have to continue to co-operate, but who retain separate interests, to work out an ongoing adjustment by which neither their common interest in production, nor their separate interests in what they put in and get out, suffer at the expense of the other.[17]

Ethically this amounts to framing Marquis of Queensberry rules for industry. We take a conflict of interests for granted, and we try to see that the fight is as fair as possible. Such views overlook the fact that conflict can only be potentially creative between equals. There can be no genuine move forward in the understanding and the ordering of things in a conflict between the weak and the strong. On the contrary, such a conflict is likely to be bitter and desperate, and the chances of creative resolution are extremely small. Of course it can be objected that unions do not meet management from a position of weakness. Brian Griffiths observes, "As one reads the various strictures of the Old Testament prophets against those who exploit their economic power I cannot help feeling that their major relevance within the UK today is to the trade union movement by the power exercised by elements within it."[18] This rather hysterical rhetoric is belied by the ease with which, in the North, all governments have been able to pass restrictive legislation, while in the South unionists are a special target of the National Security State or, as in India, of assassins hired by big business. The international trades-union movement reports that between January 1990 and March 1991, 264 union leaders were murdered around the world, mostly in Latin America. Apart from this, weakness is inherent in the very position of labour versus employers. Any conflict between the two sides takes place on the capitalist's territory, the work place. All forms of ideology, especially newspapers, are ranged against the unions. Thus we read in the news that excessive wage demands must be resisted in the national interest; strikes reflect the malign influence of "militants" and "extremists" and not the intransigence of management; and a refusal to bow to State pressure is a challenge to law and order and democracy. Where the employer has the security of wealth, labour is a perishable asset; its sellers are often poor and have no alternative means of earning a living or reserve fund. The alternative to a "free" contract is very often poverty. Transnational industries can and do shut up shop and take capital elsewhere. Individual workers can do this, but not the whole labour force, and even then "agitators" can be effectively blacklisted. More than this, the law is firmly on the side of the employer. Phelps Brown quotes the president of the National Graphical Association who told his union conference in 1980: "If we have a bad law, and there have been many in the past and we may be facing more, we have no alternative but to break it." He asks, "By what right does he set the interests of his union above the law?"[19] Faced with a similar question Isaiah of Jerusalem pronounced:

> Woe to the legislators of unjust laws,
>   to those who issue tyrannical decrees,
> who refuse justice to the unfortunate
>   and cheat the poor among my people of their rights.
> (Is 10:1)

Aquinas summarises the mainstream Christian tradition in maintaining that "if the written law contains anything contrary to the natural right, it is unjust and has no binding force ... So too laws that are rightly established, fail in some cases, when if they were observed they would be contrary to the natural right. Wherefore in such cases judgement should be delivered, not according to the letter of the law, but according to equity."[20] When law is an expression of tyranny, *morally* we have to resist it. Union suspicion of the law is only too well founded. Summing up the trial of the Tolpuddle Martyrs the judge commented that if trade unions were allowed to continue "they would ruin masters, cause a stagnation in trade and destroy property."[21] Essentially the same objections are voiced day by day around the world.

Business unionism effectively adopts the second view. It would have surprised the pioneers of the early part of this century, like the North American Joe Hill or the British Tom Mann. In response to an emerging business union attitude Mann wrote:

> It surprises me when I hear "collective bargaining" spoken of as ...
> the "first principle" of trade unionism. You may search the "objects"

of the older unions for this precious "first principle" but you will not find it. The object of trade unionism used to be to uphold the price of labour *against* the encroachments of the employers, not in agreement with them . . . We are under the guns of the enemy. We "make peace" with him because he has us by the throat.[22]

Not Competition but Cooperation

Hill and Mann represented a different strand of unionism which looked to the emergence of a *different kind of society*, in which workers controlled production and determined economic policy rather than being subject to managerial control and the fluctuations of the market. The Rochdale pioneers began the Cooperative movement in 1844 not just to counter the exploitation of factory shops but to establish the possibility of trading otherwise than on a profit basis. It spawned a worldwide cooperative movement which has sought not only to implement just trading policies but to extend popular education and empowerment.[23] The ultimate goal of the third kind of unionism, as of most people's movements in the world today, is to replace competition by cooperation as the rule of societal life, and to ensure that the purpose of production is the satisfaction of human need. In marked contrast to his predecessor, quoted above, John Paul II strongly affirms "the priority of labour over Capital" and, for all his opposition to liberation theology, espouses this form of unionism. Unions, he says, are not just instruments of class struggle but are "a mouthpiece for the struggle for social justice," their concern is "prudent concern for the common good."[24]

In defending competition two appeals are invariably made. It is said that it stimulates invention and production. The assumption is that human beings are naturally competitive, enjoy competition, and that it does them good. The phenomenon of the sports industry seems to confirm this and to imply that competition is indeed the spice of life. The second defence of competition appeals in some ways to an opposite view of human nature. According to this view human beings need incentives, without which they never stretch themselves fully, and a graded system of salaries and rewards provides these. The implication of this need is that people are fundamentally unmotivated and idle and to support this the advances of the capitalist, competitive West are sometimes contrasted with the lack of scientific and political progress of societies where competition was eliminated, for instance through the caste system. A theological ethic must oppose such a view with its own anthropology, rooted in Christology. Christ is first and foremost, in Barth's phrase, "the man for others." From this perspective "every humanity which is not radically and from the very first fellow-humanity is inhumanity."[25] This is not just an affirmation but a denial. What is *denied* is that it is proper for human beings to "stand on their own two feet"—another prominent aspect of competitive ideology. According to Nietzsche, human dignity consists in being independent. The authentic human being for him is the lonely, noble, strong, proud, natural, healthy, wise, outstanding, splendid man. This is opposed by Christian morality, which he also calls "typically socialist teaching," which teaches that the truly human may be both weak and gregarious. Because Christianity proclaims that what hangs on the cross is divine, therefore it is a religion and morality of slaves, of failures, of those who go under. "What I do not like at all about this Jesus of Nazareth and his apostle Paul," Nietzsche writes, "is that they put so many things into the heads of *little* people, as though *their* modest virtues were of some value. The price was too high; for they brought into disrepute the far more valuable qualities of virtue and manhood, opposing a bad conscience to the self-esteem of the excellent soul, and betraying even to destruction the noble, generous, bold, excessive inclinations of the strong."[26] By contrast, Barth maintains, in the light of the Son of Man, through whom we must understand ourselves, an action cannot be truly human if it refuses to ask for help. Cooperation, in other words, is fundamental to our humanity. And thus these propositions of dogmatics bear directly on ethics. "Work under the sign of . . . competition will always imply as such work in the form of a conflict in which one man encounters another with force and with cunning, and there cannot fail to be innumerable prisoners, wounded and dead. Work under this sign will always be an inhuman activity, and therefore an activity which, in spite of every conceivable alleviation or attempt at relief and order, can never stand before the command of God."[27] Herbert McCabe points out that what is wrong with capitalism is that it is based on antagonism, between employers and employees, between capitalists, and therefore between nations, an antagonism which it is the function of pluralist rhetoric to disguise. The break down of ethical consensus in contemporary Western society is in no small measure due to the influence of this concealed antagonism. But this means that Christianity is deeply subversive of capitalism because it announces "the improbable possibility that men might live together without war; neither by domination nor by antagonism but by a unity in love."[28] To the extent that trade unionism represents an attempt to move in the direction of cooperation rather than competition, we have to say that it is more in tune with the drift of God's politics than its opposite. Its failure is when it adopts the standards of the market and opts for a selfish sectionalism, making the maintenance of differentials its chief aim. Unionism in that case has nothing distinctive to offer.[29]

RESISTANCE

In the vivid words of Tom Mann, unions resist because "employers have them by the throat." This description would be familiar to many millions of people today: prostitutes in the sex trade, Latin American workers, black workers, villages at the mercy of corrupt government officials. The classic means of resistance by unionised labour has been the strike, and at the height of union unrest in the North, during the mid-sixties to mid-seventies, Christian ethicists spilled much ink debating its morality.

The word *strike* is a metaphor borrowed from the practice of striking sail and refers, of course, to the withdrawal of labour power by those who have only that to bargain with. Strikes are always a double-edged weapon as they are only effective when inconvenience is caused, but inconvenience arouses antagonism. For conflictual accounts of society they do not, in principle, represent a problem. It is rather like recognising the legitimate rights of a Parliamentary opposition. The determination of governments in the past decade and a half to crush unions and to impose restrictive legislation on the right to strike shows that this conflictual view is not widely shared by those in power. Perhaps part of the reason for this is that many unionists, like Hill and Mann, understood them on a much broader base than merely attempting to improve pay and conditions. Engels saw strikes as "the first attempt of the workers to abolish competition, thereby threatening the existing social order."[30] "Every strike reminds the capitalists that it is workers and not they who are the real masters," wrote Lenin. "Every strike reminds the workers that their position is not hopeless, that they are not alone." Allen Hutt quotes a militant as saying: "The great advantage of a strike is that it increases the enmity between labourers and capitalists, and compels workmen to reflect and investigate the cause of their sufferings. The fruit of such reflection would be violent hostility to the capitalist class."[31] This threatening stance is clearly also the view of government, press, and judiciary.[32]

Much Christian reflection on strikes has been in the interests of "reconciliation" and the need for moderation, though how employers contribute to this is left obscure. Such arguments presuppose either the unitary or pluralist frames of reference. Another ploy is to try and understand strikes on the analogy of the "just war." F. Schmidt proposed that criteria for a just strike would be that there must have been wrong done, such as a refusal to pay agreed wages, ruthless exploitation, or serious threat to life or health; they must be a last resort, after all other means are exhausted; and the scope, means, and duration must be proportionate to the wrong suffered.[33]

Invoking the Just War analogy is a very dubious procedure. Apart from the ludicrous implication that refusing to work for some period of time is analogous to killing people in war, the different situations addressed by the theory as originally framed and as applied to strikes disqualify its use. The Just War theory arose to evaluate limited and particular conflicts; it is not suited to assess a conflict endemic in the very structure of a society. Schmidt's criteria reflect an acceptance of the pluralist position. A just strike must have a just cause, but how do we decide what this is? Where the 1891 encyclical *Rerum Novarum* left the right to strike extremely unclear, John Paul II affirms that workers "should be assured the *right to strike*, without being subjected to personal penal sanctions." It is a legitimate but extreme means. "It must not be abused; it must not be abused especially for 'political' purposes."[34] The problem with this is that, as the pope must have known from his experience in Poland, it is difficult to make a sharp distinction between the economic and the political. Politics involves the structuring of the way people live, and political decisions are therefore at the same time personal and religious ones. We cannot separate the religious and the political, the personal and the political, sport and the political, or the industrial and the political. All these divisions are forms of a false dualism we have to overcome. The question rather is the fundamental possibility of a pluralist society where the plurality embraces opposite views of how society should be structured. The church prays week by week for the common good, but can there be a common good between exploiters and exploited? This is what Dussel calls the "Babylon principle," the fact that "this world" (Jn 18:36) is systematically organised around domination. The ethical position is not to call for reform but for a complete change in the way production is organised. We have argued that unions can be a positive good, to the extent that they exist as a sign that work can be organised cooperatively rather than in competition. Strikes can never be a positive good in the same way, but they may be a secondary good in various ways. Essentially they are a continuation of Jeremiah's protest:

> For from the least of them to the greatest of them, every
> one is greedy for unjust gain . . .
> They have healed the wound of my people lightly, saying
> "Peace, peace," where there is no peace.
> (Jer 6:13-14)

Strikes are frequently met with cries for respect for the rule of law and order, but "if order carries prescriptive overtones, and has to do with the way things *should* be and not just with the way they are, then the position could well be reversed in the case of a strike versus an unjust society. The strike, then, far from being damaging, may introduce an element of order into disorder or at least draw attention to the disorder which exists." A just strike then would oppose a false form of industrial peace, a distorted form of order, or a form of tyranny.[35] Tyranny according to the OED is oppressive or unjustly severe government, or arbitrary or oppressive exercise of power. Does the institutionalisation of inequality count as oppression or not?

I have devoted this amount of space to strikes because they have engaged the concern of Christian theorists, many of them tacitly on the management side. Means of resistance are to some extent culturally bound, and also related to the ruthlessness of the opposition one is facing. India is especially imaginative in its resources for resistance, as Gandhi's marches, hunger strikes, and other forms of nonviolent action show, not to mention the Chipko movement. His methods were successfully taken up by Martin Luther King. It is unlikely, however, that Gandhi would have had any success against Stalin, or against the National Security State, regimes which hold on to power through systematic murder. Nevertheless, even here women and men of immense courage and imagination keep resistance alive, whether through the circulation of Samizdat material, or the silent protest of the Mothers of the Disappeared, or getting information out to international human rights organisations. The organised labour movement has also looked for alternative ways of voicing claims and demands, which avoid the hardship inevitable in any kind of strike action.

Given that Christianity is not a theory but a praxis, a practical challenge to the world, what do we do about the class war? There is no alternative, says McCabe, to practising the Sermon on the Mount, which is a vision of human maturity. But it is difficult to see how the ruling class can be persuaded to relinquish rule without some use of violence. Such violence has no place in a truly liberated society, nor in the kingdom, but we are not yet there. "There is a paradox," he writes, "but no contradiction, in having an enemy who must be destroyed and yet who is not in any ultimate sense *the* enemy, but the one for whom Christ dies; there is a paradox, but no contradiction, in fact, in loving your enemies."[36] At their best the kinds of people's organisations we have been reviewing exist not only as a challenge to a false peace and a distorted form of order, but to further the practice of this paradox. Commonly, unionism has been only too glad to be coopted into the system, to understand itself within the Babylon principle, not least in the racism and sexism practised within it. Similarly, every strike over differentials can be considered a victory for capitalism. Where, however, as with the women of Sri Lanka, who seek solidarity with any who are on the side of life, and refuse to anathematise, then they can articulate the ethic of the alternative, of solidarity and resistance, of a different kind of order. They can be a manifestation of the Jerusalem principle, rejection of the individualism which divides people and sets them against each other, affirmation that humanity consists in working together. If there is any truth in the gospel at all, then such affirmations are not utopian. The gulf between oppressed and oppressor can be crossed by abolishing the distinction, by allowing all to be prophets (Nm 11), which is to say to share in the shaping of their own destiny.[37] The role of the church in such movements is nothing to brag about, but we can at least take encouragement from the fact that the spokespeople in three of the five groups mentioned at the beginning of the chapter were Christian inspired. Repeated failure cannot make us cynical if we live by the reality of betrayal, death, and resurrection, as we do in a faith which finds central liturgical expression in the eucharist. The church is, after all, a grassroots people's organisation of solidarity and resistance, of celebration and struggle, of hope in the midst of despair. Least of all can we refuse our birthright.

8

The Price of Life

*Cash payment never was, or could except for a few years be, the union-bond
of man to man. Cash never yet paid one man fully his deserts to another;
nor could it, nor can it, now or henceforth to the end of the world.*
— Thomas Carlyle

The dictionary offers us the definition of a wage as a payment to a person
for service rendered. This definition is very close to that offered by Aquinas,
very much in passing, in his discussion of merit. A reward, he says (*merces*,
"wage"), is something repaid to someone in return for work as a sort of
price for it. The qualification *"quasi quoddam pretium"* expresses his sense
that there is something peculiar about this particular exchange. *Things* have
their price, but labour is not an ordinary commodity, but the life of those
made in the image of God, their time, energy, potential. This life is grace —
something given *gratis*, and therefore strictly speaking priceless. How then
is it to be priced? By way of acknowledging the difficulty Aquinas goes on
directly to talk of justice:

> Thus just as the payment of the just price for goods received from
> someone is an act of justice, so too the payment of a reward for work
> is an act of justice. Now justice is a kind of equality, as is clear from
> Aristotle. And so justice holds simply between those who are related
> by simple equality; but in the case of those who are not related by
> simple equality, justice does not hold simply, although there may be
> some mode of justice in such a case, as when we speak of the right
> (*jus*) due to a father or master, as Aristotle says later on.[1]

Aquinas here raises fundamental questions about society and justice
which will have to be addressed in any theological assessment of the issue
of wages.

A JUST WAGE?

Most discussions of wages or pay take the institution of wages for
granted. Homo sapiens, however, has certainly existed far longer without

wages than with them, and may do so again. The period of the payment of
wages may come to seem an aberration, as early twentieth-century liberals
looked on slavery. Wage relations probably emerged in neolithic times, with
the diversification of crafts. If the biblical texts are anything to go by,
oppression was involved from the very beginning, as there are frequent
warnings against injustice in the payment of wages:

> You shall not oppress your neighbour or rob him. The wages of a
> hired servant shall not remain with you all night until the morning
> (Lv 19:13).

> You shall not oppress a hired servant who is poor and needy, whether
> he is one of your brethren or one of the sojourners who are in the
> land within your towns; you shall give him his hire on the day he earns
> it, before the sun goes down (for he is poor and sets his heart upon
> it); lest he cry against you to the Lord and it be sin in you (Dt 24:14-
> 15).

> To take away a neighbour's living is to murder him; to deprive an
> employee of his wages is to shed blood (Sir 34:21-22).

These sentiments are echoed in the letter of James (5:1-6), but there
was a potentially much more devastating challenge to the whole institution
of wages in the teaching of Jesus himself. The parable of the eleventh-hour
labourers (Mt 20:1-16) was doubtless directed at the relation of Jews and
Gentiles, but it also bears on the question of God's economy, what Paul
came to see as the rule of grace. The concluding verse, "Am I not allowed
to do what I want with what belongs to me?" is not, as Hengel says, "a
classic definition of property," valid up to the present day, but a demon-
stration of God's quite different order. "So the last shall be first, and the
first last" (Mt 20:16). The parable calls into question the whole system of
remuneration, and shows that in the light of God's generosity (v. 15), his
gift of life, that system is entirely arbitrary. Beyond the distributive justice
we take for granted is the justice (righteousness) of God, which responds
to need and not to deserts. The foundations of meritocracy are radically
challenged by the ethic of justification by grace, and every notion of the
deserving poor is done away with. Correspondence to this would be a society
designed to meet peoples needs and not to reward their strength.

Behind the failure to take up the economic implications of the Christian
scripture ethic lies a fundamental pessimism about human possibility, as
we find it, for instance, in Augustine. The attempt to shape society by
Christian principles, and the evolution of doctrines of the just wage, just
profit, and just war all began from the assumption that, as Duncan Forrester
puts it, "there exist in human nature an aggression and an acquisitiveness
which are inherently sinful and must be curbed if something approaching

a Christian social life is to be possible."[2] The just wage then, like the just war, was not really just, but the best we can do in difficult circumstances, taking into account human greed and envy, and trying to curb these with the constraints of eternal damnation. The theologians who elaborated the theory tried to establish four basic principles.[3] First, pay should equal the value of the work each worker does, and this value should be at the highest level current technical and social conditions permit. It is assumed that pay at this rate constitutes an incentive for productive work at the highest level the worker can achieve. There must be equal pay for equal working capacity, though how this is determined is not made clear. A labour contract was understood as parallel to the contract for hire of other durable commodities, and as a contract between equals. Secondly, a just wage enables persons to maintain the standard of living they are accustomed to. Fogarty glosses with the comment that "a Just Wage is one which allows an employee of normal earning capacity . . . to earn enough to keep himself and his wife and children at the standard customary in his social class." Phelps Brown maintains, by contrast, that the doctrine was more closely linked to the perceived value of services. "The pay of workers in a given occupation, averaged over a number of years, provides a standard of living that confers on the occupation a certain status . . . the principle of the Just Wage takes the status as an index of the normal wage, in order to protect the worker from exploitation by particular employers and from buffeting by the fluctuations of the market."[4] What this overlooks, however, is the degree to which medieval society understood itself hierarchically, a hierarchy which reflected the ordering of the cosmos, and which was fundamental to the theology of Anselm. This society believed very firmly in what Mrs. Thatcher calls "a right to inequality." Thirdly, justice was understood in relation to the common good. Wages should be consistent with the overall resources of the community and should be set to serve the interests of all. In order to be in the public interest pay must be fixed by the common estimate of the community, "arrived at by a social process which gives a voice and influence to every party concerned."[5] Traditionally, the common good has also been understood hierarchically. The image of the collaboration of the parts for the good of the whole may be a dominant image for the Scholastics, but the parts are not assumed to be equal. Finally, if at all possible, compensation between conditions should be avoided. Thus there will be cases where dangerous or dirty work demands extra pay but major discrepancies between pay, rank, and prestige will prove sources of irritation. This is equivalent to Elliott Jacques's "Felt Fair Pay."[6] He found from surveys that trouble arose in factories and work places when actual pay went more than 10 percent below what employees felt to be fair. Jacques took into account factors such as whether the employee was showing adequate care, working fast enough, and distributing time reasonably between more and less pressing elements of the job. He did not take into account such things as physical effort, danger, and poor working conditions.

The Just Wage theory, like all economic theories, emerged within a particular social and economic structure. It presupposes, says Fogarty, "the family which lives by cooperating with others but not in dependence on them." It applies, that is to say, to the move between a peasant and a market economy, at a time when the apparatus of the State was crude and minimal. As we have seen, it takes a hierarchical ordering of society for granted. This is evident in the endorsement of the theory by a succession of papal encyclicals from *Rerum Novarum* onwards. John XXIII saw fit to affirm, in 1961, that the remuneration of work must not be left to the laws of the market. The standards are those of "justice and equity," worked out in terms of what a person needs to live a "truly human life," the contribution of the worker, the financial state of the firm, and "the requirements of the common good of the universal family of nations of every kind, both large and small."[7] This encyclical, *Mater et Magistra*, began with a summary of *Rerum Novarum* and shares with it the view that equality of dignity is consistent with inequality of outcome, and that a hierarchical ordering of society is God-given. Although it goes on to advocate worker control of industry it still manifests the defects of much Scholastic thinking in being a-historical and therefore insensitive to changes in social and economic conditions. *Laborem Exercens* is more sensitive to these, seeing wages as a practical means of realising "the first principle of the whole social and ethical order," that of the common use of goods. Although the deep suspicion of Socialism of a century earlier is no longer manifest, and there is recognition that the system is imperfect, the morality of the wage system as such is not questioned. It is this which Marx challenges with his theory of surplus value.

WAGES AS RELATION

Marx makes a distinction between labour and labour power: "What economists call the value of labour is in fact the value of labour power, as it exists in the personality of the labourer, which is as different from its function, labour, as a machine is from the work it performs."[8] Labour power is what the worker sells; labour is what creates value, what creates a product to be sold. In capitalism the value of labour is always less than the value it produces, for the capitalist always makes labour power work longer than is necessary for the reproduction of its own value. Suppose someone is paid $20 per hour, based on the fact that what he or she has produced is worth $50. Even when all the other costs involved in production are allowed for, there is still an immense discrepancy between the value of labor and the value of the product, indicated by the generation of profit. Marx speaks of this as part of the "mystification" necessary to capital. Whereas in slave labour all the slaves' labour is unpaid, in wage labour unpaid labour appears as paid: "The money relation conceals the unrequited labour of the wage labourer." The exchange between capital and labour presents itself as no different to buying or selling any other commodities. The thing which interests the capitalist, however, is to receive as much labour as possible for as little money as possible. "Practically, the only thing that interests him is the difference between the price of labour power and the value its function creates . . . he never comes to see that, if such a thing as the value of labour really existed, and he really paid this value, no capital would exist, his money would not be turned into capital."[9] Thus wages always involve both theft and exploitation, and Marx noted that "the essence of the evil" of wages was "that my activity becomes a commodity, that I become utterly and absolutely for sale." Nevertheless, he ironically noted a number of advantages which followed from the establishment of wage labour:

Firstly: thereby everything patriarchal falls away, since haggling, purchase and sale remain the only connection, and the money relationship the sole relationship between employers and workers.

Secondly: the halo of sanctity is entirely gone from all relationships of the old society, since they have dissolved into pure money relationships. Likewise all so-called higher kinds of labour, intellectual, artistic etc. have been turned into articles of commerce and have thereby lost their old sanctity. What a great advance it was that the entire regiment of clerics, doctors, lawyers etc. hence religion, law etc ceased to be judged by anything but their commercial value.

Thirdly: as the workers realised through the general saleability that everything was separable, dissoluble from itself, they first became free of their subjection to a given relationship. The advantage both over payment in kind and over the way of life prescribed purely by the (feudal) estate is that the worker can do what he likes with his money.[10]

So the impact of wage labour helps to de-mystify capitalism and gives the worker consumer freedom, though this is very strictly limited. All these "advantages," however, stand under the judgement of the fundamentally alienating nature of wage labour. Moreover, the capital which makes one person free to employ the labour of another is itself the product of violence. The presupposition which Scholastic theory makes is that capital is legitimately acquired, but this is not the case. Further, it presupposes that there is real freedom on both sides of the wage contract, and this is again not the case. Those who sell their labour do so because they have no choice if they wish to live, and all the instruments of ideology are used to convince people they have no choice. The hierarchy of values in force in society persuades people that managers and owners should enjoy greater well being and higher social status. Western justice is fashioned after the contract of bargain and sale, and the prevailing distribution is accepted as non-revisable. Miranda comments that "the abyss of immorality which exists in the

Western idea of justice is strictly unfathomable; it sets up as an ideal the systematic profanation and humiliation of the human being."[11]

HUMAN EQUALITY AND EQUAL PAY

The labour theory of value has never gone unchallenged. Utility and scarcity were also recognised as determining what people would be prepared to pay for products, and in the work of Jevons and Marshall this was developed into the theory of marginal utility, the theory that it is the utility of the last and least wanted item that sets the value of all. The more freely available something is, the less people will pay for it, and vice versa. The price necessary to induce the supply is in equilibrium with the price commanded by the least urgent need, and we have the law of supply and demand. These factors affected wages. "Where a homogeneous working force was assumed and differences in skill and diligence were overlooked, as among the untutored masses of the factory, pay was set by the value of the contribution to output and revenue of the last available worker."[12] The marginal return could go down to subsistence levels but, where labour was not abundant, the supply and demand curves could intersect above that. These theories would point to the tapping of scarce resources as a source of profit. Frank Knight argued that profit was a reward for innovation and assuming risk.[13] None of these theories alter the fact that it is not only scarcity and utility but also the amount of labour involved which determines the price of something, and that, for there to be a profit, there must be a gap between what is charged for a product and the wages of the labourer. But how is remuneration for different kinds of work calculated? This is an even profounder mystery than the origin of profit. Noting that an hour's hard work might involve more labour than two hour's easy business, Adam Smith commented that "it is not easy to find any accurate measure either of hardship or ingenuity."

> In exchanging indeed the different productions of different sorts of labour for one another, some allowance is commonly made for both, it is adjusted, however, not by any accurate measure, but by the higgling and bargaining of the market, according to that sort of rough equality which, though not exact, is yet sufficient for carrying on the business of common life.[14]

As Phelps Brown remarks, this argument "begs the question of whether there is in fact any common stuff of labour to be measured." This was a question Marx did not go into. In concerning himself with the "expropriation of the expropriators," he was concerned with capital, rather than with high salaries. His precept for wages was that they should be proportionate to the quality and quantity of the work performed, but these are extremely rough and ready guidelines. It is this particular mystery which is the subject of Phelps Brown's magisterial study.

Does high pay follow from status or status from high pay? Economists and sociologists will be inclined to give different answers. The economist tends to regard the equilibrium of supply and demand as determining the incomes available for different kinds of work. The reasons that people do not automatically migrate to better paid jobs have to do with obstacles to entering those professions (such as racial or sexual discrimination or closed-shop agreements), keeping the number of jobs scarce by insisting on high wages, and a whole host of other factors such as regional immobility, lack of knowledge, or limitation of personal qualities. The economist does not see different rates of pay as constituting a structure, but as emerging through the free play of the market. There are, however, difficulties for this view. Why is it, as J. S. Mill asked, that really exhausting and repulsive labours are the worst paid of all? Would not one expect those jobs for which there were fewest applicants to be the best paid? Prompted by this kind of difficulty the sociologist comes with quite different questions and assumptions, looking at the way people act by custom, obligation, or conviction. Both sociologists and some economists involved in wage bargaining feel that status determines pay. Thus Barbara Wootton argued, "All wages are to be explained more in terms of conventions than as the result of strictly economic factors ... The conventions which makes the pattern of wages whatever it happens to be at any given time are sociological in a broad sense, rather than economic."[15] Class and gender determine income to a large extent, and this is linked to the exercise of power. Social inequalities are in part deliberately created or maintained by those who have the power to do so for their own benefit. This maintenance of social inequality is part and parcel of the social construction of gender difference, as feminists like Lynne Segal have argued.

Are there, perhaps, reasons for inequality built into the very structure of human beings? Are we by nature hierarchical animals? Phelps Brown notes that for 99 percent of our existence we have been hunter gatherers, and the evidence is impressive that such societies are egalitarian and cooperative rather than structured and competitive. What we know of the surviving hunter gatherers indicates that human beings are not by origin *homo hierarchicus*, with a genetically transmitted propensity to evaluate by ranking. The higher status attaching to greater earnings or wealth appears to be consequent upon the emergence of such differentiation in the neolithic revolution, and not prior to it in time or in aetiology. Similarly, the notion that an occupation is entitled to earnings adequate to maintain a certain station in life appears to arise from a de facto link between occupations and certain levels of earnings and expenditure, and not to be an independent and originating cause of earnings being what they are.[16]

Phelps Brown therefore concludes that economic differentiation came before status as a determinant of pay. In contemporary society he finds that levels of pay are determined by three factors. First, the main proportions of the pay structure are determined within the market by supply and demand, rather than by custom, convention, status, or power. Thus we can instance the enormous difference in remuneration for footballers between the early sixties and the early seventies. In the space of a decade they changed from being moderately well-remunerated professionals to superstars who could command extraordinary transfer fees. This change, we can surmise, was largely to do with the growth of the leisure industry and new possibilities for advertising through television. Again it is not, as Adam Smith surmised, the degree of skill and ingenuity involved which determines pay. The consumer is king to some extent and will not, for example, pay for the composition of elegant Latin hexameters.

Secondly, however, status does continue to be important. People believe that their relative pay is the measure of esteem in which they are held both by their employers and the community. Pay is a form of recognition, something like a badge of rank in the armed forces. Similarly, when once a de facto association between an occupation and the station in life, or level of consumption generally afforded by the earnings in it, becomes accepted, then it becomes sacrosanct by custom and becomes an independent force tending to uphold differentials. This is the equivalent of the scholastic doctrine that "no one should live unbecomingly," that the prince should be enabled to live as a prince, and the shepherd as a shepherd.

Thirdly, relative pay may be affected at particular points by the bargaining or monopoly power of trade unions. Phelps Brown does not add that employers may also affect wages by use of power, by forcing them down crudely, as after the General Strike in Britain in 1926, or after Pinochet's coup in Chile, by holding them static in a period of inflation. The moral issue arises from the way in which inequalities are generated. In the first place we can recall the origin of many class divisions in primitive accumulation—that the origin of concentrations of wealth was, and to a large extent remains, in violence. This was true of all earlier monarchies, of colonial fortunes, and is true in only a slightly less obvious way of mercantile and industrial fortunes, to the extent that they all rest on the exploitation of other people's labour. Once inequalities are established, they tend to perpetuate themselves and it is this which Phelps Brown documents. Genetic and social conditioning profoundly affects the ability to earn. Many studies have demonstrated that differences of socio-economic class are associated with differences of IQ; that development of the child's cognitive ability depends on how it is treated by its parents; and that nonmanual parents will make more efforts to secure good schooling, support their children through higher education, and acquaint their children with a wider range of possible careers. Secondly, mobility between generations is not that great; children tend to go into their parents' jobs, or jobs on the same social and intellectual level. Thirdly, access to employment may be restricted by prevailing attitudes—for instance to ethnic minorities or to women. The importance of these considerations is primary. If it is true that the wages given levels of qualification command are determined for the most part by market forces then this remains in practice morally insignificant because these "laws" operate within a pre-given framework of inequality at the mercy of the genetic and social luck of the draw. "Any one person's ability to work is compounded of his genetic endowment of cognitive ability and traits of personality; his upbringing in the home; his schooling; and his experience, and training on the job, in the early years of his working life."[17] The Puritan hostility to games of chance may or may not have been justified, but to assign people's life chances to this kind of roulette is either to believe in an amoral providence (perhaps the "invisible hand") or to abdicate responsibility altogether. Unless there is something sacrosanct about hierarchy as such, and the evidence suggests there is not, the only moral option is not to capitalise on these natural inequalities but to combat them.

INCENTIVE AND INTEREST

The most fundamental theological consideration is the understanding of society as a body. What this analogy tells us is that we are totally interdependent, so that the head does not deserve any more honour than the foot. Dustmen and sewage workers may not need the years of training which the doctor they consult needs, but if they withdraw their services the doctor too may die of disease. Recognition of this fundamental interdependence points to the inequality of pay as profoundly irrational. It is supported by the argument of conservative realism, that people will not work without incentives. Research in Stalinist economies does something to support this. Such research suggests that the rewards of status and consciousness of social usefulness do not motivate people sufficiently. Two Czech sociologists wrote:

> Inadequate pay differentials within and between occupations bring a lowering of interest and a disturbance of morale in work, a general fall in performance, a lack of interest in occupational careers and in attaining higher qualifications ... It is generally recognised that the ideological motivations to work become more effective if they are combined with the influence of a material interest; in themselves, and apart from other influences, they can determine the behaviour of ideological elites, but they are not wholly sufficient for the bulk of society.[18]

Phelps Brown therefore wonders whether sufficient people will be interested in acquiring qualifications if the rewards for them are reduced. Some would persevere out of interest in preparatory studies and the prospect of independent or absorbing or socially useful work, but the question is whether enough would. But the same argument can be mounted still more cogently for high compensation for mind numbing menial work. In an uncharacteristically speculative moment Phelps Brown suggests that the sense that higher qualifications should be more highly paid may not be merely conventional, but may rest upon "a categorical judgement of fairness that goes deep in human nature." Only a very small society, he supposes, could be so indoctrinated that people would be willing to work hard with little material reward. He notes that even China and Cuba, where intensive efforts have been made to inculcate a collectivist morale, have retained a wage structure explicitly differentiated according to productivity.[19]

The appeal to a categorical judgement of fairness is vague and less compelling than the evidence for the influence of custom and convention which Phelps Brown himself charts. Jacques's "Felt Fair Pay" also seems to rest on custom and convention which can change, as in the football example, as society changes. Even should there be such a thing, it is certainly challenged by the gospel. According to this the gifts we have are not for our own private gain but for the common good. Scholastic theologians would agree, but where a hierarchical vision of reality was taken for granted by them it must be replaced by an egalitarian one. Egalitarianism follows from the fact that all are one in Christ. This does not apply only to the church because *ecclesia* is the seed bed of a new humanity—it is about realising what humanity, and therefore human community, ought to be. Radical egalitarianism is part of critical utopianism. This bears, naturally, on pay. It reveals all differentials in pay as essentially arbitrary. It will be objected that to carry such egalitarianism into the sphere of reward is unjust—how can you pay someone who has worked for one hour the same as someone who has worked for twelve? The answer is that the biblical concept of justice goes beyond distributive justice, important though that is. The Scholastic discussion is framed in terms of equity, but equity is not enough. Equity between existing classes perpetuates the status quo, as it does today in trade union demarcation disputes. Justice, however, as it is understood by the Magnificat, is about realising God's purposes for all human beings by raising the lowly and humbling the mighty.

This is because, as David Jenkins has said, we cannot be fully human until all are fully human.[20] That situation, the kingdom of God, is what we mean by justice. It is not a remote dream far beyond the bounds of history, but something we pray to come on earth. It is the subject of Jesus' parables, as also of the parable of the eleventh-hour labourers. Jesus' command to his disciples is: "It shall not be so amongst you" where "you" is the small group who begin to take God's revolution "into all the world." It is the revolution of grace, not of merit and deserving, or of parity and weighing out between individuals. This revolution of sharing is signified each time we celebrate the eucharist, which is itself a practice of equality that is a very small first step towards the realisation of a new society.

PART THREE

THE COMMON TREASURY

9

The World as Private Gain

The first one who, having enclosed a piece of land, took it upon himself to say, "this is mine," and found men foolish enough to believe it, was the true founder of civil society. What crimes, wars, murders, miseries and horrors would Mankind have been spared by one who, uprooting the stakes or filling in the ditch, had cried out to his fellows: Beware of listening to this impostor: you are lost, if you forget that the fruits belong to all and the land to no one!
— Rousseau

In the hunter gatherer society which has constituted the vast majority of human history such property as there is is held in common. The Fall, the emergence of private property, meaning possession and the exclusive right to the disposal of something, probably emerges only with settlement and the division of labour, with the production of surplus and with conquest. This is what Marx calls the "original sin" of primitive accumulation.[1] All written history presupposes this development.

VIEWS OF PROPERTY IN THE HEBREW SCRIPTURES

Biblical views of property are profoundly marked by three experiences — the experience of slavery in Egypt, the period of the Judges, and the period of the monarchy. The story of slavery, which lay at the foundation of Israel's narrative identity, taught Israel that human labour might be a form of property like any artifact. Reflection on this experience lay behind the antipathy to slavery in Israel which is found so strongly in the Deuteronomic legislation and reappears in Revelation. The climax of the tremendous condemnation of Rome is that she traffics in "slaves, that is, human souls" (Rv 18:13). This origin of Israel in slavery meant that the complacent identification of some human beings as by nature slaves was always impossible to them.

In complete contrast to this was the period of the Judges, which may have lasted as long as two hundred years. When the tribes (who were probably culturally and ethnically disparate, including Canaanite peasants) came into Canaan they found the land dominated by small Canaanite city states, ruled by kings, and the struggle with these may have lasted more than a century. The tribes divided the land among themselves, existing politically as a federation with a tribal council and economically as a peasant economy. Within the tribal group, government may have been by council and differences of wealth were probably not marked. To some extent this period became for later ages a golden age, before the emergence of a class society. To the extent that this society was classless and egalitarian it lived, as it were, before the Fall. The ideology of this period (whether it was contemporary or not is not the main thing) denied absolute ownership rights to any individual on the grounds that the land belonged to God: "The land shall not be sold in perpetuity, for the land is mine; for you are strangers and sojourners with me" (Lv 25:23). Those who work it do so as stewards and not for their own gain. This could be extended to cover the whole earth:

> The earth is the Lord's and the fulness thereof,
> the world and those who dwell therein (Ps 24:1).

> I will accept no bull from your house,
> nor he-goat from your folds.
> For every beast of the forest is mine,
> the cattle on a thousand hills . . .
> the world and all that moves in the field is mine.
> (Ps 50:9-12)

According to this ideology there can be no absolute rights to private property. All human beings are no more than God's tenants, and in the use of their property have to conform themselves to God's standards. In a verse which Jesus quoted, the psalmist maintained that "the meek shall possess the land and delight themselves in abundant prosperity" (Ps 37:11). Isaiah predicts that the coming anointed one will not be seduced by riches but "with righteousness he shall judge the poor, and decide with equity for the meek of the earth" (Is 11:4). This standpoint became one of the key elements of the patristic view of property.

All this changed with the coming of the monarchy, at first the result of military necessity (1 Sm 13:19). A sour comment on the workings of the monarchy from the Deuteronomic editors of 1 Samuel notes that the king will take again and again, give the stolen property to his supporters, and that the end of absolute rule will be slavery (1 Sm 8:10-18). In the centuries following the institution of the monarchy trade developed, cities became more important, and the division between rich and poor grew. Royal circles appealed to Canaanite royal ideology, according to which the king was a son of god and entitled to do as he pleased. The story of Naboth (1 Kgs 21), later the subject of stirring homilies by Ambrose, illustrates the clash between old and new ideologies. Naboth farms his portion of the *nachalah*, the land bequeathed to Israel, which is inalienable and which he therefore refuses to surrender to the king. Here speaks the voice of the old tribal Israel, the free peasants who share the land and meet as equals. Appealing to Canaanite understandings of royal power Jezebel has him murdered and presents the land to the king. The story is a small illustration of Marx's contention that the history of primitive accumulation "is written in the annals of mankind in letters of blood and fire." At this point Elijah intervenes, as the spokesman of the old values: "Have you killed, and also taken possession?" (1 Kgs 21:19). Taking possession, claiming something for personal use, fails to recognise that all the land is held in trust to YHWH, that each Israelite farms a small portion as a tenant. Such action brings disaster on those who practice it. It is ultimately unsustainable. Far from being the expression of a primitive world view, the growing ecological crisis shows that endless killing and taking possession, the rapacity of capitalism, does in fact bring disaster, not only on those who practise it but on the whole planet. The later prophets continually attacked such practises. They see that the luxury of the rich is built on violence and spoil. Thus Amos attacks those who build houses of stone and plant vineyards on the proceeds they have made from the oppression of the poor (Am 8:4f.). Isaiah pronounces doom on those who join "house to house and field to field until there is no more room" (Is 5:8). Jeremiah proclaims, "Shame on the person who builds his house by not-justice and completes his upstairs rooms by not-right" (Jer 22:13).

Two things followed from this view. The first is that strictly speaking there is no such thing as charity, the rich helping the poor. The Hebrew word translated "almsgiving" is in fact *tsedequah*, "justice" (Prv 10:2; Dn 4:24; cf. Mt 6:1-2). Justice is restoring to the poor what is theirs. But secondly, the Deuteronomists and others who worked on programmes for reconstruction emphasised the need of the Jubilee law, by which alienated property was restored to its original owners, so doing away with poverty altogether. Every seventh year all debts were to be remitted and all slaves freed (Dt 15:1f.); every fiftieth year any land alienated by poverty, debt, or any other reason was to be returned to the original owner or his heirs (Lv 25:8f.). If these provisions were followed, said the Deuteronomists, "there will be no poor among you" (Dt 15:4). This attitude to property, according to which the earth is the Lord's, made to be a common property for all, is very different from the content with sufficiency which Aristotle recommended. Property and wealth is a good—so long as it is shared, not cornered and hoarded and used by one section to oppress another. The vision of peace and prosperity was of a society without slaves where every family dwelt "under its vine and under its fig tree" (1 Kgs 4:25; Mi 4:4; Zec 3:10). The right to own what we shall call individual property is conceded by the warnings in the Decalogue against coveting (Ex 20:17 = Dt 5:21). In a society where everyone owns their "ox, ass, field, and house," coveting could only lead to aggrandisement. It is at the root of the unnecessary division into classes.

JESUS AND THE CLASSICAL TRADITION

Little more than a century after Jeremiah we find an intensive debate about property among the Greek philosophers. Plato recognised the divisive force of the words *mine* and *thine* and proposed that the Guardians of the Republic should have all things in common.[2] Aristotle reviewed three possibilities: that land might be privately owned, but the produce stored for common consumption; that ownership and cultivation should be common, but the produce parcelled out for private use; and that the land and its produce should be held in common. The first was his preferred option. He noted the universal truths that human beings find difficulty in living together and that there is pleasure involved in owning something. Selfishness is deplorable but "some partiality for such things as oneself, property, etc. is almost universal." Moreover, it was private property which enabled one to do a kindness or lend a helping hand, which was a source of infinite satisfaction. He believed, however, in moderation. Property in itself could not be the goal of the good life — humans need just enough to make that possible. The only property which is needed is such as is "necessary for life, capable of being stored, and useful for the community of the household and city."[3] Where Plato thought of the state as a unity, Aristotle envisaged it as a plurality held together by education.[4] It was, however, the Stoics whose views of property had the greatest impact on later Western thinking. The Stoics believed that all rational creatures had a spark of the divine Logos in them, and since the whole of nature is subordinated to the common Logos all share in its rights. They shared with the Cynic philosophers an emphasis on the virtue of *autarkeia*, self-sufficiency, which taught satisfaction with those things which were essential. Stoic arguments were particularly common in the early Fathers. We find an echo of Plato as well as strong Stoic arguments in this passage from John Chrysostom:

Mark the wise dispensation of God! That he might put mankind to shame, he has made certain things common, as the sun, air, earth, and water . . . whose benefits are dispensed equally to all as brethren . . . observe, that concerning things that are common there is no contention, but all is peaceable. But when one attempts to possess himself of anything, to make it his own, then contention is introduced, as if nature herself were indignant, that when God brings us together in every way, we are eager to divide and separate ourselves by appropriating things, and by using those cold words "mine and thine." Then there is contention and uneasiness. But where this is not, no strife or contention is bred. This state therefore is rather our inheritance, and more agreeable to nature.[5]

This kind of Stoic teaching was a very strong influence on most of the early Fathers who concerned themselves with the issue of property.

While Stoicism was important among the Roman upper class, the development of the Roman law of property was more fateful, in that one way or another it entered into the law of most Western nations. The conflict between plebs and patricians dates from the beginning of the Roman state and is related to ownership of land. Ownership meant *dominium*, the unrestricted right of control over something, "to have, to hold, to use, to enjoy." Ownership could be acquired by transfer before a magistrate, first possession of something, the creation of something, or by uninterrupted possession over a number of years.

Jesus' attitude to property was critical. "Do not be anxious about your life," he warns, or about food and drink or clothing. "Seek first his kingdom and his righteousness, and all these things shall be yours as well" (Mt 6:33). In the parable of the talents (Mt 25:14f.; Lk 19:11f.) he continues the Hebrew scriptures' teaching of property as a form of stewardship. In various ways he also echoes the prophetic critique of riches. According to Luke, blessings on the poor were followed by woes on the rich (Lk 6:24f.). The story of the rich man and Lazarus (Lk 16:19f.) and the warning of the impossibility of the rich man's salvation (Mk 10:25) may indicate that Jesus condemns riches because of the injustice that accompanies them. On the other hand, he also sees the connections between riches and idolatry, because riches claim an ultimate allegiance: "No one can serve two masters ... You cannot serve God and mammon" (Mt 6:24). At the same time Jesus was not a Puritan; he enjoyed good things, though it is probably going too far to speak with Hengel of Jesus' "free attitude towards property."[6]

Hengel takes the view that it was the imminence of the parousia, rather than specifically ethical considerations, which accounts for the attitude toward property in the early church. This fails to do justice, however, to the central importance in the Christian scriptures of the image of the church as the body, in which all serve each other, and to the persistence of the criticism of riches in the Fathers. Chrysostom has already been cited, but there are fierce denunciations of the evil attending riches, and the right of all to God's earth, in Clement of Alexandria, Cyprian, Ambrose, Basil of Caesarea, and Augustine. Chrysostom located the origin of property very clearly in "primitive accumulation": "How is it that you are rich?" he asks, in a famous passage. "From whom did you receive your wealth? From your grandfather, and even his father? By climbing the genealogical tree are you able to show the justice of this possession? Of course not; rather, its beginning and root have necessarily come out of injustice."[7] Commenting on Luke 16:9 ("make friends for yourselves by means of unrighteous mammon") Jerome says, "All riches come from injustice. Unless one person has lost, another cannot find. Therefore I believe that the popular proverb is very true: " 'The rich person is either an unjust one or the heir of one.' "[8] "You are not making a gift of your possessions to the poor person," says

Ambrose, preaching on Naboth. "You are handing over to him what is his."[9] Similarly, taking up the Stoic and prophetic theme, "God willed that this earth should be the common possession of all and he offered its fruits to all. But avarice distributed the rights of possession."[10]

Aquinas was well aware of these texts and cited them as possible reasons for considering ownership wrong, but he disputes it, giving a basically Aristotelian answer. It is lawful, he says, *procurare et dispensare*, which has been translated "to care and to distribute" rather than the obvious "to procure and dispense."[11] Like Aristotle, Aquinas believed that private property encouraged people to labour and look after their affairs better, and that it led to fewer quarrels than common ownership, the view often referred to as the utility defence of private property. However, "man ought to possess things not as his own but as common, so that he is ready to communicate them to others in their need."[12] Aristotle's emphasis on moderation becomes a warning against the sin of covetousness. The desire for more than we need dehumanises us and leads to the disintegration of civil society.[13] Making a distinction between natural law and positive law, which went back to the Roman distinction between *ius naturale* and *ius civile,* Aquinas finds that common property is a natural right, but private property is justified by positive law, which is a matter of common consent.[14] Later appeals to positive law involved what we may call the contract fallacy, which supposed that all parties to a contract meet as equals. This approach to positive law was combined with another which went back to Augustine — the belief that, although the law of the emperors was unjust, such laws were necessary to keep the effects of sin at bay.

While nodding in the direction of Aquinas's solution, Leo XIII saw the right to private property as part of natural law. He claimed that "to possess property privately as his own is a right which a man receives from nature." He supported this claim by appealing to a rag bag of arguments: the need to have things to hand to protect our lives and propagate the species, our ability to plan for the future, the fact that, however obtained, "the earth does not cease to serve the needs of all."[15] "It is amazing that some people dissent from arguments as powerful as these," comments the astonished pope. John XXIII reaffirmed that "the right of private ownership of goods, including productive goods, has a permanent validity. It is part of the natural order, which teaches that the individual is prior to society and society must be ordered to the good of the individual." It is defended as a guarantee of the essential freedom of the individual and an indispensable element in a true social order.[16] The more recent *Laborem Exercens*, however, puts the emphasis firmly back on the priority of common use. The arguments of *Rerum Novarum* are summarised rather vaguely as the need to respect personal values, and it is strongly emphasised that "the right to private property is subordinated to the right to common use, to the fact that goods are meant for everyone."[17]

LOCKE, HEGEL, AND MARX

Contemporary liberal defences of private property appeal to the rather complex discussion in Locke's *Treatises on Civil Government*. Three of the standard arguments in defence of private property are found in his writings. On the one hand, we find strong affirmation of the equality of all people, and the rights of common ownership going back to both biblical and Stoic traditions. When he turns to the question of property, however, he advances what is now called the labour theory of the defence of private property. He took over the distinction between natural and positive law, applying the first to what we obtain by our labour, and the second to exchanges involving money. On his reading of natural law we all have property in our own person, and when we take something from the state of Nature by the labour of our hands then that becomes our property.

> Though the earth and all inferior creatures be common to all men, yet every man has a "property" in his own "person." This nobody has any right to but himself. The "labour" of his body and the "work" of his hands we may say are properly his. Whatsoever, then, he removes out of the state that Nature hath provided and left it in, he hath mixed his labour with it, and joined to it something that is his own, and thereby makes it his property.[18]

There are three codicils to this account. First, this passage already reveals Locke's profound individualism. He has no sense that labour can only be a common enterprise, that in society we are all bound up in the bundle of life together. Here the significance of what was happening in America at the time cannot be underestimated. In the beginning, he says, "all the world was America, and more so than is now." He imagined individual settlers taking over virgin territory, each one an entirely independent unit. The logic of such a vision was that those who had not so acquired territory must have failed though their fecklessness or idleness. From the Puritan tradition Locke took the idea that poverty was a sign of moral shortcoming.

> The poor might deserve to be helped, but it must be done from a superior moral footing. Objects of solicitude or pity or scorn, and sometimes of fear, the poor were not full members of a moral community. Here was a further reason . . . for continuing to think of them as less than full members of the political community. But while the poor were, in this view, less than full members, they were certainly subject to the jurisdiction of the political community. They were in but not of civil society.[19]

The moralising approach to work and property added another justification to the traditional defences of private property. Locke pointed out that the person who appropriates land and cultivates it "does not lessen but increase the common stock of mankind" because "he, that encloses Land and has a greater plenty of the conveniency's of life from ten acres, than he could have had from an hundred left to Nature, may truly be said, to give ninety acres to Mankind."[20] This has come to be known as the labour desert defence of private property. Thirdly, he is inclined to agree with Aristotle that "the measure of property Nature well set, by the extent of men's labour and the conveniency of life." However, money changed all that. Money corresponds to positive law rather than to natural law, and there the rule of sufficiency is overridden and we may take more than we need. This is not the result of greed but is necessary for commerce. Locke sees quite clearly, without justifying it, that inequality of possessions is necessary for merchant capitalism.[21]

An independent defence of property, known as the liberty argument, also underlies the whole argument of the *Treatises*. In part, at least, Locke was responding to a reactionary defence of absolute monarchy, which taught that people were completely subject to the crown. Locke argued, by contrast, that a State was a common agreement for the defence of property. Where individuals have no property at all, we find despotism. Shared political power is found "where men have property in their own disposal."[22] He is thinking, of course, of the landed gentry, those who withstood Charles I, and who invited William of Orange to England. This argument, dubious and disputed even at the time, has been repeated endlessly in vastly changed social and economic circumstances. Private property is no defence against the totalitarianism of the modern state, especially where this exercised through large monopolies and control of the media. This needs quite other defences. It was an argument devised for landlords, as the history of enclosures in Britain showed.[23]

A more complex, and today fashionable, defence of private property derives from the view of work as self-realisation developed by Hegel and taken over by Marx. According to Hegel the right of property derives from the fact that we shape things by our will:

> I as free will am an object to myself in what I possess and thereby also for the first time am an actual will, and this is the aspect which constitutes the category of property, the true and right factor in possession. If emphasis is placed on my needs, then the possession of property appears as a means to their satisfaction, but the true position is that, from the standpoint of freedom, property is the first embodiment of freedom and so is in itself a substantive end.[24]

It follows from this that the denial of a right to private property "violates the right of personality." Property is the embodiment of personality. The fact that people are different and vary in their gifts makes any argument for equality impossible. It ignores "the whole compass of mind, endlessly particularized and differentiated, and the rationality of mind developed into an organism." Needless to say what has happened here is that the individual has been deified.[25]

Marx was familiar with what we may call the somatic argument from Max Stirner, and caricatured it entertainingly in *The German Ideology*:

> Stirner refuted the communist abolition of private property by first transforming private property into "having" and then declaring the verb "to have" an indispensable word, an eternal truth, because even in Communist society it would happen that Stirner will "have" a stomach ache. In exactly the same way here his arguments regarding the impossibility of abolishing private property depend on his transforming private property into the concept of property, on exploiting the etymological connection between the words Eigentum and eigen and declaring the word "eigen" an eternal truth ... All this theoretical nonsense ... would be impossible if the actual private property that the Communists want to abolish had not been transformed into the abstract notion of "property."[26]

Marx's own view of property is remarkably close to Aristotle's, with the momentous exception that he is vividly aware of the social nature of all property:

> An isolated individual could no more have property in land and soil than he could speak. He could, of course, live off it as substance, as do the animals. The relation to the earth as property is always mediated through the occupation of the land and soil ... by the tribe, the commune, (or some other social formation) in some more or less naturally arisen or already historically developed form. The individual can never appear here in the dot-like isolation in which he appears as mere free worker.[27]

Nevertheless, Marx believed that the new ordering of society would give the producer "individual property based on the acquisitions of the Capital era: i.e., on cooperation and the possession in common of the land and of the means of production."[28] Communism therefore, according to Marx, is not about abolishing individual property but about the possibility of individual property which is not alienating, about reintegrating having and being.

CHARITY OR JUSTICE?

A view very close to Hegel's defence of property, which we have called the somatic or self-realisation view, has recently been developed at length as a Christian defence of property by Luke Johnson in his book *Sharing Possessions*.[29] He is concerned to support the "mandate" that we must do good with our possessions but at the same time to challenge the notion that property should be held in common. The first plank of Johnson's argument against common property is that there is no one central line on property to be found in scripture. Both total renunciation of possessions, and alms-giving and hospitality seem to be recommended there. We have to understand that scripture is not a rule book, that in any case its demands cancel one another out, and that "they appear incapable of being fulfilled in this complex, contemporary world." We need therefore to move to what he calls a theological understanding of possessions, and there are two aspects to this. On the one hand, possessions are understood as an extension of our body, our exteriority: "It is in the ambiguity of our somatic/spiritual existence as humans that we properly locate the mystery (!) of human possessions."[30] "We regard tools as the extensions of our bodies. We say that clothes make the man, the style is the person, you are what you eat. We perceive that our possessions, the things we have and use, extend our bodies and *ourselves* into the world and into the lives of other persons . . . possessions are symbolic expressions of ourselves because we both are and have bodies."[31] The somatic argument is strong on the significance of the individual human person and the individual call from God. But, as David Jenkins has said, the ideal of the individual is a myth, and a dangerously dehumanising one at that.[32] It is again part of idealist, essentialist thinking which conveniently abstracts from where things come and at what cost. But, and here we make the second move, these symbolic expressions of ourselves can be either idolised or used in faith. Idolatry is a form of possessiveness, a form of covetousness which fails to acknowledge life as a gift from the Creator. In a characteristic move, Johnson maintains that idolatry is not primarily of material things, but of spiritual. He tells us that "the elimination of all material possessions but the body by no means eliminates the idolatrous spirit within the human heart."[33] Naturally, therefore, faith is not primarily to do with anything material: "The poverty of Jesus is to be found first in his faith; it is, properly speaking, a theological poverty. He is the one among us who has refused to identify his life in what he had, but sought his life in God's will." When we acknowledge our life as gift then we are freed from the tyranny of possessing and can see things rather as a gracious gift from God. Without this theological poverty even giving all our goods away may be simply idolatry. *With* such poverty, however, we need not cling to our possessions as a means of self-definition but can use things freely. We are certainly called to share what God has given as a gift — that is the mandate — but how we are to do this is determined by the discernment of the Spirit. What this discernment amounts to today is — almsgiving.

The two main dangers of property identified by the biblical writings are idolatry and domination. "I am not accusing the rich," said John Chrysostom in a sermon, "nor do I begrudge them their wealth . . . Money is called *chremata* (from *chraomai*, "to use," "make use of") so that we may use it, and not that it may use us. Therefore possessions are so called that we may possess them, not they possess us. Why do you regard the master as a slave? Why do you invert the order?"[34] Meeks comments: "The mystery of idolatry is that persons reflect what they possess. Idolatry is being possessed by a possession and thereby refusing God's claim on oneself and shirking one's responsibility toward others in the community. Idolatry is the loss of freedom."[35]

Not only is there shirking of responsibility but actual domination, and ideological evasions to cover this up. Justifications of private property are always abstract and essentialist. Arguments that charity is the correct form of Christian relation to property overlook the injustice by which property was acquired in the first place. Johnson wants to defend almsgiving as respecting "the complexity of ever changing human circumstances and the continuing validity and awesomeness of God's mandate" and at the same time respecting "legitimate rights of property owners." Faced with similar arguments Ambrose reminded his congregation that the poor person was the rich person's equal: "Since therefore he is your equal, it is unjust that he is not assisted by his fellow men; especially since the Lord our God has willed this earth to be the common possession of all and its fruit to support all. Avarice, however, has made distribution of property rights. It is just, therefore, that if you claim as your own anything of that which was given to the human race, indeed to all living beings, in common, you should distribute at least a part among the poor."[36] Chrysostom says that not to share one's resources with the poor is robbery, and Augustine, preaching on Haggai 2:8 ("Mine is the silver and mine is the gold") says that "those who offer something to the poor should not think that they are doing so from what is their own."[37] Charity rests on inequalities of possession which abstract from the injustice by which riches are acquired and from the fact that the earth is "a common treasury for all." Johnson's main target is the principle of community of possessions, Aristotle's third option, which is not here being defended. The style of his appeal, and its practical effect have to be noted, however. Sober realism is contrasted with unrealistic idealism. We must celebrate not an ideal picture of humanity generating programmes of societal reform but the command of God leading to self-sacrifice. The obedience of faith must not be substituted by a human project. Faith in programmes of structural reform fail to take seriously the power of sin and idolatry.[38] Thus theological legitimation is sought for continuing exactly as we are—what Marx spoke of contemptuously as "sprinkling holy water over the heartburnings of the aristocrat." Johnson maintains, correctly, that there is no Christian economic structure to be found in the Bible and that the Christian social ethic has to be repeatedly reforged, but he uses these perceptions to smuggle in laissez faire individualism in the guise of obedience to the word of God. Rather than the attempt to work for change being sin and idolatry there is a better case for maintaining that the failure to attempt the structural change which can actually make people's lives better is sin and idolatry. Idolatry is not first and foremost the worship of the creature but service of those things which destroy life.

REDEFINING PROPERTY

The individual property Marx defends fulfills that delight in possessions which Aristotle speaks of. This does not have to be justified with high flown "somatic" arguments but is something to do with what Meeks calls "the promise of freedom," at least to the extent, as Aristotle says, that we are free to give to others. Further, if property is understood as what is necessary to life, then there are certain rights to property. Macpherson has argued that behind the notion of exclusive possession lies another idea of property, the right not to be excluded from the means of labour.[39] He argues that property rights have become so central to our society that it is only if human rights are treated as property rights that they will be taken seriously. These include a right to a job and a right to revenue, which should take the form of guaranteed annual income or negative income tax. The transition from market capitalism to regulated and managed capitalism will mean that the narrowing of property to the idea of exclusive possession can be reversed and more emphasis put on "individual property in the means of a full and free life." Property must be understood as both gift and trust. As *trust* it is not ours to corner or hoard, to "use for private gain" or to destroy recklessly. Patristic teaching on sufficiency or moderation has an extraordinary relevance to a consumer society indifferent to the vast numbers of the world's poor and to the destruction of earth's nonrenewable resources. "If each one would take that which is sufficient for one's needs," said St. Basil, "leaving what is in excess to those in distress, no one would be rich, no one poor."[40] There is a law of nature, says Ambrose, "that one can seek only what suffices for nourishment." "Seek sufficiency, seek what is enough, and more do not seek," says Augustine.[41] Such sufficiency, however, cannot be preached by the rich to the poor. The attempt to establish equality through the levelling of possessions, warns Johnson, wrongly continues to use possessions themselves as a measure of worth and identity. This point of view is very comfortable for possessors, but less comfortable for those who are not. As a possessor, Johnson high-mindedly refuses to judge others' worth through possessions. If he took somatic existence more seriously he might reflect that houses, wages, facilities which are extensions of the somatic existence of white North Americans, can also be an extension of the existence of others. If possessions enhance the quality of life they should be available to all. Moreover, he overlooks the fact that property as the right to dispose of what we have necessarily disadvantages some:

Not everyone is equal in skill and energy. Exclusive and disposable property rights lead to some getting more than others. The more one gets the easier it is to get still more. This results in a constant transfer of part of the powers of the non-propertied to the propertied. Many persons in a market society upholding this right will be constantly submitted to the threat of inhuman existence.[42]

This is especially the case given that the dice are loaded at every throw as the evidence amassed by Phelps Brown's study of pay comprehensively illustrates.

As *gift*, property is certainly to be welcomed, but the essential perception is that property is a social relation like the concept of rich and poor. Robinson Crusoe on his island was neither rich nor poor. I am only rich or poor, a possessor or indigent, in relation to others. In the same way rights can never be purely individual but express a relation. Property arises in the relation between our work and what is given us in work, creation. Except in small peasant economies this requires a highly complex set of relations. These relations have to express the fact that, as the Fathers never tired of repeating, the earth is God's gift to all, given to be shared and enjoyed equally. But what is it which is given? For centuries the Latin translation of the Bible promised human beings *dominium*—which was then understood through Roman law. But what is shared is not the right to exploit, but responsibility.

Is it possible to make significant changes in property relations? Macpherson correctly insists that changes in economic structure already imply different understandings of property from those implied by the heyday of market or industrial capitalism. There have been countless changes in the pattern of property relations over the centuries; nothing is unchangeable. We need a vision of what we are moving towards, however, because the future bears on the present and gives it shape. It calls into being what H. Gollwitzer has called "concrete utopias," structures which are not the kingdom but which we can aim for and arrive at. Such a utopia might be Marx's individual property within a socialised framework, and in particular within the common ownership of the means of production. A generous reading of *Mater et Magistra* might construe it in the same way. We cannot simply go on talking about the right to private property, says John XXIII. "We must also insist on the extension of this right in practice to all classes of citizens." He went on to reemphasise the "social function of private ownership." As he defines it, in reference to earlier encyclicals, this remains within the framework of charity from the rich. If this insistence came within a framework of real, rather than notional, equality there would be a real rapprochement between this and radical socialist views. Taking the social function of property seriously certainly means limits to individual property and therefore to the freedom of the individual to do whatever he or she likes. But freedom is a social relation. My freedom is at the expense of your freedom. What we have to move to is a situation where our freedom is mutually creative. In all sorts of areas, music or sport for example, human beings recognise that real creativity and achievement need the coordination of individual freedoms. What is needed is the extension of this coordination of individual freedom to the ownership of property, and ultimately to the tenure of the whole inhabited earth. Far from being a utopian dream, this is an urgent necessity if the poor of the Third World are ever to come into their own, and if poverty is to be eliminated, as it could be. And what, after all, is the alternative? To believe, smugly, that "I'm all right, Jack" is both to neglect the urgent warnings of ecologists and to turn our backs on our own humanity, which we cannot have at the expense of others. What is at stake is neither a utopian view of property nor a political dogma, but our humanity. Once again, we find ourselves before two ways, and the choice is anything but academic.

10

The Spoil of the Poor

The spoil of the poor is in your houses.

—Isaiah 3:14

The year 1990 saw the publication of the first World Bank report on poverty for ten years. It shows that although consumption per capita rose in some countries by almost 70 percent between 1965 and 1985, and life expectancy, child mortality, and educational attainment have improved in many countries, still more than one billion people around the world were living in abject poverty on incomes of less than $310 per year. Under present conditions more than fifteen to twenty million people die yearly from malnutrition and hunger related-diseases, including twelve million children — the equivalent of a Hiroshima every two days, as Susan George notes. Even on the best predictions the Bank estimates that 700 million will still be living at this level at the turn of the century; it has to be noted that poverty has increased rather than decreased in many countries in the past ten years. The 1980s have been called the lost decade in the fight against poverty. The Report notes that incomes fell and poverty increased in Sub-Saharan Africa and Latin America. The report of The United Nations Children's Fund (UNICEF), in 1989, *The State of the World's Children*, begins as follows:

For almost nine hundred million people, approximately one sixth of mankind, the march of human progress has now become a retreat. In many nations, development is being thrown into reverse. And after decades of steady economic growth, large areas of the world are sliding backwards into poverty.

Throughout most of Africa and much of Latin America, average incomes have fallen by 10% to 25% in the 1980s. The average weight-for-age of young children, a vital indicator of normal growth, is falling in many of the countries for which figures are available. In the 37 poorest nations, spending per head on health has been reduced by 50% and on education by 25%, over the last few years. And in almost half of the 103 developing countries for which recent information is available, the proportion of 6 to 11 year olds enrolled in primary school is now falling.[1]

All over the Third World real wages, health standards, and expenditure on education are actually falling. Why is this? Brian Griffiths, writing to defend the Christian morality of capitalism, is convinced that the arguments that Western market policies are in any way to blame for this problem are "almost entirely untrue." "It is quite wrong to suggest that the international trading system is a sort of jungle in which the strong systematically exploit the weak . . . The Third World has certain legitimate grievances against the First World but at best these are marginal in explaining Third World Poverty."[2] Structures like the General Agreement on Tariffs and Trade (GATT) and OECD Codes of Liberalisation are, he believes, fundamentally sound. Multinational corporations are found to make a positive contribution to third-world economies. The causes of third-world poverty are cultural differences, political factors such as corruption and incompetence in third-world governments, and the adoption of non-monetarist economic policies. The West is not in any sense guilty for what is happening in the Third World. Our sole responsibility in the First World or Northern block of nations is to foster wealth creation, oppose subsidies to French and German farmers, and give to private charity. Unfortunately there are compelling reasons for thinking that this Pilatical washing of hands will not do.

The remote origins of the present situation lie in colonial policies, and India may be taken as an example of how these worked.[3] In the first place there was a great drain of resources from colonial to colonising countries. From the mid-eighteenth century there was an immense outflow of capital, and after 1870 the volume of annual interest remitted abroad on foreign investment exceeded the annual inflow of fresh capital.[4] Thus Britain was a net importer of capital from India in the last quarter of the nineteenth century. Investment of new foreign capital was made from the profits of past investments.[5] Still more important was the change in the nature of imports and exports. The highly profitable Dacca muslin trade, worth Rs 3 million in 1787, had stopped altogether by 1817. India's export of cotton goods collapsed and she became a net importer. By 1850 India absorbed a quarter of Lancashire's cotton exports. By 1904 cotton products constituted 39 percent of India's total imports. Food exports likewise rose, at the expense of the local population.[6] "Under the cheering appearance of a brisk grain trade lies concealed the fact that the home and villages of a cultivating nation are denuded of their food to a fatal extent . . . Even on the eve of great famines the export of food goes on as briskly as ever."[7] Traditional peasant economies were destroyed by the introduction of huge plantations for tea and cotton. Where for centuries peasants had been able to sustain their families by work on their own land they became wage labourers on the big estates, unprotected, unlike factory workers, by industrial legislation. Vociferous support of free trade and the abolition of tariffs in India were matched by protectionist policies at home, with duties of up to 80 percent on Indian cotton goods, and the import of silks and taffetas prohibited. Had such restrictions not existed "the mills of Paisley and Manchester would have been toppled in their outset, and could scarcely have been again set in motion, even by the great power of steam. They were created by the sacrifice of Indian manufacture."[8] Industry was established but in a very lopsided way, concentrating on semi-finished goods, raw materials, and consumer industries. In this way, while colonized countries were integrated into the world market, they were created as an underdeveloped periphery dependent on a developed centre. The effects of these policies can in no way be overlooked when considering the present facts of third-world poverty.

The proximate origins of the present situation can be found in the reconstruction of the world economy after World War II. This reconstruction set out to establish a world central bank (to become the International Monetary Fund), a world development agency (the International Bank for Reconstruction and Development or World Bank), and an international trade organization. The latter was never instituted, but the gap was filled by the General Agreement on Tariffs and Trade which was, however, largely a trading agreement between the members of the Organisation for Economic Cooperation and Development (OECD), the twenty-four wealthiest nations. The free trade policy which was advocated never worked to full advantage vis à vis the Third World. The purpose of all these organizations was to develop world trade, and behind them lay a belief in the market economy. Market economies need customers, and in order for third-world countries (or less-developed countries) to be able to purchase the products of the First World they needed to "develop." The aim of development was, in the words of Senator McGovern, that "the people we assist today will become our customers tomorrow." As an American Aid administrator put it in 1964, "Our basic, broadest goal is a long range political one ... An important objective is to open up the maximum opportunity for domestic private initiative and to insure that foreign private investment, particularly from the United States, is welcomed and well treated." President Truman was even more explicit: "All freedom is dependent on freedom of enterprise ... The whole world should adopt the American system ... The American system can survive in America only if it becomes a world system."[9] The desire for development was shared by most third-world countries, which saw it as the obvious route to raise their standard of living. To develop meant acquiring heavy industry and all the infrastructure it requires, and this needed money. Development was funded partly by government aid, partly by investments of transnational companies, and partly by loans from banks. The aim was that these countries would pass through the five stages identified by Walt Rostow, one of the United States government's main advisers during the Vietnam war: the traditional economy, the preconditions for take off, take off, the drive to maturity, and the age of high mass consumption. Of the host of factors which have prevented this happening we shall pick out six.

The first is the continuation of the protectionism we have already seen in the colonial era. Commitment to free trade has never allowed third-world exports to damage first-world markets. In 1986 an article in *The World Economy* noted that "the breakdown in the GATT system is nowhere more evident than in trade relations between developed and developing countries. Here an undeclared trade war is in progress."[10] Products subject to restriction climbed from 20 to 30 percent in the United States and the EEC between 1980 and 1983. Four hundred trade bills designed to prevent imports and protect home products were introduced in the United States Congress in 1985 alone.[11] In order to meet third-world objections to GATT principles of nondiscrimination and reciprocal trade liberalisation, which could only work between equals, the "generalised system of preferences" was introduced in 1969. It was supposed to help developing countries to export their manufactured and semi-manufactured goods by granting tariff preferences, but its force has been almost totally evaded by the imposition of quotas and other restrictive legislation. The European Community specifically excludes the three principal third-world exports — metals, agricultural products, and textiles — from the scheme. The situation in the United States is only very marginally better.[12] The multifibre agreement, which aimed to protect the textile industries of the North against cheap imports from the South, has so far resisted all attempts to change it. The verdict of Belinda Coote, writing for Oxfam, is sombre:

> The GATT is often accused of being a club that regulates world trade to suit the interests of its most powerful members, particularly those of the USA and the EC . . . The evidence to support these criticisms is overwhelming.[13]

It has not even managed to avoid the prospect of trade wars among its leading members, and the 1992 round of GATT negotiations foundered on acrimonious recriminations about protectionism and punitive tariffs. Needless to say, the concerns of the Third World scarcely appear on the agenda.

A further aspect of trade, again stemming from the nature of colonial investment, is that there cannot be competition between the commodity exports of the Third World and the manufactured goods of the First World. Demand for commodities grows only slowly and competition increases; they are sold on the market whereas tractors and turbines are sold on a cost plus basis.[14] The Report of the World Commission on Environment and Development in 1987 maintained that "among the many causes of the African crisis, the workings of the international economy stand out."

> Within the last decade, many sub-Saharan countries have been hit by adverse trends in commodity terms of trade and external shocks such

as higher oil prices, fluctuating exchange rates, and higher interest rates. Over the last 10 years, the prices of major commodities such as copper, iron ore, sugar, ground nuts, rubber, timber and cotton have fallen significantly. In 1985, the terms of trade of sub-Saharan countries (except oil-exporting countries) were 10 percent below 1970 levels ... The economic difficulties of sub-Saharan countries have had devastating social impacts. Declining per capita food production has contributed to growing undernourishment. The recent drought placed some 35 million lives at risk in 1984/5, and as the drought receded some 19 million people continued to suffer famine.[15]

The introduction of artificial substitutes, sometimes prompted by a hike in third-world commodity prices—corn syrup for sugar, synthetics instead of cotton, plastics instead of timber—in turn affects the prices of raw materials. The *Economist* in 1985 estimated the "poor man's gift" to the rich through low commodity prices at $65 billion dollars. An example of the link of IMF policies to a slump in commodity prices is the fate of copper. In 1975 the major copper exporting countries—Chile, Zambia, Zaire, and Peru—had to ask for IMF help. The IMF imposed devaluations on all four countries, which led to over-production, which in turn forced the price in real terms below the 1975 level. In April 1987 GATT figures showed that the percentage of world trade held by third-world countries dropped from 28 percent to 19 percent between 1980 and 1986, while the trade of the rich countries increased proportionately. At the same time imports from third-world countries fell from 29 percent to 19 percent. This, despite the demand that the poorer countries must increase their exports. The World Bank report notes that protectionism has reached the level of the early postwar years. In 1989 the United States warned Brazil, India, and Japan that it might take unilateral steps to protect its own trade by using its Super 301 legislation. In 1986 Julius Nyerere told the National Centre for Cooperation in Development in Brussels:

> This year the rains in Tanzania were quite good. The peasants in our major cotton-growing regions have more than doubled their cotton crop compared with that of last year. We are desperately short of foreign exchange with which to buy essential imports, and cotton is one of our major exports; we were therefore pleased about this big output increase. But the price of cotton on the world market dropped from 68 cents a pound to 34 cents a pound on a single day in July this year. The result for our economy—and the income of the peasants—is similar to that of a natural disaster: half our crop, and therefore of our income, is lost.[16]

A third factor is, as Griffiths points out, the behaviour of third-world elites. Much of the money loaned to these governments is put straight back into Western banks to earn interest for the powerful who have embezzled it. The case of Ferdinand and Imelda Marcos is only the most spectacular of this kind. In 1986 Morgan Guaranty estimated that 70 percent of all loans to the ten principal debtors in Latin America had taken this route. Money has been squandered on pharonic projects for the ruling elite.

Vast differentials between rich and poor call for the apparatus of the national security state, and it is estimated that 20 percent of third-world debt can be attributed to spending on arms. At the same time currently 43 percent of "aid" to the South is military. A clear example from among many of the murderous link between monetarism and repression is Pinochet's Chile where these policies were applied with rigour. The immediate result was repression, and vast human rights abuses. As the 1980s progressed Chile experienced an "economic miracle" as exports climbed and diversified. The cost of the miracle has been failing health; dangerous, insecure, and overlong hours of work; pollution; and ecological devastation. When the fish stocks of the coastal waters, fished by fleets supplying the multinationals, are exhausted, the foreign companies will move on and the people will be left stranded. "Their traditional way of life, and their livelihoods, will have been destroyed. This will be not only a local tragedy but ... a national catastrophe."[17] As far as dangerous work practices go, an editorial in the highly respected magazine *The Economist* leaves us no doubt about transnational managerial views. Under the heading "Don't Green GATT" it warns the new president of the United States that he will be met with all sorts of "old fashioned arguments" about "saving jobs and seeking fairness," which might delay a GATT deal. No, the president must realise that Free Trade is the ally of good environmental policy. The environmental standards appropriate in developing countries may well be lower than in those which are developed. Those in the Third World must express their preference either for first-world standards on pollution or for better health care and education. They cannot have both.[18]

A fourth factor relates to technology, which Singer and Ansari believe to be crucial. They argue that the imbalance between rich and poor countries cannot be corrected by the operations of the market. Salvation for third-world countries lies in the development of indigenous scientific and technological capacities within the developing countries—precisely the programme of the Allende government in Chile. The issue of appropriate technology has been radicalised by Vandana Shiva. She argues that there is an important distinction between poverty as subsistence and misery as deprivation. Western observers, the officials of the IMF for example, declare any nonparticipation in the world economy to be poverty, whereas it may in fact be prudent subsistence. The Ethiopian famine, in which 100,000 people died, was partly created by the attempt to remove culturally perceived poverty. "The displacement of nomadic Afars from their traditional pastureland ... by commercial agriculture (financed by foreign companies) led to their struggle for survival in the fragile uplands which degraded the ecosystem and led to the starvation of cattle and the nomads."[19]

A fifth factor is the role of transnational corporations, which now control between a quarter and a third of total world output and which account for 30 percent of all world trade within themselves. Griffiths's view that the transnational corporations are major benefactors to the Third World is disputed by Singer and Ansari. They argue that, in the first place, their investment is concentrated in a very small number of countries but that, secondly, the overall objective of these companies is maximization of profit. "A development process that is being sustained by organizations interested primarily in profit maximization is organically different from a development process in which the public sector sets the pace. The former is likely to generate tendencies that accentuate income equalities within the developing country ... The direct effect of the multinational's investment is largely confined to the employment of a small, elite, semi-skilled and highly skilled labour force, the members of which earn incomes that are substantially higher than the incomes of the domestic labour class."[20] They are correspondingly interested in products for which there is already a lucrative world market and which are available only to the wealthy minority in developing countries. "By introducing the ideology of Western consumer society TNCs [transnational corporations] have neglected the pressing basic needs of the mass of underprivileged persons of the developing countries."[21] The companies have a dominant nationality, and funds tend to flow from the firm as a whole to the citizens of the parent country, who hold the bulk of the shares. In the period 1974-77 for instance, net earnings from British overseas investment in developing countries averaged £675 million ($1013 million), whereas the annual net flow of new British investment to the developing countries was only £400 million ($600 million). Further, "the global strategy of a multinational may necessitate the adoption of policies or actions that may be detrimental to the interests of the domestic enterprise or public authority of the country concerned." So-called Free Trade Zones, of which there are now more than eighty operating in thirty countries, offer transnationals cheap nonunion labour kept in check by harsh anti-strike legislation, a range of subsidies, and unrestricted repatriation of profits.[22] In the face of major disasters, such as Bhopal, the host country finds it has very little legal power over the transnational company. Part of the logic of transnational operation is that the companies may "freeze a host country into an existing and unacceptable international division of labour" through their monopoly of the markets. The technology of transnational industries could theoretically spill over into local industries but in general this has not happened. Research and development is primarily made with a view to the requirements of the developed countries. Much of the new technology has nothing to contribute to third-world countries and may, as in the development of synthetics, be positively harmful. Transnational investment can lead to the squeezing out of local firms and consequent increase in the concentration of economic power whose priorities are not dictated by the overall good of any country's population but rather by the amount of profit to be made. Where conditions become uncomfortable the companies can uproot and move elsewhere.

Investment by transnationals often diverts finance and energy away from the rural areas where most people live. Where it does not, however, as in the agribusiness of the Green Revolution, the effects can be in the literal sense disastrous. The introduction of soya bean cultivation in Brazil, for example, has downgraded the quality of the local diet by occupying formerly food-producing land and causing prices to rise. The introduction of cash crops throughout Sub-Saharan Africa has taken the most fertile land away from direct food production. "In this way, they not only exploit the food crisis, but are significantly responsible for it in the first place."[23] The high technology export-crop model of agribusiness increases hunger because "scarce land, credit, water and technology are pre-empted for the export market. Most hungry people are not affected by the market at all ... The profits flow to corporations that have no interest in feeding hungry people without money."[24] Unsympathetic methods of agriculture, using chemical fertilisers and pesticides, and high levels of water consumption drain water tables and ruin the best land, while those who used to work on it are forced into poverty in the cities. The effects of the Ethiopian famine have already been noted. In the Dominican Republic, where the American giants have put huge investments into sugar, food prices have doubled over ten years so that many Dominican families are reduced to one meal per day.

Forests, too, have become cash crops, though the profits made from the sale of timber are not replaced by the cattle ranches which take their place, as the land quickly becomes infertile.

Finally, the argument that multinational investment is in any sense *necessary* to growth (even if this is assumed to be a good thing), is repudiated by the South Korean experience. South Korea has developed its economy by the execution of a strongly state-interventionist economic strategy and not merely by adopting monetarist policies, as Griffiths would like to insist.

Far and away the most important factor, however, is debt. The present debt crisis of third-world countries began when OPEC countries deposited their new oil wealth in Western banks. Since idle money loses against inflation, the banks needed to find countries to take loans. At first interest rates were low or even negative, but they leapt in the 1980s when the United States pushed up world interest rates as a response to trade and budget deficits. The World Commission report already mentioned notes that "major changes in international conditions" made debts contracted in the early 1970s unsustainable.

> A global recession restricted export markets, and tight monetary policies forced up global interest rates to levels far exceeding any in living memory ... A flight of indigenous capital from developing countries

compounded the problem. The ensuing crisis forced governments into austerity policies to cut back imports. As a result, Latin American imports fell by 40 percent in real terms over three years. The consequent economic contraction reduced per capita gross domestic product by an average of 8 percent in the eight main Latin American countries. Much of the burden was carried by the poor, as real wages fell and unemployment rose. Growing poverty and deteriorating environmental conditions are clearly visible in every major Latin American country. Further, the lack of new credit and the continuing burden of debt service forced these countries to service their debts by running trade surpluses. The net transfers from seven major Latin American countries to creditors rose to almost $39 billion in 1984, and in that year 35 percent of export earnings went to pay interest on overseas debt. This massive drain represents 5 to 6 percent of the regions gross domestic product, around a third of the internal savings, and nearly 40% of export earnings.[25]

As a result of this, and the application of monetarist policies, there was a recession in which the price of raw materials, on which third-world economies depend, collapsed.[26] Debts incurred were so large that they needed new loans to finance them. To qualify for new loans the IMF insists on "adjustment programmes." These insist on the abolition or easing of exchange and import controls, devaluation of the local currency, anti-inflation policies of cuts to public spending, high interest rates, and pegging wages. These policies have kept Western banks solvent, involving huge transfers from the southern to the northern hemisphere. The World Bank calculated that the transfer of capital from the Third to the First World in 1986 was $15 billion. The human cost of this to third-world countries is tremendous. Some of these effects are documented by Susan George in *A Fate Worse than Debt*. In Morocco IMF loans were used to develop export crops like citrus fruits, and this meant importing food. Food imports rose 220 percent between 1970 and 1983. In the early 1970s Morocco depended on outside funds for 23 percent of her projects. By 1984 this figure was 76 percent. In 1970 debt accounted for 18 percent of GNP; in 1984 for 110 percent. IMF austerity measures led to riots in which hundreds of people were killed. Throughout Latin America real wages have fallen. In Mexico the agricultural wage is back to its 1965 level. In Bolivia, a country where in 1987 169 out of every 1000 babies died before they were a year old, only 1.94 of the government's budget is spent on health while more than half of its legal foreign earnings goes to pay off its $3.7 billion debt. In Jamaica the adoption of monetarist policies led to a drastic drop in health standards so that in 1982 it had its first polio death in thirty years. In Thailand debt rose from 125 million dollars in 1980 to 9.89 billion in 1985. Much of the borrowed money was put into tourism, a leading feature of which is prostitution. Poverty is the push factor which involves the approximately one million girls involved in this. "Poverty, patriarchy and the debt crisis have conspired to exploit them as a human 'cash crop.' "[27]

In responding to these facts the functionaries of the IMF maintain a stance of principled ideological neutrality. The former managing director of the IMF, Jacques de la Rosiere, has said that "an international institution such as the Fund cannot take upon itself the role of dictating social and political objectives to sovereign governments." As Susan George comments, "If the Fund believed, which it patently does not, that economic growth can also result from greater social equality, access to education, health care and other basic services, fairer income distribution, etc. it could perfectly well make such objectives part of its programmes. On the contrary, exactly those countries that have most insisted on maintaining social objectives ... have had the greatest difficulties in coming to terms with the IMF."[28] Countries which refused to toe the monetarist line have been severely disciplined and the availability of IMF loans has been heavily politically biased. Allende's Chile was refused a loan made freely available to the fascist Pinochet regime. Socialist Vietnam was refused one but South Africa granted one almost equal to its increase in military spending immediately after Soweto. The Somoza regime in Nicaragua was granted one; the Sandanista was not. The then Treasury Secretary, Donald Regan, commented, "The IMF is essentially a nonpolitical institution ... But this does not mean that United States' political and security interests are not served by the IMF."[29] Correspondingly, United States-backed Contra forces in Nicaragua inflicted economic damage on Nicaragua estimated at $600 million, aside from the money the country was obliged to divert to defence. The extraordinarily repressive regime in El Salvador was given standby credit in which normal IMF conditions on interest rates, subsidies, and the prices of agricultural goods were ignored. Countries whose economic policy conflicts with IMF policies are manoeuvered into impossible situations. This has most recently happened with Alan Garcia's Peru. A study of IMF policy concludes that it "intervenes massively in the economic, social and political structures of deficit countries."[30] In fact, Susan George concludes, "The debt crisis is a symptom ... of an increasingly polarized world organized for the benefit of a minority that will stop at nothing to maintain and strengthen its control and its privilege."[31]

New arrangements in 1988 for African countries and for "middle income countries," the so-called Brady Initiative, have done something, but the World Bank report notes that debt service for African countries will continue to cost 5 percent of Gross Domestic Product. "Alternative profit opportunities and doubts about the prospects for debt-distressed countries ... have accelerated the exit of commercial banks."[32] The rescheduling of debt and provision of debt relief is still tied to "stringent macroeconomic management and continued progress with the adjustment programme."

Any response to the problem of third-world poverty has to take account of the interdependence of the contemporary world. Singer and Ansari note that the imbalance between the rich and poor countries cannot be corrected by means of an automatic, self-operating market mechanism. "The cliché that 'each country has the primary responsibility for its own development' is a half truth. The statement that we are 'all members one of another' comes nearer the truth, since the world economy forms an interdependent system. Economic interdependence is inescapable in the modern world."[33] Such interdependence cannot be reduced to the "free play of market forces." The trickle down of wealth which this is supposed to produce does not work globally, any more than it does in national economies, as the World Bank report emphasises. Rather, the net effect of pursuing monetarist policies over the past thirteen years is the growth of the gap between rich and poor on both the global and the domestic scene. Susan George comments that three decades have passed during which the magic of the free market has had time to operate. "We witness, rather, a fiasco: unmanageable debts, stagnant trade, a permanent slump in commodity prices, tragic hunger and poverty on a hitherto unheard of scale. Even the terminally myopic can see that the emperor has no clothes."[34] The reasons for this fiasco, perhaps better described as wickedness, is the compulsion to put growth and profit (which involves lifestyle), before everything else. These are the two fetishes to which millions of human lives are sacrificed. There is nothing fated about economics. Priorities are debatable. We can choose how we allocate resources and which policies we adopt. The net effect of giving absolute priority to profit is death, in two ways. It means death because it has meant the propping up of governments which rule by torture and the death squad, run by dictators such as Somoza, Pinochet, and Marcos. The wars these governments wage against their own populations are known as low intensity conflict, a euphemism for tens of thousands of murders by death squads.[35] The funding of these conflicts is primarily to defend the market economy, as the fanatical opposition to the Sandanista regime in Nicaragua made clear. But secondly there is also *financial* low intensity conflict. A Brazilian Labour leader speaking in 1985 described this in these terms:

> Without being radical or overly bold, I will tell you that the Third World War has already started — a silent war, not for that reason any the less sinister. This war is tearing down Brazil, Latin America and practically all the Third World. Instead of soldiers dying there are children, instead of millions of wounded there are millions of unemployed; instead of destruction of bridges there is the tearing down of factories, schools, hospitals and entire economies ... It is a war by the United States against the Latin American continent and the Third World. It is a war over the foreign debt, one which has as its main weapon interest, a weapon more deadly than the atom bomb.[36]

As with any war, there can be an end. The solution Susan George favours to this genocide by debt includes orienting the economies of third-world countries toward the satisfaction of their own people's real needs, building up a strong agricultural sector as a basis for growth, and making primary health care, literacy, education, and the promotion of women the main aims of social policy. The 1990 World Bank Report goes some way towards this in making the two main pillars of policy for the next decade labour intensive growth geared to appropriate technology and institutions and adequate provision of social services, including primary education, basic health care, and family planning. It continues to insist, however, that "credible macroeconomic measures are of primary importance" and these include "adjustment programmes." The Brady Initiative on debt rescheduling is still guided by the imposition of monetarist policies rather than the election of democratic and representative governments as Susan George proposes.

The kinds of alternative proposals advocated by third-world pressure groups, and by individuals and groups within the Third World who do not toe the IMF line, need not be regarded as merely utopian. If the political will is there, alternatives are possible, but we have to be clear that what is challenged is profit and power. The present system keeps the North awash in capital and maintains the United States and her dependent elites' dominant position. To change this system we need not only resistance in the South but "strong and sustained popular pressure" in the northern countries. It is here that the church has a role to play, as one far from negligible voice in the debate about policy, especially as it has strong grassroots representation both North and South. The last thing the church in the North can do is to play Pontius Pilate and wash its hands of the whole problem. As Paul wrote to the Christians in Rome: "You who boast in the law, do you dishonour God by breaking the law? For as it is written, 'The name of God is blasphemed among the Gentiles because of you'" (Rom 2:23-24).

There are at least three fundamental considerations which demand church pressure for a different economic order.[37] The first is suggested by Singer and Ansari's allusion to St. Paul in reminding us that we are "members one of another" (Eph 4:25). From there we are led to Paul's further reflections on this theme:

> God has composed the body, giving the greater honour to the inferior part, that there may be no discord in the body, but that the members may have the same care for one another. If one member suffers, all suffer together; if one member is honoured, all rejoice together (1 Cor 12:24-26).

Paul's respect for weaker members would entail some kind of global planning which rested on a revision of priorities. This means that economic development cannot be left to the free market. In fact, as the acrimony of the GATT negotiations spells out with tragi-comic seriousness, there is no such thing. There is only a market controlled by the rich and powerful for their own benefit. But that control can be changed—*and has to be changed.*

In the encyclical *Pacem in Terris* John XXIII noted very clearly that "the moral order . . . demands the establishment of some sort of world government."[38] Furthermore, this is a specifically church issue, since Christians in the North grow richer at the expense of those in the South. Thus if there is any sense in which we are still one body, that body is divided among "active thieves, passive profiteers, and deprived victims." Rectifying this situation should be the concern of the so-called ecumenical movement. The unity of the body is not primarily about institutions but, as it was in Corinth, about seeing that the poor are not despised in the household of God.

Secondly, the principle of the remission of debts, the Jubilee year, is a fundamental part of our scriptures, and we pray for it day by day (*opheilema*, translated "trespasses," in fact means "debts"). Jesus himself specifically addressed the question of debt and advocated its remission (Mt 18:24f.). The idea that this teaching might have import for our personal behaviour but no bearing on what society does rests on the entirely artificial individualism we have already criticised. Of course, secular or non-Christian governments cannot be expected to try and run their policy according to the Sermon on the Mount, but in deciding what kind of policy it should be advocating the church is certainly guided by it. The church cannot single-handedly put these policies into practice, but it *can* contribute through the "education of desire" and through the practical suggestions of prophecy. What the remission of debt might actually amount to is indicated by Susan George's idea of creative rescheduling. In no sense need the idea of remission be the stuff of fairy stories, though failure to reschedule might well be the stuff of apocalyptic.

Thirdly, the priority of life is part of the church's founding charter. Political regimes and economic policies which lead to death cannot be connived at by the church, far less offered spurious theological justification. That such justifications are offered has led Ulrich Duchrow to propose that the global economy is a confessional issue for the churches. "If the heresy of the 'German Christians' in the time of the Nazi Third Reich was their blasphemous misuse of Christ's name to extend the power of the German Aryan 'master race' the question put to us today is . . . Where is Christ's name being directly or indirectly (mis)used to justify and maintain the power of the white race, especially that of its wealthy and powerful representatives, by every available kind of propaganda, economic manipulation and military and other forms of violence."[39] The theological issues this raises will be dealt with more fully in the final chapter, but for the moment we can note Duchrow's proposals that *first* churches must see their own financial practices as a theological problem and that *second* they need to study both the ideologies of the present system and its effects both at home and abroad. As an advocate of *life* the church is a resistance movement against *death*. Its existence as such is the hermeneutic of the gospel which constitutes Christian ethics. The building of a new kind of social order might, like judgement, begin with the household of God. It could do so by addressing the issues of the global economy.

11

The Longing of Creation

Where were you when I laid the foundation of the earth?
Tell me, if you have understanding . . .
On what were its bases sunk,
or who laid its cornerstone
when the morning stars sang together
and all the heavenly beings shouted for joy?

—Job 38

By now the story of how the holes in the earth's ozone layer were discovered is widely known. In 1975 American scientists postulated a link between chlorofluocarbons (CFCs), the raw material of all sorts of insulating material from hamburger containers, to walls, to refrigerators and ozone loss. Two years later restrictions on the production of CFCs were proposed but resisted by the European Community, which produces nearly half of world CFC output. In 1984 British scientists in Antarctica, who had been measuring a steady decline in the ozone layer for ten years, but had not believed their data, found what seemed to be a hole in it. In the United States, scientists at the National Aeronautics and Space Administration (NASA) were sure there was no such thing; satellite readings had never revealed it. As they retrieved and checked over their data they found their computers had been programmed to reject the findings — on the assumption that the instruments must be wrong.[1] The story is a parable of contemporary attitudes to the planet. We take the earth for granted. We have lived with it so long; it has protected us, and nurtured us. Surely things can't go this seriously wrong? The situation has been aptly compared to that on the Titanic after she grazed the iceberg; no one fussed or worried. Here they were on a ship which was the product of the very latest technology, double hulled, and unsinkable. At the end, all that was left was for the band to play *"Nearer My God to Thee"* with dignity as they settled below the icy seas.

142

PEOPLE AND THE PLANET

For the vast majority of human history people have had no option but to respect their environment. The questions God put to Job from the whirlwind summed up their position vis à vis the nonhuman creation. In humble awe the psalmist asked

> When I look at your heavens,
> the work of your fingers,
> the moon and the stars that you have established;
> what are human beings that you are mindful of them,
> mortals that you care for them? (Ps 8:3-4).

Humans were only too aware of their limited strength, skill, and wisdom over against the mystery of creation. Over millennia human beings throughout the world, from the Arctic to the Sahara, evolved a dazzling range of cultures which lived in respectful symbiosis with the environment. Clothing, housing, diet—all drew on what was locally available. All peoples drew on skills slowly and cumulatively developed, though the "neolithic revolution," when agriculture was first practised, seems to have been a critical turning point. The wisdom of these countless centuries of experience is what sustained all peasant societies, and all forest dwellers and aboriginal populations, until the coming of industrialisation. In many areas of the world, and for many millions of people, this wisdom has not been lost, and symbiotic life patterns which go back to the dawn of human time still govern ways of life. But they are under imminent threat. Alternative tourist agencies seek ever remoter places to stimulate jaded appetites, and tourism brings with it all the baggage of the late twentieth century. Governments needing to raise foreign exchange cut down forests and dam rivers. As this happens the ancient ways of living together with nature are destroyed, often taking native populations with them.[2]

We must not romanticise preindustrial society. Reading medieval or earlier history is harrowing not just because of the "inhumanity of man to man," but because of the chronicle of famine and pestilence, drought, flood, crop failure, and disease. We can scarcely imagine what the Black Death, which may have wiped out a third of the population of Europe, meant to people. "However great the terrors of war were to ordinary people," writes the medieval historian Richard Southern, "undoubtedly famine and disease were the main sources of despair."[3] Very gradual improvements in health led, over many centuries, to the elimination of plague from Europe by the end of the seventeenth century. Equally gradual improvements in technology led to houses which were less draughty, more weatherproof, and to better sanitation. Health began to improve, and people began to live longer. These improvements are responsible for that change from the *memento mori* culture of the early sixteenth century, to the self-confidence of its end. The growing confidence of the late seventeenth century, and the downright optimism of people like Adam Smith, reflect an accurate perception that in some ways things were improving. Population statistics show that people were living longer; infant mortality, though still terrible, fell. Smith lived exactly at the turning point from symbiosis to domination. The development of steam power and of sophisticated technology, scarcely a twinkle in anyone's eye at the beginning of the century, took off and has not ceased since. Success bred a new attitude to nature. At the end of the eighteenth century Paley could still argue for God from the marvel of creation, and Goethe and Wordsworth could find the Divine Spirit in "rocks and stones and trees." By the middle of the next century the most dismal of all philosophies, Positivism, had replaced Hegel's theory of the immanent development of Spirit. By the end, the Jesuit poet Gerald Manley Hopkins, looking sadly out over industrial landscapes, could only acknowledge that everything "wore man's smudge and bore man's smell."

The intellectual origins of this development have been much discussed. In a famous paper Lynn White traced it to medieval Christianity's attitude to nature, which appealed to the Genesis command to "have dominion" over the earth. Religions shape values, and values shape cultures, White argued, and the values Christianity inculcated were aggressive, dominating, and exploitative.[4] Caroline Merchant has highlighted the chilling interrelationship of sexual and scientific rhetoric with that of torture and the inquisition among the early philosophers of science, and especially Francis Bacon. According to him nature, conceived as feminine, must be bound into service, made a slave, conquered and subdued, and hounded to reveal her secrets. Her womb must be entered and penetrated. The scientific revolution of the Renaissance effected a paradigm shift from viewing nature as Mother Earth to a female slave to be subjected to bondage and raped.[5] Her argument is persuasive, and yet to look only to these intellectual attitudes is to oversimplify. We must rather understand both late medieval Christianity and the project of Baconian science as expressions of the new self-confidence we have noted, *in part bred by more efficient technology*. We find the beginnings in the sixteenth century, but the full flowering comes later. The sixteenth century is not only the period of the conquistadors but of humanists like Erasmus and Socinus, not only the period of increasingly effective guns, but of the invention of the water closet and of sewage arrangements which drastically improved community health. In someone like John Donne we have *both* the swagger of "Renaissance man," dividing the world with his compasses, jestingly bidding the "unruly sun" not to bother him and his mistress, *and* the anguished religious person at the mercy of sudden death and fully aware of his puny limitations. What happens in the next two hundred years is that the unity of science and religion is increasingly severed. Already for Hume religion is pathetically dishonest nonsense; for Bentham it is beneath discussion. The human person is no longer a unity of body and soul, but a machine. This intellectual development cannot be understood aside from the growth of a world market and the founding of colonial empires. Self-confidence; new technology; the drive of the market; new ways of conceiving the world. None of these can be separated from the others. And this brings us to our point: a momentum is established. At first it feels like bravely battling uphill, against all odds. This is the atmosphere of the early circumnavigators and of scientists like Copernicus, Galileo and even Kepler. In one way or another all these people did what they did at risk to their lives. We cannot read Hakluyt's *Voyages* or the story of Galileo's encounter with the Inquisition, without admiring their courage. Another two hundred years and there is the sense that moral and material progress stretches before human beings like the open road. This is the sense of Hegel, of the Victorian entrepreneurs, of Huxley, and even of Marx. But speed continues to accumulate. One hundred years later we begin to realise that the vehicle is out of control, travelling at a lunatic speed, careening off the road. We look around for the brakes and realise that none were incorporated in the model. The assumption had been, the faster the better. We have gone, as Meadows and Randers put it, *beyond the limits*.

THE EARTH MOURNS

"The earth mourns," said the prophet Hosea long ago, "and all who live in it languish" (Hos 4:3). He spoke out of that profound sense of human beings bound up with the bundle of life which marks all ancient cultures. Human wickedness affects not only themselves, but all creation. The facts of how this has happened in hitherto unimaginable ways in the twentieth century are documented in hundreds of reports, silting up over the past thirty years. The facts are familiar, but it is nevertheless important that we review them briefly before continuing the discussion. In doing so we can follow the psalmist.

The heavens, the works of your hands (Ps 8:3).

The ozone layer, damage to which has already been noted, protects us from harmful radiation.[6] Without it we develop skin cancer. But more important, it is a vital part of what makes the earth able to support life; the effects of its large-scale destruction are simply incalculable. Even if CFC depletion stopped tomorrow, a century would be needed for the ozone layer to be restored. Given this, and given the scientific evidence for what is happening, resistance to the creation of CFCs can only be described as reckless. Profit, and the need to retain jobs, is what accounts for such recklessness. Business generated by products incorporating CFCs is simply too profitable to give up. A 1997 deadline for withdrawal has been overruled in favour of the year 2000.

Equally important is the impact of carbon dioxide in global warming, the so-called greenhouse effect. The emission of carbon dioxide is natural. It traps heat and keeps the planet warm; we could not survive without it. When natural processes are augmented by 450 million motor vehicles, however, responsible for 13 percent of global carbon emissions and 25 percent of world oil consumption, not to mention the industries which supply consumer needs, the temperature of the earth increases unnaturally, again with unknown effects. Winds, rains, and ocean currents will shift in strength and direction, and sea levels will rise. "Whatever the consequences might be, there is no question that humanity's emissions of greenhouse gases are filling up atmospheric sinks much faster than the planet can empty them. There is a significant disequilibrium in the global atmosphere, and it is getting exponentially worse."[7]

YHWH prepares rain for the earth,
makes grass grow on the hills (Ps 147:8).

L. S. Lowry's industrial landscapes are among the best known evocations of the first half of the present century. People scurry about in the mill towns of northern England, past soot grimed buildings, blackened by chimneys belching smoke at every corner. As postwar governments moved to get rid of smog all over the Western world, domestic fires disappeared and factory chimneys were heightened as much as six times. There was clean air once more. Or was there? Very soon the problem of acid rain was diagnosed, rain which brought down sulphur dioxide and nitrogen oxide, damaging lakes, and forests, and historic buildings. Led by the Scandinavian countries, many states have agreed to reduce nitrogen oxide emissions, but the United States, Britain, and Poland have refused. Such policies are too expensive domestically, and the damage is far away. It is always possible to shelter behind the argument that theories are "inconclusive."

You make springs gush forth in the valleys;
they flow between the hills,
giving drink to every wild animal (Ps 104:10).

Human conflicts have largely been about control of resources: land, seaboards, more recently about oil. In the future, it is predicted, conflicts will be about water.[8] Through the processes of evaporation and precipitation, 40,000 cubic kilometres of water are transferred from the sea to the land each year. As human populations rise, there is less water to go around. Countries which receive fewer than 1000 cubic metres per person are considered water scarce. Already twenty-six countries, home to 232 million people, are water scarce, and their number is growing. Aquifer reserves of water, untapped before the middle years of this century, are being recklessly exhausted in countries such as Saudi Arabia and Libya, while realization of the problems involved in draining them has led to the shrinking of the once great beef industry in Texas. The loss of aquifer recharge from land degradation has caused major problems in India, so that even areas of high rainfall are perpetually short of water. The Indian scientist Jayanto Bandyopadhyay warns: "Water is only a renewable resource if we respect the ecological processes that maintain and give stability to the water cycle."[9] Throughout the world the need for quick fixes has led to the ignoring of this warning. As populations grow, so the need for food, and therefore more irrigated land, grows. The answer for decades seemed to be to build dams, but the effects of many of these call this solution into question. Sometimes irrigation projects have spread waterborne diseases. The prevalence of biharzia climbed from 15 percent to 80 percent after the completion of the Gezira project in Sudan. In India local people and environmentalists have fought the construction of the vast Naramada dam complex, arguing that it will not benefit the majority of the people it aims to serve and will lead to waterlogging and salinization. Wherever great projects like this have gone through it has proved that technical know-how is not the be all and end all. The most spectacular illustration of this is in Russia's Aral Sea, where the diversion of tributary waters for irrigation purposes led to a 40 percent shrinking of the sea's surface, the death of all fish in the sea, and the end, therefore, of a once flourishing fish industry. The Aral Sea is now the most polluted lake on earth, and typhoid, hepatitis, and cancer have all increased among the communities who live around it. Symbiotic living has been replaced by the arrogant confidence of the engineer who assumes that human ingenuity and constructive skill will provide an answer to everything. But ingenuity without wisdom turns out to be catastrophic, something ancient Greek writers already knew very well. They described it as *hubris*.

The trees of the Lord (Ps 104:16).

The great forests are the lungs of the world.[10] We rely on them to stabilize climate and to keep the hydrological cycle functioning. But they are shrinking by more than 17 million hectares a year. Two hundred million hectares, an area the size of the United States east of the Mississippi River, have been lost since 1972. Locally the destruction of forests leads to increased floods and droughts, silting up of rivers, and the destruction of fish breeding areas. Because these forests are home of half the biological species on earth, their destruction is a primary cause of the loss of biodiversity. In addition, the forests are still home to an estimated 140 million forest dwellers, whose way of life is threatened. The burning of forests also contributes significantly to global warming.

In the case of acid rain or global warming it has been the industrialised countries which have formed veto coalitions to oppose measures to reduce

damage. In the case of the world's forests it is the heavily indebted countries
of the South, which account for 62 percent of the world's remaining forests,
which form the veto coalition. Malaysia in particular has insisted that no
forest agreement can be negotiated until developed countries commit themselves to reduce energy consumption.[11] Once again self-interest — the need
for hard cash or foreign exchange — lies behind a recklessness which can
damage the whole earth.

Yonder is the sea, great and wide,
creeping things innumerable are there . . .
There goes Leviathan that you formed to sport in it (Ps 104:26).

The whale can be taken as representative of numerous endangered species, from the African elephant, killed for its ivory, to butterfly species
becoming extinct because their habitat is destroyed.

Israel was not a sea-going people. So far were they from any utilitarian
approach to its riches that the only purpose they could think of for whales
was that God created them to play with in the evening. It was a beautiful
image of a creation made primarily for joy. Commercial whaling could
only begin when ships were big enough and strong enough to cope with
the icy seas that whales favour. The hardships and dangers of whaling in
the eighteenth and nineteenth centuries generated a moving volume of
songs and stories. Many men lost their lives on "the weary whaling
grounds." The coming of steel ships and the harpoon gun changed all
that. Whales were now sitting targets and were hunted ruthlessly. By the
mid-sixties the blue whale was in danger of extinction; only two thousand
of them were left. Strong pressure for many years failed to stop the major
whaling nations, especially Japan. "A long history of scientific evidence
was subordinated to the political and economic interests of the whaling
nations as the International Whaling Commission's Scientific Committee
routinely produced data and analysis supporting the continued commercial exploitation."[12] Over the past twenty years, international pressure
has succeeded in enforcing a moratorium, though the three principal
whaling nations have threatened to withdraw from the IWC if it continues. What possible gain can there be to cultures in which whale meat
conventionally forms part of the diet to extinguish that resource? The
short-term outlook and blinkered intransigence are paradigmatic of
human responses to such threats in many areas. "Scientific" evidence
can be manipulated until it is too late, and we can then claim that we
were misled. But we have already learned from Rubem Alves that there
is no such thing as pure science, only science funded by this or that vested
interest.

The earth lies polluted
under its inhabitants;
for they have transgressed laws,
violated the statutes,
broken the everlasting covenant.
Therefore a curse devours the earth (Is 24:5).

For the nineteenth-century theologian Schleiermacher, Isaiah's everlasting covenant referred to an eternal pact between theology and reason.
The course of the intervening two centuries have called this interpretation
into question. The everlasting covenant, as this appears in Genesis, is about
the interrelationship of all living things under the sign of God's presence,
the rainbow. It is, in part, technical reason which has led to the breaking
of this covenant, human *hubris*, lack of what the Hebrew scriptures speak
of over and over again as wisdom.

On a wet autumn afternoon in 1987 a pathetic group of perhaps forty
mothers pushing children in prams made their way up ancient Oxford's
main shopping street to the Town Hall to make a protest. The previous
week a young mother who had left her baby outside a supermarket while
she went to do her shopping returned to find her baby dead, poisoned by
carbon monoxide fumes released by the newly deregulated buses. This happens even in so-called advanced countries, where health care is available
and pollution laws are in force. In Mexico City coin-operated oxygen
machines are needed, and pregnant wives of foreign businessmen or dip-
lomats are sent away to have their babies. To spend a day in Bombay is
the equivalent of smoking ten cigarettes. In Bangkok the presence of two
million cars has made lead poisoning endemic in the city's children.

The problems caused by industrial pollution are even more widely dis-
seminated. In the Rhine, though fish are once more to be found, chloride
levels remain high, coming from the salt mines in Alsace, as do nitrogen
levels from the use of chemical fertilizers. Cadmium, which does not break
down chemically, is now embedded in the river bottom. Nuclear power
stations, with a life span of perhaps only thirty or forty years, produce waste
which may last for millennia and which cannot be rendered harmless.
"Every day one million tons of hazardous wastes are generated in the world,
90% of them in the industrialized world."[13] Most of these involve artificially
synthesized chemicals; there are no natural organisms to break down such
chemicals. Accidents involving these toxins occur every day. Chernobyl is
only the dramatic symbol of something which is going on, on a small scale,
daily. One of the worst aspects of this waste is that much of it is exported
to third-world countries for ready cash, a process which the Dutch minister
of the environment properly spoke of as "waste colonialism." Such "accidents" and the "side effects" of pollution are not the necessary results of
progress but spring rather from a fundamental disregard both for people
and for the planet.

THOSE GREEDY FOR GAIN

Those who make their highest priority the amassing of wealth and possessions receive a sombre warning in the first chapter of Proverbs. They exploit others, but properly speaking the ambush they set is for themselves, says the writer:

> Such is the end of all who are greedy for gain;
> it takes away the life of its possessors (Prv 1:19).

If we ask what the cause of the ecological problems we have outlined is, then the answer is absolutely clear. It stems from the interrelationship of the market's need for growth and the consumer's need for more. It is true that the world's exploding population is also a problem of the utmost magnitude. Northern analysts often suggest that this is a third-world programme which "they" have to get in order. If not, then, to go back to the example of the Titanic, we need a lifeboat ethic. It is certain that the earth is finite (though the rhetoric of the market ignores that) and is therefore only capable of sustaining a population of a certain size. Each country must regard itself as a lifeboat which can only carry a certain number of people, argues Garrett Hardin.[14] We must find ways of dealing with any surplus if we are not to threaten the life of the entire planet. Aid therefore should be directed to those countries with the greatest chance of survival, while others are abandoned to famine. This is supported by the situation ethicist, Joseph Fletcher, who maintains that "any action, however 'criminal,' can be right depending on the situation." He says that although he hates the idea, he cannot resist the lifeboat logic.[15] The malleability of ethics is explained in terms of the myth of the expert. We learn in another context that "in every specialism there are situations which appear unacceptable and inexplicable to the lay person and yet the professionals involved have clearly understood and evaluated the ethical implications."[16] There is more than an echo of the Third Reich in this justification of the "unacceptable and inexplicable."

More drastic still is the argument of Christopher Manes, who wishes to go back beyond the neolithic revolution. He maintains that the only ecologically acceptable lifestyle is that of hunter gatherers. Since such a society can only support a very small population, we have to recognise that the vast majority of the world's population is ecologically redundant.[17]

These totalitarian solutions can only be addressed rationally by analysing the relation of population and consumption. If population is taken first, in what follows, it is not because that is taken to be the key issue, as opposed to consumption—rather the reverse. It is consumption patterns which have to be addressed before the problem of overpopulation can be solved.

Be fruitful, and multiply, and replenish the earth (Gn 1:28).

It was Parson Malthus who first raised the alarm about population growth in 1798.[18] He wrote in the first industrialised country and theorised what was evident to all — that people were living longer and that there were a great many more of them. More people mean more people, as growth is exponential. Malthus foresaw disaster and recommended withdrawing all support from the poor as a way of dealing with this situation. What Malthus did not appreciate was the connection, now proven to exist, between prosperity and security on the one hand, and birth rates on the other. As northern hemisphere countries acquired prosperity, their birthrates fell. This fact is crucial in considering the present population explosion, most of which takes place in the South.

World population has more than doubled since 1950, to the present figure of 5.4 billion. Projections for the future vary, but it is expected to be between 10 and 12 billion by 2050. The lifeboat ethicists have a point in that such growth rates put a huge strain on resources — on water, on forests, on the whole food chain. More people are born into the degradation of absolute poverty. The question is how this problem is to be tackled. The 1991 *State of the World's Children* report argues that four factors are necessary for lower birth rates: economic and social progress, improvements for women, family planning programmes, and reduced infant mortality. All these factors work together:

> Women's advancement (and especially secondary education) makes family planning more likely; family planning reduces both child deaths and child births; slower population growth can assist economic progress; economic progress can lead to lower birth rates.[19]

The report speaks of a "cat's cradle of synergisms," which makes it impossible to single out one factor over others. The empowerment of women is obviously crucial. Women's groups in India which began with family planning have ended by extending their brief to community health, literacy, and the environment. Family planning, meanwhile, has been shown to be unfeasible where under 5 mortality rates are above 100 per 1000 births. For that situation to be altered, better living conditions, better diet, and better water are needed. These problems *can* be addressed; positive movement in this synergism can begin. But only if the North plays its part. We need to listen to the voice of Amos, long ago:

Hate evil and love good,
and establish justice in the gate (Am 5:15).

Though population growth is occurring primarily in the South, it is the North which is responsible for the ecological destruction which affects us all. Humankind can be roughly graded into three economic groups, which vary greatly in terms of consumption. The world's poor number approximately 1.1 billion, live on grains and lentils, get here and there by walking, and cook and warm themselves on wood fires or by using cow dung. The middle-income group earns between $700 and $7,500 per family member. They have sufficient grain, and clean water; they travel by bicycle and bus; and they own a few consumer durables. The rich, on the other hand, have an income of more than $7,500; they have a diet of meat, fast food, and soft drinks; they travel by plane and private car; they are part of the throw-away society.[20] With 24 percent of world population the North consumes 64 percent of all meat, 81 percent of all paper, 80 percent of all iron and steel, is responsible for 70 percent of all carbon dioxide emissions, and owns 92 percent of all cars. It is the consumer society, numbering again 1.1 billion, which is responsible for most environmental damage. As an example, it is estimated that the average Swiss "pours 2000 times more toxic waste into the environment than the average Sahelian farmer ... If levels of waste and consumption do not change the 57 million extra Northerners expected during the 1990s will pollute the Earth more than the extra 911 million Southerners."[21]

> The furnishings of our consumer life-style — things like automobiles, throwaway goods and packaging, a high fat diet, and air conditioning — can only be provided at great environmental cost. Our way of life depends on enormous and continuous inputs of the very commodities that are most damaging to the earth to produce: energy, chemicals, metals, paper.[22]

It is this pattern of consumption more than population growth which is putting the planet at risk. To go back to the picture of the slow growth from symbiosis to a vehicle out of control, global economic output was greater in the 1980s than in the entire period of human history until 1950! We have to ask why this is so.

The answer is not far away. It can be found in the advertisements and editorials of every business magazine, from *The Economist* to *Business Week*. Growth is the deity which is adored, whose service requires any sacrifice. The chief executive of Coca Cola extols growth as an experience of heaven: "When I think of Indonesia — a country on the Equator with 180 million people, a median age of 18, and a Moslem ban on alcohol — I feel I know what heaven looks like."[23] He points out that his company has conquered the globe as neither Napoleon, nor Hitler, nor Lenin managed to. Such growth is completely at odds with the demands of the global ecosystem. "To the extent that constraints on economic expansion are discussed on the business pages, it is in terms of inadequate demand growth rather than limits imposed by the earth's resources. Lacking an understanding of the carrying capacity of ecological systems, economic planners are unable to relate demand levels to the health of the natural world."[24] Economists still believe in the possibility of technological "fixes" whereas ecologists realise that economics forms a narrow subset of the global ecosystem. Until this vital shift of view is achieved, putting ecology before economics, there is little chance of altering present ruinous consumption patterns.

Growth is needed for profit, of course, but to sustain growth it is necessary to work on the human psyche. Consumerism appeals to elemental aspects of the human being. It is natural to desire comfort, devices which will save us toil, greater mobility. As consumer durables accumulate, a collective culture develops around them, defining who is in and who is out. Advertising capitalises on this: unless you drink, or smoke, or eat this product you are not sexy, attractive, potent. Satisfactions, especially sexual ones, are implicitly promised but never realised. There is always a further horizon where the ultimate experience might finally be awaiting us. There is always room to upgrade equipment. Technology moves so fast that cars, hi-fi, video machines are out of date almost as soon as they are marketed. The promise is always of something better.

You are what you own is the universal advertising slogan, promoting everything from shampoo to jeans to luxury cars. This leads to a quite systematic distortion of values. Human longings and instincts are valuable only insofar as they can be exploited for market growth. The question is not what people need, but what they can be persuaded to think they need. Thus capitalism is rooted in a world of illusion, a general voyeurism determines the human instinctual culture, and those who are neither young, nor beautiful, nor successful are marginalised.[25] In the advertising culture it is no longer "man" who is the measure of all things, but sexual orgasm. Advertising promises us that all products will either finally deliver that to us or simulate it. If prophecy is the proper education of desire, this is its demonic opposite, a negative education of desire freed of all moral constraint. Iris Murdoch has argued consistently that if attention to reality is the heart of the moral life, then fantasy is the heart of its opposite.[26] The satisfactions promised us by the advertising culture are entirely illusory. They do not exist. They do not exist because true sexual satisfaction is only found in relations of *love*, relations which integrate the erotic into that shared common project Paul speaks of as agape. By the same token the substitute satisfactions promised us by the consumer world fail because they do not stand in relation to a common social project. The only ultimate satisfaction is life together, in peace and justice, with others.[27] The market needs not only to forget this, but to cause others to forget it, for it needs the spending power of individual *consumers* (the sinister euphemism for people in adspeak). The logic of the market was stated with brutal clarity by one of its principal spokeswomen: "There is no such thing as society."[28]

LEARN WISDOM!

Wisdom cries out in the street;
in the squares she raises her voice ...

"How long, O simple ones, will you love being simple?"
(Prv 1:20f.).

"Simple" here, of course, means "slow-witted." Today it is addressed to those of us who believe that the consumer lifestyle can last forever. The earth is, as the seventeenth-century Diggers loved to say, a common treasury for all. If the human family is one, then there can be no moral ground for treating one part of it differently from another. For the planet to survive, the consumption patterns of those of us in the North cannot be maintained. Just as there are strategies for dealing with population growth, so there are strategies for dealing with consumption. Some of these are technical — involving increasingly efficient energy uses. More important still is the moral counter revolution which is called for.

Durning quotes from Aristotle the remark that "human avarice is insatiable." It is worth looking at what Aristotle *actually* said. The Greek word in question is *orexis*, "appetite." Aristotle had a good deal to say about this, and he recognised it as a life force in both humans and animals.[29] Unbridled appetite, however, he regarded as a sign of immaturity:

> The name self-indulgence is applied to childish faults . . . children live at the beck and call of appetite, and it is in them that the desire for what is pleasant is strongest . . . In an irrational being the desire for pleasure is insatiable and tries every source of gratification, and the exercise of appetite increases its innate force, and if appetites are strong and violent they even expel the power of calculation. Hence they should be moderate and few, and should in no way oppose reason — and this is what we call an obedient and chastened state — and as the child should live according to the direction of his tutor, so the appetitive element should live according to reason.[30]

We live in a society where the childish craving of appetite is not disciplined but rather encouraged in every conceivable way. We are like spoiled children who, if we do not get our way, throw a tantrum. If we are to survive, there is no option but for us to learn from the best parts of our tradition, to learn what Aristotle called "temperance" (*sophrosune*, translated in the Christian scriptures as "sobriety"), rational control of the appetite. Most people already recognise this very clearly with regard to drinking and diet. We recognise the way that a drinking problem can destroy individuals and their families. We have associations, self-help groups, doctors, psychiatrists, for those who cannot control their craving for drink. But we have not acknowledged that consumerism is a related disease — that we cannot control our cravings for everything the world has to give us. The difference is that while alcoholism destroys individual lives, our corporate disease stands to destroy the life of the planet. A certain amount technology can do, and must do. The development of realistic forms of solar energy, for example, is an urgent technical imperative. But the root problem is moral. Aristotle's "temperance" means concretely that enough is enough. We have already all that is required for the realisation of a full and satisfying human life: the resources to feed everyone, to relieve people from the worst and most degrading forms of toil, to provide creative forms of leisure, to guarantee high levels of health care. It is not a question of putting the brakes on human inventive skill, but of *directing* that skill so that it is no longer at the service of the market, but serves instead the interests of the whole human family and the whole planet.

It is here the church has a role to play, not as the only voice, but as one important voice in the ethical debate. With the people of Israel we must "learn wisdom." We simply have to recognize that greed is destructive, and that only through cooperation, justice, and sharing can life be sustained. There are only two other alternatives. One is that those of us in the North play the Pied Piper, leading the world's children away to destruction. The other, unfortunately more plausible, is that advocates of Fascist lifeboat projects will gain power and declare war on the Third World, or at least, let the people of the South starve. Nazism could then be seen as a trial run for what would truly be a "final solution." But that would also, truly, be the destruction of the human essence.

PART FOUR

TWO WAYS

12

Two Ways

What amount of wealth we should produce if we are all working cheerfully at producing the things that we all genuinely want; if all the intelligence, all the inventive power, all the inherited skill of handicraft, all the keen wit and insight, all the healthy bodily strength were engaged in doing this and nothing else, what a pile of wealth we should have! How would poverty be a word whose meaning we should have forgotten! Believe me, there is nothing but the curse of inequality which forbids this.

—William Morris

The concern of Christian ethics is fullness of life, and this means that economics is at the heart of ethical concern for, as Hilaire Belloc remarked, the control of the production of wealth is the control of human life itself. It is the argument of this book, as it was the argument of the Deuteronomists, that two ways lie before us, a way of life and a way of death, a way of equality and a way of domination, a way of corporate justice and a way of concealed tyranny, a way of global nurture and a way of global suicide. The way of death is the prevailing economic system, built on cynicism and whistling for destruction, content to enjoy power and affluence at the expense of the Third World and of future generations. The way of life calls for conversion, turning around, making new options, as it did for the people who listened to the Deuteronomic preachers. Then it was the future of Israel which was at stake; now it is the future of humankind and of the planet.

BY THEIR FRUITS ...

In 1984 the Catholic Bishops of the United States issued a pastoral letter strongly condemning many aspects of the modern capitalist economy. According to them "the fundamental moral criterion for all economic decisions, policies and institutions is this: They must be at the service of all people, especially of the poor."[1] The justice of a community, they argued, is measured by its treatment of the powerless in society. According to these criteria the level of inequality both in America and globally is "morally inacceptable."

This document was answered by a letter from prominent Catholic lay people. They advanced five different arguments in the defence of contemporary capitalism. Pointing out that the word *capitalism* comes from *caput*, "head," they maintained that "the cause of the wealth of nations is inventive intellect, the creativity of the human intelligence seeking to decipher the wealth hidden in creation by the Creator himself." In this way capitalism is a sharing in God's creation. This they then interpreted by an appeal to contemporary theories of creation and evolution on the one hand, and Schumpeter's famous defence of the role of the entrepreneur on the other. "The path of the free economy is marked, like that of God's creation itself, with what Schumpeter has called 'creative destruction.' " Thirdly, they maintained that only a market system respects the free creativity and liberty of every human person. Fourthly, the ethics of private property and of self-interest were derived from scripture — the former from a law of nature, legitimized by the command "You shall not steal" and the latter from the Golden Rule ("Love your neighbour *as yourself*"). Finally they appealed to the actual results of the market. Because countries based on private property and market systems, incentives, and the discipline of profit have raised the living standards of their poor, "We judge markets to be by far the most successful social device ever discovered . . . 'By their fruits ye shall know them.' "

The argument of this book has been that this claim is not justified. We found that, in the phrase of Braverman, capitalism has meant the systematic degradation of work, the reduction of human beings to an "appendage to a machine." Work has been organised according to a division of labour which divorces conception from execution, the former of which is committed to a managerial class and denied to others. The system is predicated on the inequality of life chances, which means a growing gap between rich and poor both in Western countries and globally, the holocaust of those who die by starvation when there are adequate resources for all, and the widespread employment of death squads in countries committed to the market economy. It is predicated on the systematic divorce of ethics and economics — the subjection of social policy to the fetish of "economic man." It is predicated, finally, on the cornering and hoarding of earth's resources for a tiny minority and their denial to the majority. All of these policies involve a reckless destruction of the earth. By their fruits you shall indeed know them.[2]

The world view generated by capitalism is marked by a manifold *dualism*, between fact and value, ethics and economics, freedom and equality, the individual and society, work and leisure. It rests on a view of the human which gives absolute priority to *self-interest*, what Adam Smith called "the uniform, constant, and uninterrupted effort of every man to better his condition." This leads to a situation where self-interest is seen as a moral principle, in contradistinction to almost every other ethical system. Older societies depended upon religious and social obligation, but in the market society we take account of others only insofar as they serve our interests. The baker does not bake good bread to serve his customers well. "The baker does not have to bake 'good' bread or serve his customers 'well'; he has to avoid serving his customers so badly that he drives them away. The coincidence of interest becomes a matter of precise calculation and the development of a market economy enables us all to take part in the calculation."[3] The effect of organising society around such a principle is that disintegration of community which is so obvious a feature in all Western societies, and the collapse of ethical discourse remarked by Alasdair MacIntyre follows directly from it. Where we have no common goal we have no common good, and without an end, a *telos*, there can be no ethic. This collapse can be instantiated from two of the principal defenders of the capitalist order, Friedman and Hayek.

Friedman interprets the Declaration of Independence – that all men are created equal and endowed by their Creator with unalienable rights – as meaning that "every person is entitled to pursue their own values." But Jefferson, and the other framers of this Declaration, presupposed and spoke out of a society where an immense tradition about values was taken for granted – the seventeenth-century New England conscience was not yet dead. After two hundred years of the promotion of self-interest as the only value, there is no longer grounds for such an appeal. The Friedmans demonstrate this in their manifest failure to understand what the word *ethical* means. Inequality of outcome, they point out, may come from the inheritance of property or from genetic inheritance. The Friedmans ask, "From the ethical point of view, is there any difference between the two?"[4] But the ethical question is about what we *do* with our talents, however we receive them – whether we use them for private gain or for others. In an example of repulsive triviality they conclude that we benefit from unfairness – we all like looking at Marlene Dietrich's legs, for example.[5] Moreover, if the winners repaid the losers this would take all the fun out of the game. So the world economy is a great game, a divine sport – in which the losers are the thirty million who die from starvation each year to guarantee Mr. and Mrs. Friedman's "fun."

Hayek likewise fails to understand values in any meaningful sense. He says "strictly speaking scales of value can exist only in individual minds." This they precisely do not. Values presuppose traditions and ongoing discussions. There can be no values in Hayek's solipsist world, and his conclusions substantiate this. Susan George points out that hoarding, blackmarketing, and smuggling in situations of scarcity are only rational forms of behaviour for profit maximizers, the heroes of private enterprise.[6]

The primacy of self-interest is linked to methodological individualism which is "the respect for the individual man *qua* man ... the recognition of his own views and tastes as supreme."[7] Such individualism, says Hayek, does not assume that people are egoistic or selfish, simply that the range of their concern and knowledge is necessarily limited. This wilful blindness recalls the reply of Scrooge when asked for charity for those in need at Christmas. When told that many would rather die than go to the workhouse, Scrooge replies: " If they would rather die they had better do it, and decrease the surplus population. Besides — excuse me — but I don't know that." "But you might know it," reply his interlocutors. "It's not my business," Scrooge returned. "It's enough for a man to understand his own business, and not to interfere with other people's. Mine occupies me constantly. Good afternoon, gentlemen!" Hayek is in good company.

The collapse of ethics under the weight of market assumptions is very properly underwritten by a nihilistic metaphysic. We have seen that Hayek justifies the market through the theory of spontaneous order. Justice consists in following this order. Far from being the affirmation of fullness of life, it is essentially impersonal, abstract, and negative. It can only tell us what not to do, and what is unjust. It cannot tell us what is just. Market forces are lauded precisely because they do not distribute things according to human will. The word *redistribution* is a euphemism for imposing a distribution on an impersonal will. Social justice is impossible — it imposes a made order on the given. What is "natural," and therefore right and just, is subjection to market fluctuations and humility before these are demanded. According to Hayek, "The basic orientation of true individualism consists of humility with respect to the procedures (of buying and selling)."[8] We dare not question market laws. According to the law of supply and demand, when food is scarce prices should increase. This means that some will be left without food and consequently will die. According to entrepreneurial metaphysics, they die as a result of a dictate of nature. To intervene and control prices and distribution of food so that everyone survives would be an act against nature. Price control breaks the social contract and leads to the loss of freedom, and what is life worth without freedom?[9] Market forces are, as Douglas Meeks points out, like the *deus absconditus*, and they are known like the God of natural theology by deductions from effects in the market to their presumed cause. Smith's "invisible hand" functions as a secularised providence. Behind Smith's vision lay the world of Newtonian mechanics with its concept of the universe as ruled by differential equations. The self-regulating economy was the correlate of the self-regulating universe of Deism.[10] Deism is above all the religion of the self-satisfied, those who are in positions of power and need to change nothing. It is the theology of the self-confident mercantile capitalism of the early eighteenth century. The difference between this theology and modern secularised providence is that the narratives which underlay the thought of the eighteenth century, which spoke of guilt, forgiveness, and compassion, have largely passed away. Hayek's spontaneous order is the brutal deity of Social Darwinism.

A sophisticated theological defence of capitalism has been developed by the American theologian Michael Novak, and published by the American Enterprise Institute, and it is instructive to look at his metaphysics. The great virtue of capitalism, for Novak, is pluralism, the freedom of each individual to do what he or she chooses. Such pluralism entails, he recognises, feelings of anomie, alienation, and purposelessness, but such experiences are not to be feared: "Of course free persons will feel alienation!" In a pluralist society there is no sacred canopy; rather, "At its spiritual core, there is an empty shrine." This emptiness is defended by an appeal to the ancient tradition of apophatic theology, the notion that no concept is adequate to God. The anthropological correlate of this theology is absolute individualism. Although humans are social animals, says Novak, it is still more profoundly true that they are ultimately alone.[11] This vision of a non-defined transcendence which "each person must define for himself" is radically at odds with the biblical vision of God who is fullness of life and makes blazingly clear demands on God's people. The metaphysical heart of Novak's theology is the void so sharply analysed by Bonhoeffer as he looked at the Third Reich. "The void towards which the west is drifting," he wrote, "is not the natural end, the dying away and decline of a once flourishing history of nations."

> It is . . . a rebellious and outrageous void, and one which is the enemy of both God and man . . . It is the supreme manifestation of all the powers which are opposed to God. It is the void made god. No one knows its goal or measure. Its dominion is absolute. It is a creative void, which blows its anti-god's breath into the nostrils of all that is established and awakes to a false semblance of a new life while sucking out from its proper essence, until at last it falls in ruin as a lifeless husk and is cast away. The void engulfs life, history, family, nation, language, faith. The list can be prolonged indefinitely, for the void spares nothing.[12]

This void, Novak makes clear, is what we are led to by the dominance of market capitalism. Politically the claim is that all state functions must be transferred to private enterprise. What we have in fact are civil governments which wield their power through the use of police and military apparatus. The slogan is, "The social state enslaves, the police state liberates." Hinkelammert quotes the head of the Chilean Secret Police at the height of its imposition of monetarist policies who said: "National security is like love: there is never enough of it."[13] The metaphysic of entrepreneurial capitalism is needed to justify this use of state terror against the enemies of free enterprise.

From a biblical standpoint what is involved in these systems is very clearly idolatry, a position cogently argued for by Hinkelammert in a paper read at the fiftieth anniversary of the Barmen declaration in 1984. In the Christian scriptures idolatry of money (Mt 6:24, 1 Cor 5:10, Col 3:5), of the law (Gal 4:8f., 5:1; Mk 2:1f.), and of oppressive political power (Rv 13:11f., 14:9f., 16:2, 19:20) are singled out. All idolatry leads to the destruction of persons and of nature, which is why it is impossible to serve both God and Mammon, where *serve* means "be the slave of." The way the market is spoken of illustrates this idolatry in a rather pathetic way. The market is endowed with personal qualities as were the attributes of God in post-exilic Judaism. There is a medical rhetoric—we take the pulse of inflation, demand infusions of income, and the news reports at the end of a day of trading that "the pound has had a calm day." The need for these medical analogies springs from the other major rhetorical source—warfare. The magazine *Businees Week* tells us that managers must practise superaggressive marketing, the captains of industry marshal their troops; books on management tell us that they must (with wearying constancy) occupy the commanding heights, and we learn that they must kill off rival corporations in order to survive. The enemies to be combatted are social values, government spending on the elderly, the poor, and the sick, the demands of the labour unions, and Green economics.

Faced with the Baal prophets of his day Elijah demanded that people make a choice:

"How long will you go limping with two different opinions? If the Lord is God, follow him; But if Baal, then follow him." And the people did not answer him a word (1 Kgs 18:21).

Part of the ideology of the market is that there is no alternative, but this is false. There are realistic alternatives, which many groups are working hard on. There is a second way.

THE WAY OF LIFE

Writing in 1884 Edward Aveling and Eleanor Marx described socialism as follows:

Let us state in the briefest possible way what socialism means to some of us. (1) That there are inequality and misery in the world; (2) that this social inequality, this misery of the many and this happiness of the few, are the necessary outcome of our social conditions; (3) that the essence of these social conditions is that the mass of the people, the working class, produce and distribute all commodities, while the minority of the people, the middle and upper classes, possess these commodities; (4) that this initial tyranny of the possessing class over the producing class is based on the present wage system and now maintains all other forms of oppression, such as that of monarchy, or clerical rule, or police despotism; (5) that this tyranny of the few over the many is only possible because the few have obtained possession of the land, the raw material, the banks — in a word, of all the means of production and distribution of commodities . . . (6) lastly, that the approaching change in "civilised" society will be a revolution . . . The two classes at present existing will be replaced by a single class consisting of the whole of the healthy and sane members of the community, possessing all the means of production and distribution in common.[14]

Seven years after this was written Leo XIII warned the faithful that socialism was greatly unjust and that it would "do violence to lawful owners, divert government from its proper tasks and cause utter confusion in the state." Not only did it want to do away with property, but it threatened male headship in the family. "The door would be thrown open to mutual envy, detraction and dissension. All incentive for individuals to exercise their ingenuity and skill would be removed and the very founts of wealth dry up."[15] A century later he would doubtless feel that his worst fears had been confirmed, but that society, at least in the West, was back on the right track.

The problem with revolutions, as Hannah Arendt reminds us, is that they devour their own children. The socialist dream of the early Marxists became the nightmare of Stalinism. The attempt to create a more equal society led to Lubyanka and the camps and Tiananmen Square. Must this be the upshot of any more humane society, of a society which banks on altruism rather than self-interest, on cooperation rather than competition and putting Number One first? Can we so organise society that the characteristics most rewarded are not "greed, avarice, cheating, competitiveness, and aggression"?[16] Can we recognise that the only genuine "economic man" is a *social* creature? Can there be a revolution which does not devour its own children? These are the questions to which the new Deuteronomists are addressing themselves, and they do so in terms of quite specific proposals, for prophecy not only educates the desires but is concerned also with the concrete. They are inspired partly by a passionate conviction about human equality, transcending the bounds of gender, race, and class, and partly by the knowledge that, as we have seen, the planet cannot sustain present levels of growth, either of population or consumption. In the phrase of James Robertson, all of these groups and thinkers seek a Sane, Humane, and Ecological (SHE) economy, characterised by attitudes which are conserving, enabling, and politically participatory.[17] Following roughly the outline of topics we have addressed, the agenda of the new Deuteronomy would be something like the following.

As we have seen, our understanding of work will have to change, so that the present alternatives of useful work or useless toil, of being engaged either in conception or in execution, are minimised and people can once again be subjects of their labour. To be sure, toil cannot be completely eliminated but it can be both vastly reduced and *shared*, so that it is not largely allocated to one group in society. The vertical division of labour between line and staff can give place to a situation where managers are accountable to and *interchangeable with* other workers, and the gender division of labour can be largely done away with. In these ways work can be redeemed.

Secondly, economics can be reconceived, freed from the bondage of the ridiculous laws of positivist imagination. Instead of self-interest, rights and obligations will be at the heart of the new economics, and the central concern will be enabling people to meet their needs and develop themselves. The new vision of the economy, which will replace that derived from Adam Smith, will be enabling and conserving. Rather than the model of unlimited growth the new order will see "the whole of economic activity as a single continuing cyclical process, consisting of countless interrelated cyclical sub processes, with the wastes from each providing resources from the other."[18] The economic system will be envisaged as an organic part of the natural world and not as a machine external to it. Both Gorz and Robertson emphasise that the new economic order must not be hampered by the clichés of the struggles of the past century. There is nothing intrinsically, wrong with enterprise, initiative and ownership. What is wrong is when these are harnessed to profit, power, self-aggrandisement, and inequality. There is scope for both initiative and cooperation in many areas — in production and consumption, housing, land, savings, and finance.

Fundamental to the new economics will be that *decentralisation* which makes democracy in production possible. The local economy, Robertson suggests, will be the central focus of interest, rather than the national or multinational economy.[19] Local economies may even be able to use local currencies, related to national ones. Central planning for things like transport, energy, and heavy industry will remain a necessity. Given that fact, the task in an alternatively structured society is to see that bureaucracy does not get in the way of responsibility and accountability, and that, if private ownership of the means of production is abolished, industries owned by the community are answerable to both workers and consumers. Planning is inescapable, and is essential to the survival of the planet. The World Commission notes that conservation pricing requires that governments take a long-term view in weighing the costs and benefits of various measures. "Spontaneous order" will lead to the apocalypse which would be the consummation of metaphysical nihilism. Governments of all political persuasions have in fact made use of the "Input-Output" analysis of Wassily Leontief since he introduced it in the 1930s. His tables were designed to show what sections of each industry sold to each other and received from each other and thus to enable rational predictions of needs for materials. Computer technology has enabled the practical application of such planning.[20] Planning means knowing where we are going, having goals in view. It is one of the deepest human needs. The question is not whether or not we should have planning but who plans, for what, and for whom.

The new economic order involves rethinking *money* and *taxes*. Taxes would not be on personal income but on land (as proposed long ago by Henry George), on activities that pollute and damage the global environment, on activities which exploit international resources such as ocean fishing and sea bedmining, on imports between one nation and another, and on international currency exchanges. The development of the credit card system has already familiarised us with the idea that "money" is basically an exchange of information, a way of facilitating the exchange of goods and services. This needs to be rethought in terms of a fair and efficient scoring system. Like work, the money system could be *redeemed* through a recognition of the proper function of money as enabling people to transact with one another and act conservingly. "There is a difference between a price system which is designed merely to give signals to producers about relative demand and supply, and one which is used to create material incentives and so economic differentiation between people."[21]

The redemption of money will involve—as Deuteronomy, the medieval theologians, and Luther all insisted—the abolition of usury. The charging of interest, it has been shown, involves a significant transfer of wealth to the richest groups of a country's population.[22] This systematic transfer of money from those who need it most to those who need it least is one of the factors pushing the world towards catastrophe. It fuels the urge of the very rich, including the huge industrial and financial corporations, to compete with one another purely for the sake of economic wealth and power. It lulls the moderately well off into a complacent sense that all is well with economic life. By artificially increasing the financial pressures on the less well-off and the poor, it deepens their economic dependency. In each of these ways it stimulates an unnecessarily high level of economic activity and the ecological damage which results.[23] Thus interest is opposed for the very reason it was opposed by the medieval church—because it harms life.

Along with many others (including Milton Friedman) Robertson argues for the provision of a basic income for all, financed by the new tax system. The scheme is feasible but rests on the assumption that human beings are basically trustworthy and not workshy, and that it is not only the whip of poverty which makes them work.[24] Levels of wages can be established between maximum and minimum rates, "the distance between them being determined by the principle that persons at the floor would not be excluded through lack of resources from freely participating in the same social activities as those at the ceiling." There should be no stratification of society on the basis of income levels (or any other criteria).[25]

Finally the destructive ideology of necessary growth would be replaced by recognition of the need for limits to growth. There has to be a recognition that the earth is not "an inexhaustible cornucopia." Countries will be encouraged to seek self-sufficiency in things like food and energy. Repair, recycling, reuse, and reconditioning will be as important as manufacturing. Limits to growth also imply both institutional limits and limits to our personal expectations. "A SHE economic path will shift the priorities to human needs, social justice and ecological sustainability. It will not aim for no growth, but for healthy growth instead of cancerous growth. It will aim for equilibrium or steady state economics, in the sense of preferring activities that can be sustainable."[26]

These changes partly presuppose and partly entail very different views of human community. In particular we have to reject the credo of individualism. Human progress, as the World Commission notes, has always depended on the possibility of cooperation. Far from being a socialist daydream, cooperation is now recognised as essential for survival. Turning his back on a false idea of "man come of age," Stephen Verney argues that "if the Renaissance can be understood as a period when we in Europe broke out of a hierarchical order into an age of individualism—if at least the emphasis of that collective change was from dependence to independence—then we might understand our own generation as a time when the emphasis must be on interdependence—we must stop behaving like irresponsible adolescent individualists."[27] This does not mean reducing every person to a grey uniformed worker but rather, as socialism was always meant to be, the "liberation of individuality through the social cooperation of equals."[28] In turn, the recovery of community is the necessary presupposition for the recovery of virtue.

These changes would necessarily involve some degree of loss for the rich and powerful, and in today's global economy this applies between the countries of the northern and southern hemispheres. Does this mean that, as the advocates of anarcho-capitalism maintain, we have to make a choice between freedom or equality? It has been one of the contentions of this book that what is meant when this option is proposed is simply the freedom of the strong, the freedom to continue to enjoy privilege. But freedom for one at the expense of another is not truly freedom. The freedom we seek is from want and oppression, freedom to create and participate fully in society. These freedoms cannot be exercised except by people who are equal. "Equality does not mean identity. It means the removal of the pervasive material inequalities which characterise capitalism; and the removal of barriers or discriminations based on race, age, sex, sexuality, disability and so on."[29] Thus, as Tawney argued, freedom and equality imply each other.

None of the proposals outlined above is utopian. Here and there, as in the longstanding association of cooperatives in northern Spain, or in some of the movements referred to earlier, anticipations of such schemes exist in practice. At the moment they are forced to exist under the hegemony of the market, but the need to generalise their practice must be understood not as impractical idealism but rather a sober programme for survival. The point is whether there is the political will to implement them. Even Robertson, who is an optimist, raises this question:

People with more power and wealth than others do not willingly give them up, and people who enjoy security and order do not willingly see them threatened. It would be foolish to underestimate potential resistance to the necessary economic transformation which we are trying to bring about. It could be disastrous to underestimate the ruthlessness with which this transformation might be suppressed even in law-abiding countries like Britain, if ever it came to be seen as a vehicle for disruptive social and political forces.[30]

So we stand before two ways, more clearly than those who listened to the discussions of Deuteronomy. The generation which came back from exile found itself, like the Sandinistas, compelled to put a disproportionate emphasis on defence and soon fell again before a world empire. The community polarised between those prepared to assimilate to survive and those prepared to resort to armed struggle. The victory of the latter finally led to Jerusalem being put under the plough, and yet it was not the compromisers who preserved the faith. Meanwhile the First International had already come into being, spreading round the Mediterranean, east to Persia and India, and north to France and Britain.[31] The First International lives by neither violence nor compromise, but by hope in the redeeming, which is to say liberating, action of the God who raised Jesus Christ from the dead. The hope by which Christians live is loyal to the earth, to the flesh which God assumed, to the creation the Triune God called into being. It is only otherworldly in refusing the methods, principles, and anti-ethics of this world, the world of the "spontaneous order" of the police and the armed forces needed to deal with IMF riots.

The World Commission on Environment and Development believed that a more prosperous, just, and secure future depended on changes in human attitude which would need "a vast campaign of education, debate, and public participation." The First International is composed of disciples, those who are taught or trained by their master, apostles who are sent by him to proclaim the good news of life in all its fullness for all people, of human sharing and solidarity.[32] If liberal individualism believes that community is simply an arena in which individuals pursue their own interests, then the church offers an alternative narrative according to which no one can be fully human unless all are fully human. The reading and discussion of scripture at the heart of the liturgy is given us as a vast campaign of education, debate, and public participation in the context of the celebration of life. To anticipate the obvious criticism, it goes without saying that the church is not merely a pressure group, but it is *also* a pressure group, a pressure group for the things of the kingdom. Its demands and hopes and dreams are rooted in faith in the infinite mystery of God, in confidence in God's redemptive love known in the flesh-taking. In the face of the problems of the global economy people are paralysed by the feeling that they can do nothing. But if the Christians of the Western world seriously committed themselves to the agenda of life for all, a very great deal could be accomplished in terms of the emergence of a new world order. The alternative, and perhaps more probable, outcome is a church under the cross.

The church has to decide whether to continue to be satisfied with the marginal "religious" role assigned to it. It can opt to discount the warnings of ecological ruin as scaremongering designed to damage profits and the way of life of Western democracy. It can opt to listen to the false priests and prophets in its own midst, crying "Peace, peace" (and "Profit, profit") like Pashur and Hilkiah long ago. But those who live by the realism of the Spirit, the new Deuteronomists, have to persist in the hope of the God of life, insisting on the International, insisting on both freedom and equality, insisting that iron laws or spontaneous order are nothing but ideological fantasies aimed at retaining power. In the struggle for fullness of life we are called to make a clear option on the side of the God of life and against the Baals of profit and power. There are two ways—and we must choose.

Notes

Introduction

1. A. MacIntyre, *After Virtue,* 2nd edition, London, Duckworth 1985. Henceforth cited as AV.
2. *Our Common Future,* Oxford University Press 1987, pp. 1,2. Henceforth cited as OCF, and referred to in the text as the "World Commission."
3. According to the World Commission the quarter of the world's five billion population who live in the developed world have an energy consumption seventeen times as high as those who live in the poorest countries.
4. AV, p. 254.
5. Ibid p. 216. The discussion of narrative, p. 208ff., is extremely illuminating in relation to Deuteronomy.
6. M. Mies, *Patriarchy and Accumulation on a World Scale,* London, Harvester 1986, p. 230.
7. R. Kothari, *Environment, Technology and Ethics* in *Ethics of Environment and Development,* ed J. R. and J. G. Engel, London, Belhaven 1990, p. 35; H. Skolimowski, *Reverence for Life,* ibid p. 97; "A new ethic, embracing plants and animals as well as people, is required. . . . The long term task of environmental education is to foster or reinforce attitudes and behaviour compatible with this new ethic." International Union for the Conservation of Nature and Natural Resources, *The World Conservation Strategy: Living Resource Conservation for Sustainable Development* (Gland, Switzerland: IUCN, 1980), Section 13.1.
8. E. P. Thompson, An Open Letter to Leszek Kolakowski, in *The Poverty of Theory,* London 1979.

1. Choosing Life

1. Greek *ethikos* means "pertaining to character." This was translated into Latin by Cicero as *moralis.* AV, p. 38. *Ethical* and *moral* thus originally mean the same thing, though we shall want to distinguish between them. An ethos includes "the whole fabric of social relations in which the members of a community are enmeshed, by which they are influenced for good or ill, and which can make people turn inward on their fantasies (including violent and aggressive ones), or turn outward to see their fellows as persons with claims on their behaviour." I. Fairweather and J. McDonald, *The Quest for Christian Ethics*, Edinburgh, Handsel 1984, p. 248.
2. AV, p. 61.
3. AV, chap. 2.
4. Alasdair MacIntyre has for many years addressed this problem. He insists that we can recognise that we need to learn from other traditions, and that there

171

are aspects of all traditions which are untranslatable, and still argue for the proper hegemony of one particular tradition. "Only those whose tradition allows for the possibility of its hegemony being put in question can have rational warrant for asserting such a hegemony. And only those traditions whose adherents recognize the possibility of untranslatability into their own language-in-use are able to reckon adequately with that possibility." MacIntyre, *Whose Justice? Which Rationality?*, London, Duckworth 1988, p. 388.

5. For a brilliant discussion of the relation of ethics and aesthetics, see Terry Eagleton, *The Ideology of the Aesthetic*, Oxford, Blackwell 1990. Where ethical theory has been relativised by its subsumption under the aesthetics of art for art's sake, Eagleton wishes to insist that aesthetics is in itself ethical discourse because it concerns what we do in and with the body.

6. Skolimowski, p. 98.

7. AV, p. 54.

8. P. Haas, *Morality after Auschwitz*, Philadelphia, Fortress 1988, p. 233.

9. Analogies to this attempt might be found in the apartheid state or in some contemporary Latin American attitudes to the poor.

10. *Rerum Novarum*, May 1891, Denzinger 3265ss, 35th edition, Freiburg, Herder 1973.

11. The point of natural law is to allow us to derive an 'ought' from an 'is', to use Hume's terms. *Treatise on Human Nature* III.i.1 Hume's meaning in this famous passage is hotly contested. Cf. W.D. Hudson, *The Is-Ought Question*, London 1964.

12. Stoicism became effectively theistic, and this made the *rapprochement* with Christianity possible. Cf. the two articles in E. Troeltsch, *Religion in History*, Edinburgh, T & T Clark 1991.

13. See, for example, the opening chapters of Calvin's *Institutes*, and the fierce debate on this issue between Barth and Brunner, published as *Natural Theology*, London, Geoffrey Bles 1946.

14. F. Hayek, *Rules and Order*, London, RKP 1973.

15. S.Th 1a 2ae 91 arts 1 and 2. I use the Blackfriars edition, 1964, published in conjunction with Eyre and Spottiswoode, London.

16. M. Mellor, *Breaking the Boundaries*, London, Virago 1992.

17. For a comprehensive restatement of natural law theory see J. Finnis, *Natural Law and Natural Rights*, Oxford University Press 1980.

18. Principally in E. Levinas, *Totality and Infinity*, trans. Lingis, The Hague, Nijhoff 1979; *Otherwise than Being or Beyond Essence*, trans. Lingis, The Hague, Nijhoff 1981; *Collected Philosophical Papers*, trans. Lingis, The Hague, Nijhoff 1987. I do not claim to offer a correct reading of Levinas, whose work I find in equal measure baffling and inspiring, but use it as a jumping off point.

19. Levinas, *Totality*, p. 45.

20. E. Levinas, *Ethics as First Philosophy*, in *The Levinas Reader*, ed S. Hand, Oxford, Blackwell 1989, p. 83.

21. Levinas, *Totality*, p. 79.

22. There are law codes from Akkadia (19th c), Sumeria (c. 1865), and Babylon (the code of Hammurabi c. 1792-1750 BC), all of which probably look back to the Code of Ur-Nammu of Ur (c. 2000 BC).

23. As we see today only too vividly and tragically in communities as disparate as Somalia, Sri Lanka, and Bosnia.

24. Levinas, *Totality*, p. 254ff.

25. The possibility of communication across cultures, and above all the possibility of translation of languages and mutual understanding, are arguments for strong analogies between cultures. Extreme forms of cultural relativism commit us to a position of mutual unintelligibility which is profoundly implausible.

26. Levinas, *Totality*, p. 145. The argument could equally appeal to the rather different perspective of Charles Taylor, for whom "our deepest moral instincts, our ineradicable sense that human life is to be respected," constitutes our access to the world in which ontological claims are discernible. *Sources of the Self*, Cambridge 1989, p. 8. What Levinas discusses in terms of the face Taylor calls an "inescapable framework."

27. Deontology is that form of ethics which stresses the absolute demand of duty; from Greek *dei*, "it is right," "necessary."

28. I owe this observation to Nigel Biggar.

29. A. Schweitzer, *The Teaching of Reverence for Life*, trans. R. & C. Winston, London, Peter Owen 1966, p. 26.

30. A. Schweitzer, *Civilization and Ethics*, 3rd ed., trans. C. Russell, London, A&C Black 1946, chaps. 18 and 21.

31. K. Barth, *Church Dogmatics* III/4, p. 324. All references to Barth's *Dogmatics* (henceforth cited as CD) refer to the translation edited by T. F. Torrance and G. W. Bromiley, Edinburgh, T & T Clark 1956 and following.

32. Cf. Justin Martyr, *First Apology*.

33. Such analogies form the basis of Barth's theological anthropology. CD III/2.

34. It is to this point, at the intersection of the Christ of faith and the Jesus of history, that we look for a meeting between Barth and Levinas.

35. Levinas, *Totality*, p. 112.

36. G. Gutiérrez, *A Theology of Liberation*, London, SCM 1974, pp. 231-32 and Maryknoll, New York: Orbis Books, 1973, rev. ed. 1988.

37. B. Griffiths, *Morality and the Market Place*, London, Hodder & Stoughton 1982, p. 10.

38. The remembrance of slavery as a ground for practice, Dt 6:21f.; having a care that the neighbour is never degraded, Dt 25:3; living by the covenant with the community, Dt 5:3f. Liberty, equality, and fraternity is in fact no bad summary of the Deuteronomic ethic.

39. W. Eichrodt, *Theology of the Old Testament*, vol. 1, trans. J. A. Baker, London, SCM 1961, p. 241.

40. Lynne Segal, *Is the Future Female?* London, Virago 1987.

41. Irenaeus, *Adversus Haereses* 4.18.4. There are echoes of such views in both deep ecology and ecofeminism! The following quotations from Irenaeus are also from this passage.

42. John of Damascus, in B. J. Kidd, *Documents Illustrative of Church History*, vol. 3, London, OUP 1941, p. 73.

2. Prophecy and Wisdom

1. D. Bonhoeffer, *Ethics*, trans. N. H. Smith, London, SCM 1955, p. 3.

2. Oliver O'Donovan, *Resurrection and the Moral Order*, Leicester IVP 1986, p. 191f.

3. The idea of middle axioms has been widely used by Ronald Preston. He

traces it to a preparatory volume for the Oxford Conference on Church, Community, and State in 1937 by Visser't Hooft and J. H. Oldham. Cf. R. H. Preston, *Explorations in Theology*, London, SCM 1981.

4. Fairweather and McDonald, p. 250.

5. CD III/4, p. 13. With this objection we may compare the rough draft on fallacious questions found by Bonhoeffer's editor in his *Ethics*:

1. How does the will of God become concrete? Answer, *the will of God is always concrete or else it is not the will of God*. In other words, the will of God is not a principle from which one has to draw inferences and which has to be applied to "reality." A "will of God" which can be recognised without immediately leading to action is a general principle, but it is not the will of God.

2. How does the goodwill of the Christian become concrete? The goodwill is from the outset a concrete deed; otherwise it is not Christian will. Man is from the outset engaged in concrete action.

3. What is the will of God for this or that particular case? This is the casuistic misinterpretation of the concrete. The concrete is not achieved in this way, for it is once again already anticipated by a principle (p. 252).

Fairweather and McDonald quote Preston's characterisation of Barth's position as "act-deontology," which gives no consistent help in making moral decisions. However, their own position seems to correspond remarkably closely to Barth's save for his refusal to allow the validity of non-Christian ethics. Here as elsewhere the very different position of CD IV/3 on natural theology would doubtless have produced very different ethical results. O'Donovan criticises Barth's and Bonhoeffer's position but in conceding God's freedom to act he speaks of an "irreducible duality" between the freedom of God to act particularly in history and the generic ordering of the world. This is exactly the point they wish to make.

6. Fairweather and McDonald, p. 251.

7. Cf. J. Ellul, *The Ethics of Freedom*, Oxford, Mowbrays 1976.

8. CD II/2, p. 647.

9. E. P. Thompson, *William Morris, Romantic to Revolutionary*, London, Phaedon 1976, pp. 786-87 (citing M. Abensour, *Utopies et dialectique du socialisme*).

10. A. MacIntyre, *A Short History of Ethics*, London, RKP 1967, p. 183 (henceforth cited as SH).

11. Keynes, *General Theory of Employment, Interest, and Money*, New York, Harcourt, Brace 1936, pp. 383-84.

12. This is the dismal conclusion of Donald Hay, *Economics Today*, Leicester, Apollos 1989, p. 63.

13. W. Brueggemann, *Hope Within History*, Atlanta, John Knox Press 1987, p. 75.

14. This may not always be true of folk wisdom, but is certainly true of the upper-class wisdom we find, for example, in Ecclesiastes or Ben Sirach.

15. A. Nygren, *Agape and Eros*, trans. Hebert, London, SPCK 1932.

16. Cf. Aristotle, *Nicomachean Ethics* VIII.14 1161b. I use the edition of J. Barnes, 2 vols., Oxford 1981.

17. Levinas, *God and Philosophy* in *Collected Philosophical Papers*, p. 165. The

whole paper seems to be in dialogue with Nygren's book.

18. *Face to Face with Levinas*, ed R. Cohen, Albany, New York, State University of New York 1986, p. 25.

19. Dussell, *Ethics and Community*, trans. Barr, Maryknoll, New York, Orbis Books 1988, p. 102.

20. SH, p. 149.

21. Levinas, *God and Philosophy*, in *Collected Philosophical Papers*.

22. The Pentecost story in Acts 2 expresses the same perception.

23. See the account of the relation of the different parts of scripture in my *Redeeming Time*, London, DLT 1986, p. 25f.

3. Ethics and Economics

1. *The Penguin Dictionary of Economics*, ed Bannock, Baxter, and Davis, 4th edition, Harmondsworth 1987.

2. L. Robbins, *An Essay on the Nature and Significance of Economic Science*, London, Macmillan 1932, p. 1.

3. D. Meeks, *God the Economist*, Minneapolis, Fortress 1989, p. 10.

4. J. K. Galbraith, *A History of Economics,* Harmondsworth, Penguin 1987, p. 115.

5. Marx, *Capital*, vol. 1, chap. 18, trans. Moore and Aveling, Moscow 1954, p. 505.

6. Aristotle, *Nichomachean Ethics*, 1.5.

7. Aristotle, *Politics*, 1258b.

8. S.Th 2ae 2ae 77.4.

9. R. H. Tawney, *Religion and the Rise of Capitalism*, Harmondsworth, Penguin 1938, p. 55.

10. Luther, *Trade and Usury*, trans. Jacobs and Brandt, in *Luther's Works*, vol. 45, Concordia 1962, p. 233f.

11. M. Weber, *The Protestant Ethic*, trans. Parsons, London, Allen & Unwin 1930; Tawney, *Religion and the Rise of Capitalism*.

12. R. H. Tawney, *Thomas Wilson, A Discourse upon Usury*, London, Bell 1925, p. 106.

13. Hobbes, *Leviathan*, chap. 15, chap. 10.

14. C. B. Macpherson, *The Rise and Fall of Economic Justice,* Oxford University Press 1985, p. 9.

15. Smith, however, allowed himself to lament the fact that "all for ourselves and nothing for other people seems, in every age of the world, to have been the vile maxim of the masters of mankind" (A. Smith, *An Inquiry into the Nature and Causes of the Wealth of Nations*, Bk III, chap. 4).

16. N. W. Senior, *Four Introductory Lectures on Political Economy*, London 1852. For Senior's unsavoury advocacy of the longer working day, under the pressure of Manchester mill owners, see Marx, *Capital*, pp. 216, 383.

17. W. S. Jevons, *The Theory of Political Economy*, ed R. Black, Harmondsworth, Pelican 1970, p. 3.

18. Robbins, *An Essay of the Nature and Significance of Economic Science*, p. 155. There is a good discussion of scientific method and its implications for economics in Hay, p. 90ff.

19. L. Robbins, *Politics and Economics*, London, Macmillan 1963, p. 3ff.

20. M. Polanyi, *Personal Knowledge*, London, RKP 1958, p. 183. Cf. the discussion of "facts" on p. 167.

21. K. Popper, *Logik der Forschung*, Vienna 1935; cf. *Objective Knowledge*, Oxford 1972.

22. P. Donaldson, *10 x Economics*, Harmondsworth, Penguin 1982, pp. 162, 164.

23. R. Alves, in *Faith and Science in an Unjust World*, WCC, Geneva 1980, p. 41f.

24. E. Burke, *Thoughts and Details on Scarcity,* London 1800, pp. 31-32.

25. Meeks, p. 10.

26. Smith, *Wealth of Nations*, Bk 1, chap. 2; Bk 2, chap. 2,

27. A. Sen, *On Ethics and Economics*, Oxford, Blackwell 1987, p. 17.

28. Sen, p. 25. Nevertheless, Smith was well aware of the damaging effects of factory work. Arguing for what Marx called "homoepathic doses" of state-funded education, Smith wrote: "The man whose whole life is spent in performing a few simple operations . . . has no occasion to exert his understanding. . . . He generally becomes as stupid and ignorant as it is possible for a human creature to become. . . . His dexterity at his own particular trade seems in this manner to be acquired at the expense of his intellectual, social and martial virtues. But in every improved and civilised society(!), this is the state into which the labouring poor, that is, the great body of the people, must necessarily fall" (*Wealth of Nations*, Bk V, chap. i, art. ii). During Smith's lifetime, according to the Factory Inspectors Report of 1860, "young persons and children were worked all night, all day, or both *ad libitum*." So much for the beneficent effects of the market. Smith could accept this with equanimity because of the profound class bias of his view of society.

29. G. Stigler in *Tanner Lectures on Human Values*, vol. 2, Cambridge 1981, p. 176.

30. Sen, p. 32.

31. I am here following MacIntyre, SH, p. 236.

32. SH, p. 241. MacIntyre calls utilitarianism a "sievelike" theory. Cf. the criticisms of Taylor, *Sources*, p. 339.

33. Sen, p. 50.

34. See G. Becker, *The Economic Approach to Human Behaviour,* University of Chicago Press 1976.

35. W. Letwin, Introduction to *The Wealth of Nations*, London, Everyman 1975.

36. Meeks notes sombrely that "systems that justify themselves on the basis of a rigid, unchangeable human nature idolatrously deny the eschatological power of God the Holy Spirit to create human beings anew and transform conditions in which they live" (*God the Economist*, p. 10). At least Adam Smith (like his latter day disciple Milton Friedman) had the decency to be an unbeliever and "a great foe to parsons." For the lamentable contribution of clergy to political economy see Marx, *Capital*, p. 578, n. 2.

37. AV, p. 229.

38. Marx, *Capital*, pp. 556, 558. It is difficult to deny that "when a certain stage of development has been reached, a conventional degree of prodigality, which is also an exhibition of wealth, and consequently a source of credit, becomes a business necessity to the 'unfortunate' capitalist. Luxury enters into capital's expenses of representation" (ibid p. 557). This is the heart of T. Veblen's theory of conspicuous consumption—the need for firms and individuals to convince others of their success.

39. See Boyd Hilton, *The Age of Atonement*, Oxford University Press 1988.

40. M. and R. Friedman, *Free to Choose*, London, Pan Books 1980, p. 26.

41. Smith, *Wealth of Nations*, Bk IV, chap. 9.

42. Marx, *Capital*, p. 172. Marx was deeply contemptuous of Bentham, whom he referred to as "the arch-Philistine . . . that insipid, pedantic, leather tongued oracle of the ordinary bourgeois intelligence of the 19th century." And "Bentham is a purely English phenomenon . . . in no time and in no country has the most home-spun commonplace ever strutted about in so self-satisfied a way" (ibid pp. 570-71).

43. Donaldson, p. 55.

44. Hazel Henderson, *Creating Alternative Futures*, New York, Perigee Books 1978, p. 15.

45. Mellor, p. 197.

46. Marx, *Capital*, pp. 667-68. Cf. Friedman and Friedman, p. 23, for the hard work myth which is clearly stated, if it does not originate, in Locke. Unemployment, according to Locke, was due to moral depravity. He therefore recommended that pauper children above the age of three be set to work in workhouses.

47. Griffiths.

48. Marx, *Capital*, p. 452. Marx at this point gives but one example. "In one scutching mill, at Kildinan, near Cork, there occurred between 1852 and 1856 six fatal accidents and sixty mutilations; every one of which might have been prevented by the simplest appliances, at the cost of a few shillings. Dr. W. White, the certifying surgeon for factories at Downpatrick, states in his official report: The serious accidents at the scutching mills are of the most fearful nature. In many cases a quarter of the body is torn from the trunk, and either involves death, or a future of wretched incapacity and suffering." At this time there were eighteen hundred such mills in Ireland. Exactly similar results can be found in mills in present-day India.

49. Thirty thousand people disappeared in the eight-year "dirty war" in Argentina. Sixty thousand people died in El Salvador in a war funded by the United States in the defence of "democracy and freedom" after the assassination of Archbishop Romero in 1980.

50. Present GATT negotiations, for example, are foundering on protectionism and the desire of member countries to defend their own industries. The participants are only united in seeking protection for the trade of the richest nations against cheap exports from the poorest. During the cotton recession in 1863 the British Parliament intervened to stop the labour force emigrating at the instigation of mill owners, who were alarmed that their work force would have disappeared by the time the recession was over. See *Capital,* p. 538ff. On the other hand, the Rev. J. Townsend, who styled himself "a well wisher of mankind," preferred to leave intervention to God: "Legal constraint (to labour) is attended with too much trouble, violence, and noise . . . whereas hunger is not only a peaceable, silent, unremitted pressure, but as the most natural motive to industry and labour, it calls forth the most powerful exertions." He must have sung "God Moves in a Mysterious Way" with special gusto.

51. J. Seabrook, *The Myth of the Market*, Devon, Green Books Bideford 1980, p. 158. He points out that the reason that functional illiteracy has now reached 30 percent in the United States is not because of lax and permissive teachers but because buying and selling have become the site where action, invention, and creativity are extinguished. "The decay of human possibilities is inscribed in the very structures of the market economy." Similarly, the rise in violent crime is not "mind-

less" but a response to processes of expropriation and loss, the extinction of social hope (ibid, pp. 31-32).

52. J. Robertson, *Future Wealth*, London, Cassell 1989, p. 95.

53. P. Drucker, *The New Realities*, London, Heinemann 1989, p. 150.

54. Charles Caccia, at a WCED Public Hearing in Ottawa, May 1986, OCF, p. 38.

55. Marx, *Capital*, p. 555.

56. *Quadragesimo Anno*, May 1931, Denzinger 3725ss.

57. See Griffiths, p. 40; Friedman and Friedman, p. 23. Hayek also assumes this.

58. Marx, *Capital*, p. 712.

4. On Human Equality

1. Diana Adlam, cited in Segal, p. 48.

2. Marx, *Selected Correspondence,* London, Martin Lawrence 1935, p. 57.

3. See, for example, R. Williams, *Keywords*, London, Fontana 1976, p. 60f. In Britain the 1844 Railway Act legislated for third-*class* passengers.

4. See, for example, the dismissive account in P. Saunders, *Social Class and Stratification,* London, RKP 1990.

5. Marx, *Theories of Surplus Value*, trans. Burns, Moscow 1963, chap. 19, sect. 14.

6. Engels, *The Origin of the Family, Private Property and the State*, p. 75.

7. *The German Ideology*, p. 46.

8. A. Giddens, *Capitalism and Modern Social Theory*, Cambridge 1971, p. 38.

9. A. Giddens, *Sociology*, Cambridge, Polity 1989, p. 209. Cf. the discussion in *The Class Structure of Advanced Societies*, 2nd ed., London 1979, chaps. 5-7.

10. Ibid p. 211.

11. *The Eighteenth Brumaire of Louis Bonaparte*, sect. VII, Marx and Engels, *Collected Works,* Moscow 1976, vol. 11, p. 187.

12. So the British Tory politician Norman St. John Stevas maintains that claims that class hinders people's advancement are "an excuse for their own failures." In fact, we have "a society open to talent," and anyone can make it to the top if he or she chooses. The ideology of the self-made millionaire is even stronger in the United States. Apologists for this ideology necessarily believe that the world is largely peopled by the feckless and the useless.

13. Marx, *Capital*, chap. 6, p. 172.

14. I follow Saunders, *Social Class and Stratification*, p. 11f.

15. A. Boesak, "He made us all, but . . . ," in *Apartheid Is a Heresy*, ed J. de Gruchy and C. Villa-Vicencio, London, Lutterworth 1983, p. 3.

16. H. Gollwitzer, *Zür Schwarzen Theologie*, in *Evangelische Theologie*, Jan 1974, vol. 34, no. 1, pp. 43-69.

17. M. Weber, *Wirtschaft und Gesellschaft*, pt. III, chap. 4, pp. 631-40, in *From Max Weber*, ed Gerth and Wright Mills, London, RKP 1948, p. 180f.

18. Ibid p. 182.

19. Giddens, *Capitalism*, p. 165.

20. The primacy of an economic, and to that extent Marxian understanding of class cannot be easily dismissed. So Giddens takes Marx as a departure point in his discussion of class structure, and Westergaard and Resler use it as their main tool for the analysis of contemporary British society in *Class in a Capitalist Society*,

Pelican 1976. According to Giddens, Weber follows Marx in admitting that ownership or non-ownership of property is the most important basis of class division in a competitive market (*Capitalism*, p. 164).

21. Giddens, *Class Structure*, p. 149.

22. M. Mies, "Capitalist Development and Subsistence Production: Rural Women in India," in *Women: The Last Colony*, London, Zed Books 1988, p. 41. However, Rohini Hensman, of the Union Reform Group, points out that in South Asia, where patriarchal control within the family is very oppressive, the chance for women to engage in collective labour outside the family is sometimes emancipatory.

23. J. Westergaard and H. Resler, *Class in a Capitalist Society*, Harmondsworth, Pelican 1976, p. 129. Cf. pp. 116, 284.

24. In what follows the data are taken from Britain sharing the assumption of Westegaard and Resler that "the conditions of class and power which Britain shares with other capitalist countries, by virtue of the fact that they are capitalist, are overwhelmingly more significant than the differences among them" (p. 1).

25. In F. Field, *The Wealth Report*, London, RKP 1983.

26. *Social Trends*, London, HMSO 1990, p. 177.

27. Report in *The Independent*, 25 July 1990. Analysis of the government's low income statistics showed that the number of people living on less than half the average income has more than doubled, from 4.9 million to 10.5 million in the past ten years.

28. Ivan Reid, *Social Class Differences in Britain*, London, Fontana 1989, p. 324. Statistics for Britain in 1985 showed that male degree holders earned 70 percent more than males without qualifications, while the figure for women was 91 percent. This needs then to be set alongside data on academic attainment. As expected, the higher the class the higher the proportion with qualifications. Fifty-two percent of men with fathers in class 1 had degrees and 24 percent of women; 54 percent of men with fathers in class 6 had no qualifications and 68 percent of women. The 1988 UCCA statistics showed that social class 1, which makes up 5 percent of the population gains 20 percent of all university acceptances. Class 3, by contrast, which makes up 36 percent of the population gains only 7 percent of acceptances. Classes 4 to 5, which make up 7 percent of the population, have only 1 percent accepted.

29. Townsend, Davidson, and Whitehead, ed, *Inequalities in Health*, Harmondsworth, Penguin 1988, p. 254.

30. A. Giddens, *Sociology*, p. 215.

31. Hayek, *The Road to Serfdom*, ARK, London 1986, p. 69.

32. Drucker, *The New Realities*, p. 11.

33. Hayek, *The Constitution of Liberty*, p. 27.

34. Saunders, p. 51.

35. *Rerum Novarum*, 3265ss.

36. *The Guardian*, 20 June 1990.

37. *The Independent*, 3 August 1990.

38. R. H. Tawney, *Equality*, London, Geo Allen & Unwin 1968, p. 27.

39. OCF, p. 67.

40. Tawney, *Equality*, p. 48.

41. Aristotle, *Nicomachaean Ethics*, Bk V.

42. Hayek, *The Road to Serfdom*, p. 59.

43. Tawney, *Equality*, p. 167. Again, what is said of class here applies globally to the Third World.

44. Tawney, *Equality*, p. 229.

45. A. F. Pollard, *The Evolution of Parliament*, 2nd ed., London, Longmans 1964, pp. 183-84.

46. In A. MacIntyre, *Against the Self-Images of the Age*, London, Duckworth 1971, p. 38f.

47. Griffiths, pp. 37-38.

48. *Rerum Novarum*, 14. (Italics mine.)

49. S. Lukes, in *A Dictionary of Marxist Thought*, ed Bottomore, Oxford, Blackwell 1983, p. 341.

5. Work, Leisure, and Human Fulfillment

1. The quotation with which I head the chapter actually reads "all men." In view of the evident sympathy with early feminism of Morris's *News from Nowhere*, I feel that removing the male noun does justice to his avowed intentions.

2. Anyone familiar with the work cultures of Germany, England, and Ireland will appreciate this, and the same seems to be true in many other parts of the world.

3. J. B. Pritchard, *Ancient Near Eastern Texts*, Princeton 1950. B. Wielenga draws attention to the significance of this story. It is probable that "man" ought to be translated "humans."

4. *Politics* 1329a.

5. Ibid 1254a.

6. *Politics* 1253b. In *The Ideology of Work*, P. D. Anthony argues that the existence of slavery set up a tension between civil law and natural law, the one condoning slavery, the other not. This was doubtless the case for Roman authors like Cicero, influenced by Stoicism, but not for Aristotle. It is yet another example of the dangers of the natural law tradition (Tavistock 1977, p. 20ff.).

7. C. Mossé, *The Ancient World at Work*, London, Chatto & Windus 1969, p. 29.

8. Mellor, p. 174.

9. *Laborem Exercens,* September 1981. The pope notes that all work involves toil and sees in it a way of carrying the cross. The idea of co-creation is paralleled by the Protestant notion of cooperation with God. Cf. John Stott, "Reclaiming the Biblical Doctrine of Work," *Christianity Today*, 4 May 1979.

10. B. Wielenga, *Biblical Perspectives on Labour*, Madurai 1982, p. 49, to whom the whole of the preceding paragraph is indebted.

11. *Economics* 1344a.

12. Cf. Murray Bookchin: "Sexual differences, also biological in origin, defined the kind of work one did in the community and the role of a parent in rearing the young. Women essentially prepared and gathered food; men hunted animals and assumed a protective role for the community" (*Remaking Society*, Montreal, Black Rose Books 1989, p. 52).

13. Marx and Engels, *Collected Works,* vol. 5, p. 44. Cf. *The Origin of the Family, Private Property and the State,* Peking 1978, pp. 75, 85. Marx's marginal note to this remark was "The first form of ideologists, *priests*, is coincident."

14. K. Anderson in *Feminism and Political Economy*, ed J. Maroney and M. Luxton, London, Methuen 1987.

15. For a vivid picture of this see Thomas Hardy's *Tess of the D'Urbervilles*.

16. Mellor, p. 134, citing Marilyn Waring, *If Women Counted*, London 1989.

17. So L. Ryken in his otherwise excellent book, *Work and Leisure in Christian Perspective*, Leicester, IVP 1989, p. 192.

18. S.Th 2a 2ae 187.3.

19. Luther, Commentary on Genesis 13:13 in *Luther's Works,* vol. 2, Missouri, Concordia 1958f. (henceforth cited as LW). References to Luther are to this edition unless otherwise stated.

20. See *Luther's Works,* vol. 45, p. 40, translating the 1522 Treatise on the Estate of Marriage.

21. Inst 3.10.6.

22. Exposition of Psalm 127, LW, vol. 12.

23. *Institutes* III.10.6. I am using the translation of Beveridge, Michigan, Eerdmans 1975.

24. M. Weber, *The Protestant Ethic and the Spririt of Capitalism*, trans. Parsons, London, Allen & Unwin 1930.

25. *Christian Directory*, vol. I, London, 1673, p. 108.

26. R. Baxter, *Saints' Everlasting Rest*, London, 1650, Bk 4, chap. 12; Calvin, *Institutes,* III.10.

27. Baxter, *Christian Directory,* quoted in Weber, *Protestant Ethic,* p. 261.

28. Marx notes that "Protestantism, by changing almost all the traditional holidays into workdays, plays an important part in the genesis of capital." An interesting anticipation of Weber's thesis. *Capital,* p. 262 n. 2. I use the Moscow edition, 1954, in 3 vols.

29. J. Milton, *Tetrachordon,* in *Complete Prose Works*, Yale and OUP 1969, vol. 2, p. 597. I owe this reference, along with other references to the Puritan divines, to Ryken, *Work and Leisure in Christian Perspective.*

30. R. Baxter, *Catechizing of Families,* quoted in C. Hill, *Society and Puritanism in Pre Revolutionary England*, London, Secker and Warburg 1964, p. 166.

31. R. Burkitt, *The Poor Man's Help*, London 1705.

32. J. Clarke and C. Critcher, *The Devil Makes Work*, London, Macmillan 1985, p. 52.

33. Even in Britain it remained a familiar part of rural life until after the First World War. Cf. Laurie Lee, *Cider with Rosie*, Harmondsworth, Penguin 1962, or Bob Copper, *A Song for Every Season,* London, Heineman 1971.

34. R. Blythe, *Akenfield,* Harmondsworth, Penguin 1969, p. 41.

35. Marx, *Capital*, vol. 1, p. 604.

36. Cf. H. Braverman, *Labour and Monopoly Capital,* New York, Monthly Review Press 1974; R. Blackburn and M. Mann, *The Working Class in the Labour Market*, London 1979.

37. Swasti Mitter, *Common Fate, Common Bond*, London, Pluto 1986.

38. Gita Sen and Caren Grown, *Development, Crises and Alternative Visions*, New York 1987. Cited in Mellor, p. 252.

39. Mies, *Patriarchy and Accumulation,* p. 48.

40. B. Franklin, *Advice to a Young Tradesman* (1748); *Necessary Hints to Those that would be rich* (1736) in *Works*, vol. 2, p. 80ff., New York, Putnam 1887-88.

41. S. Smiles, *Self help,* London 1908, p. 33.

42. A. Ure, *Philosophy of Manufacturers*, London 1861, p. 424-25.

43. T. Carlyle, *Past and Present*, London 1868, p. 223.

44. Clarke and Critcher, p. 59.

45. The first music hall was opened in 1840. By 1866 London had thirty-three

music halls and there were several hundred in the provinces.

46. For this process see Clarke and Critcher, pp. 69ff., 78ff.

47. Ryken's summary of Postman's views, p. 54.

48. N. Postman, *Amusing Ourselves to Death*, London, Methuen 1985, p. 161.

49. Out of a great mass of literature cf. I. Illich, *Tools for Conviviality*, London, Calder & Boyars 1973; A. Gorz, *Farewell to the Working Class*, London, Pluto 1987, *Paths to Paradise*, London, Pluto 1985; C. Handy, *The Future of Work*, Oxford, Blackwell 1984.

50. Clarke and Critcher are skeptical of postindustrial predictions. They point out the opportunist element in predictions of this kind coinciding with huge increases in unemployment. They conclude pessimistically: "Post-industrialism often assumes a harmonious set of outcomes from these changes — a universal reduction in working time and an equally distributed set of 'rewards' in terms of time, money and opportunity. This optimism seems misplaced. The decline of work will not be equally distributed, and worklessness will continue to be viewed with suspicion and be subject to scrutiny and control" (p. 209).

51. So Tom Stonier, *The Wealth of Information*, London, Methuen 1982.

52. Cf. C. Handy, *The Future of Work*, Oxford, Blackwell 1984, p. 66; James Bellini, *Rule Britannica*, London 1981.

53. A. Gorz, *Paths to Paradise*, London 1985, p. 38f.

54. Marx, *The German Ideology*, trans. Lough, Moscow 1976, p. 47.

55. Handy, p. 130. But see Clarke & Critcher's cautions n. 50.

56. Cf. also Clarke and Critcher's view below.

57. *Rerum Novarum*, May 1891.

58. Gabriele Dietrich, "The Unfinished Task of a Marxist Conceptualisation of the Women's Question," in *Women's Movement in India*, Bangalore 1988. In 1981 John Paul II is still insisting on "the primary goals of the mission of a mother" although "experience confirms that there must be a social re-evaluation of the mother's role." *Laborem Exercens*. To date this has not been forthcoming.

59. James Robertson, *The Sane Alternative*, Minnesota, SRiver Basin Publishing Co. 1979.

60. Marx and Engels, *Origin of the Family*, p. 86. They add "this in turn demands the abolition of the monogamous family's attribute of being the economic unit of society." Whether what they have in mind is the replacement of the family by what they consider as "the great advance" of "modern individual sex love" is not clear.

61. Mellor, p. 275.

62. As summarised by S. Parker, *The Sociology of Leisure*, London, Allen & Unwin 1976, p. 19.

63. Anthony, p. 277. Cf. S. Terkel, *Working*, London, Wildwood House 1972, p. 1.

64. Under Stalin it even acquired a special name, "*Stakhanovism*," after a miner who voluntarily produced fourteen times the amount he was required to. Lenin believed that Taylorism had to be tried and adapted in Soviet industry. He noted that it was "a combination of the refined brutality of bourgeois exploitation and a number of the greatest scientific achievements in the field of analysing mechanical motions during work" (Braverman, p. 12).

65. Anthony, p. 284.

66. Marx, *Capital* 1, 173f.; *Grundrisse*, Harmondsworth, Penguin 1973, p. 611. Karl Barth follows Marx in this: "To live as man is to fashion nature through the

spirit, but also to fulfil the spirit through nature. It is the subjectivisation of the object but also the objectivisation of the subject. . . . It is the besouling of the body, but also the embodying of the soul. In this movement to and fro, from above downwards but also from above upwards, man lives as man" (CD III/4, p. 519).

67. Gorz rightly sees that toil can never be fully eliminated. The point is to share it equally, and to liberate all for more creative tasks as far as possible (*Farewell to the Working Class*, p. 94ff.).

68. I owe this point to Rohini Hensman.

69. See MacIntyre's comments on work in AV, p. 227. He correctly says that *pleonexia* is now the driving force of modern work. Cf the remarks on teleology on pp. 215, 219, and on practices, p. 187ff. Virtues are exercised in practices, which are "any coherent and complex form of socially established cooperative human activity through which goods internal to that form of activity are realized in the course of trying to achieve those standards of excellence which are appropriate to, and partially definitive of, that form of activity." The comment that bricklaying is not a practice, but architecture is, is misleading. On the contrary, bricklaying is certainly a practice as it is part of the builders skill. Cf. the comments on manual work in G. A. Sturt, *The Wheelwright's Shop*, Cambridge 1923.

70. Mary Boulton, *On Being a Mother*, London, Tavistock 1983.

71. *Capital,* vol. 1, p. 174.

72. This is what Ryken (p. 174) means by the pursuit of excellence. He writes, "Commitment to excellence in work is one of the prime moral virtues the Bible prescribes for workers. . . . Christians are called to excellence because the God they serve is excellent." The problem is that the language of excellence has been corrupted by being harnessed to meritocracy. Barth's criteria are less subject to ideological distortion.

73. CD III/4, pp. 546, 549.

74. Tertullian, *De Spectaculis* 15. Incidentally, the insight that rivalry, or mimesis, leads to violence, is close to Girard's thesis in *Things Hidden Since the Foundation of the World*.

75. Lest this be thought fanciful listen to this advocate of the game of baseball.

> The essence of religious experience, so we are told, is the "redemption from the limitations of our petty individual lives and the mystic unity with a larger life of which we are part." And is this not precisely what the baseball devotee or fanatic, if you please, expresses when he watches the team representing his city battling with another? . . . Baseball exercises and purifies all of our emotions, cultivating hope and courage when we are behind, resignation when we are beaten, fairness for the other team when we are ahead, charity for the umpire, and above all zest for combat and conquest (M. R. Cohen, "Baseball as a National Religion," in L. Schneider, ed, *Religion, Culture and Society*, New York, Wiley 1964, p. 37).

76. Clarke and Critcher, pp. 11, 145.

77. J. Huizinga, *Homo Ludens, A Study of the Play Element in Culture*, London, RKP 1949.

78. Rohini Hensman points out that in the Third World, quite apart from technology, production could be expanded, and work shared, to make an impact on the

huge numbers of unemployed. But the possibility of this would rest on freedom from structural adjustment programmes or military destabilization.

79. Gorz, *Farewell to the Working Class*, p. 136.

80. Clarke and Critcher, p. 209.

6. Ideology and Alienation

1. I am here following R. Williams, *Keywords*, p. 189f.

2. M. Fores, "Management: Science or Activity?" in *Introducing Management*, ed Elliott and Lawrence, Harmondsworth, Penguin 1985, p. 18.

3. Shakespeare is rebuked several times for failing to understand the nature of leadership. The difference between Shakespeare and Jay on this score is that Shakespeare was concerned about ethics.

4. A. Jay, *Management and Machiavelli*, London, Hutchinson 1987, p. 37.

5. Jay, p. 210.

6. Jay, p. 32. Which theology, one wonders. Neither Jewish nor Christian, for sure. The last time an appeal was made to a frankly pagan theology was in Germany between 1933 and 1945.

7. Swasti Mitter, *Common Fate, Common Bond*, London 1986, cited in Mellor, p. 161.

8. Marx, *Capital*, pp. 236, 252. Cf. the present pressure for Sunday trading in Britain.

9. Smith, *Wealth of Nations*, Bk 1, chap. 1.

10. J. Ruskin, *The Stones of Venice*, London 1853, section II, chap. 6.

11. Taylor, pp. 63, 39, cited by Braverman, who quotes also this passage from Thilliez, the engineer who introduced numerical control to the Renault factories:

> But in addition the technique of numerical control implies an effect which might be called extraordinary, on the level of the philosophy of the organization of the enterprise. It separates the intellectual work from the work of execution, just as has for a long time been the case with the fabrication of long runs on special purpose machines, and this separation allows the execution of both functions under the technical conditions best adapted to a superior organization, thus in the final accounting most profitable.

Braverman comments, in a passage worthy of Marx, "Such a separation of 'intellectual work from the work of execution' is indeed a 'technical condition' best adapted to a hierarchical organization, best adapted to control of both the hand and the brain worker, best adapted to profitability, best adapted to everything but the needs of people. These needs, however, are, in the word of the economists, 'externalities,' a notion that is absolutely incomprehensible from the human point of view, but from the capitalist point of view perfectly clear and precise, since it simply means external to the balance sheet" (p. 205).

12. Braverman, p. 171. There are obvious practical problems with Taylor's scheme. As Fores points out, the "one best way" to do a job is rarely discernible and there is also the paradox of the efficient rat catcher. A fully efficient rat catcher can do himself out of a job. According to Taylor's scheme management could soon end up unneeded.

13. B. Jameson, "Management by Uncertainty," *Management Today*, February 1979, pp. 61-63, cited by Fores.

14. Braverman, p. 87.

15. Marx, *Economic and Philosophical Manuscripts*, in McClellan, *Early Texts*, Oxford, Blackwell 1970, p. 142.

16. F. Taylor, *The Principles of Scientific Management*, New York, Harper & Row 1967, p. 46.

17. Braverman, p. 16, citing Kerr, Dunlop, Harbison, and Myers, *Industrialism and Industrial Man*, Cambridge, Mass. 1960.

18. Jay's appeal, still popular in the 1980s, is clearly to charismatic authority. Fores, however, notes that such views are often criticised for thinking too much about strategy at the expense of the tactics involved in keeping the show going.

19. M. Weber, *General Economic History*, New Brunswick, Transaction Books 1981, p. 354.

20. *From Max Weber*, p. 331.

21. Cited in Fores, p. 24. He also quotes Dale and Michelon, who maintain that "management is not an exact science like physics and chemistry. Although many things have been discovered about it, it is essential that the manager use judgement, based on good sense and experience" (*Modern Management Methods*, Harmondsworth, Penguin 1966, p. 11).

22. AV, p. 107. The argument I have summarised is developed on pp. 23ff., 74ff.

23. Jay, p. 207.

24. Jon Clarke, "Industrial Relations," in Elliott and Lawrence, p. 174.

25. Argyris, *Integrating the Individual and the Organization*, New York, John Wiley 1964.

26. Termination of employment "could be initiated by an individual or groups assigned such responsibility. ... Anyone who is to be terminated must have the opportunity to participate in all the discussions. ... The line supervisor of the employee could raise the question about the employee's capacity to meet the standards he accepted upon entrance. The employee's peers could also raise the same question" (p. 210, cited by Anthony, p. 233).

27. R. Blake and J. Mouton, *The Managerial Grid*, Houston, Texas, Gulf Publishing 1964, p. 145. Cited by Anthony, p. 235.

28. D. McGregor, *The Human Side of Enterprise*, New York, McGraw-Hill 1960, p. 4.

29. I take the following from W. Harries, *Employee Participation*, in Elliott and Lawrence, p. 181ff.

30. F. H. Harbison, in *Industrial Conflict*, ed Kornhauser, Dubin, and Ross, New York, McGraw Hill 1954.

31. R. Dahrendorff, *Class and Class Conflict in Industrial Society*, London, RKP 1959.

32. McGregor, p. 49.

33. J. Burnham, *The Managerial Revolution*, London, Penguin 1942.

34. C. Wright Mills, *White Collar*, Oxford 1956.

35. R. P. Dore, *British Factory-Japanese Factory*, London, Allen and Unwin, 1973.

36. H. Mintzberg, *The Nature of Managerial Work*, New York, Harper & Row 1979.

37. In a survey of directors, managers, and workers conducted in Britain in the mid 1970s by the Department of Employment it was found that directors were in

favour of decisions being taken by management alone, workers in favour of joint decision-making, and management split between the two groups (I. Knight, *Company Organisation and Worker Participation,* London, HMSO 1979).

38. By 1982 more than twenty of the top companies in Britain had such departments. "The government relations function in large firms based in the United Kingdom: a preliminary study" (*British Journal of Political Science* 12, 1982, pp. 513-16).

39. Jay, p. 235.

40. Anthony, p. 257.

41. In an essay on business ethics the main topic for discussion is whether or not a firm should offer a bribe. An extremely feeble version of utilitarianism (the attempt to promote human happiness) is the starting point and fundamental questions of power and value do not arise at all (K. Blois, "Ethics in Business," in Elliott and Lawrence, p. 219ff.).

42. Braverman, p. 7.

7. Solidarity and Resistance

1. Cited in H. Pelling, *A History of British Trade Unionism,* Harmondsworth, Penguin 1963, p. 22.

2. Kim Moody, *An Injury to All,* London, Verso 1988; R. Hyman, *Industrial Relations,* London, Macmillan 1977; K. Coates and T. Topham, *Trade Unions and Politics,* Oxford, Blackwell 1986.

3. Miranda Davies, ed, *Third World, Second Sex,* London, Zed Books 1987, p. 159ff.

4. Ibid p. 59ff.

5. H. Bhaskara, et al., *Against All Odds,* London, Panos 1989, p. 150ff.

6. Davies, p. 211ff.

7. Vandana Shiva, *Staying Alive,* London, Zed Books 1989, p. 67ff.

8. Pelling, p. 23.

9. The president of the Yorkshire miners said that "the National Union of Mineworkers recognizes that it is the duty of the National Coal Board to manage industry efficiently and to secure sound developments within their responsibilities. ... Equally it has always been the duty of the union to defend its members. We don't want to take away either right from either party" (cited in Peter Hain, *Political Strikes,* Harmondsworth, Penguin 1986, p. 241).

10. Moody, p. 15.

11. "Industrial Relations," in Elliott and Lawrence, p. 160f.

12. H. Phelps Brown, *The Origins of Trade Union Power,* Oxford University Press, Oxford 1986, p. 1.

13. *Rerum Novarum.*

14. Moody, p. 188.

15. J. K. Galbraith, *American Capitalism: The Concept of Countervailing Power,* London, Hamish Hamilton 1957.

16. So in O. Kahn-Freund, *Labour and the Law,* London, Stevens 1972, pp. 52-53.

17. Phelps Brown, *Origins,* p. 289.

18. Griffiths, p. 117.

19. Phelps Brown, *Origins,* p. 13.

20. S.Th. 2a 2ae 60.art.6.

21. Cited in Hain, p. 55.

22. Cited by Hyman, p. 108.

23. See Mellor, pp. 244-45, for the importance of this movement.

24. *Laborem Exercens*, September 1981.

25. CD III/2, p. 228.

26. F. Nietzsche, *The Will to Power*, trans. W. Kaufmann, New York, Random House 1962, p. 142.

27. CD III/4, p. 541.

28. H. McCabe, *God Matters*, London, Geoffrey Chapman 1987, p. 193.

29. Cf. *Laborem Exercens*: "Union demands cannot be turned into a kind of group or class egoism ... in such a situation they easily lose contact with their specific role, which is to secure the just rights of workers within the framework of the common good."

30. F. Engels, *The Condition of the Working Class in England in 1844*, London, Allen & Unwin 1968, p. 218.

31. A. Hutt, *British Trade Unionism*, London, Lawrence and Wishart 1975, p. 13.

32. Battle language is frequently used about unions and their propensity to strike. At the beginning of the '84-'85 miners strike in Britain a *Times* editorial accused the miners of having "declared war on British society." This was at a time when more than half of the population were members of the union movement. Urging the government to use greater powers in July 1984 it commented, "There is a war on."

33. F. Schmidt "The Law On Industrial Conflict in Modern Society" in R. Preston, ed, *Industrial Conflicts in Modern Society,* London, SCM 1974, pp. 28ff.

34. *Laborem Exercens,* 1981.

35. M. Taylor, "Evaluating Strikes," in *Perspectives on Strikes,* ed Preston, London, SCM 1975.

36. McCabe, op. cit., p. 198.

37. Phelps Brown, *Origins*, p. 301.

8. The Price of Life

1. S.Th 1a 2ae 114.1.

2. D. Forrester, *Theology and Politics*, Oxford, Blackwell 1988, p. 29. As we would expect, we find this view endorsed by a theological apologist for capitalism like Michael Novak. He writes: "No intelligent order—not even within a church bureaucracy—can be run according to the counsels of Christianity. . . . An economy based upon the consciences of some would offend the consciences of others" (*The Spirit of Democratic Capitalism*, Touchstone 1982, p. 352).

3. I follow M. Fogarty, *The Just Wage*, London, Geoffrey Chapman 1961.

4. H. Phelps Brown, *The Inequality of Pay*, Oxford University Press 1977, p. 121. With this principle, cf. the British Corn Production Act of 1917 which provided that the Board it set up should "as far as practicable, secure for able bodied men wages which, in the opinion of the Board, are adequate to promote efficiency and to enable a man in an ordinary case to maintain himself and his family *in accordance with such standard of comfort as may be reasonable in relation to the nature of his occupation*" (ibid p. 119, italics mine).

5. Fogarty, op. cit., p. 17.

6. Cf. S. Cameron, *Felt Fair Pay*, HMSO 1976.

7. *Mater et Magistra*, May 1961, Denzinger 3930ss.

8. Marx, *Capital*, p. 504.

9. Marx, *Capital*, p. 505.

10. Marx and Engels, *Collected Works*, vol. 6, p. 436.

11. J. Miranda, *Marx and the Bible*, London, SCM 1977, p. 25.

12. John Kenneth Galbraith, *The History of Economics,* Harmondsworth, Penguin 1987, p. 110.

13. F. Knight, *Risk, Uncertainty and Profit*, Boston, Houghton Mifflin 1921.

14. Smith, *Wealth of Nations*, Bk 1, chap. 5. He also noted that "by nature a philosopher is not in genius and disposition half so different from a street porter, as a mastiff is from a greyhound, or a greyhound from a spaniel, or this last from a shepherd's dog" (Bk 1, chap. 2). This observation ought to have practical consequences.

15. B. Wootton, Appendix to the Royal Commission on Equal Pay, 1946, cited by Phelps Brown, p. 19.

16. Phelps Brown, *Inequality,* p. 326.

17. Ibid p. 328.

18. Strmiska and Vavakova, cited by Phelps Brown, *Inequality*, p. 137.

19. Phelps Brown, *Inequality*, p. 330.

20. D. Jenkins, *The Contradiction of Christianity*, London 1976.

9. The World as Private Gain

1. Cf. Rousseau: "From the moment one man began to stand in need of the help of another; from the moment it appeared advantageous to any one man to have enough provisions for two, equality disappeared, property was introduced, work became indispensable, and vast forests became smiling fields, which man had to water with the sweat of his brow, and where slavery and misery were soon seen to germinate and grow up with the crops. Metallurgy and agriculture were the two arts which produced this great revolution. The poets tell us it was gold and silver, but, for the philosophers, it was iron and corn, which first civilised men and ruined humanity" (*Discourse on the Origins of Inequality*, pt. 2).

2. Plato, *Republic*, Bk V.

3. Aristotle, *Politics,* 1256b29-30.

4. Aristotle, *Politics*, 1263a,b.

5. Homily XII on 1 Tm 4, NPNF, vol. 12.

6. M. Hengel, *Property and Riches in the Early Church*, London, SCM 1986, p. 180.

7. Chrysostom, in 1 Tm, *Patrologia Graeca* 62, col 562-63; cited by Miranda.

8. Jerome, "Carta 120," *Patrologia Latina* 22, col 984.

9. Ambrose, "De Nabuthe," *Patrologia Latina* 14, col 747.

10. Ambrose, *Patrologia Latina* 15, col 1303.

11. Miranda, p. 1.

12. S.Th 2a 2ae 66.2.

13. S.Th 2a 2ae Q 118 arts 5 and 8.

14. Cf. also Augustine, *In Ioannis Evangelium* 6.25, cited by Avila, *Ownership: Early Christian Teaching*, Maryknoll, New York, Orbis Books 1983, p. 111.

15. *Rerum Novarum*, 5-8.

16. *Mater et Magistra,* May 1961.

17. *Laborem Exercens,* September 1981.

18. Locke, *Second Treatise on Civil Government,* chap. 5.26.

19. C. B. Macpherson, *The Political Theory of Possessive Individualism,* Oxford University Press 1962, p. 227.

20. Locke, *Second Treatise,* para 37. Added only in the fourth edition.

21. Locke, *Second Treatise,* 48. Cf. Macpherson, *The Political Theory of Possessive Individualism,* pp. 205ff.

22. Ibid chap. 15,174.

23. Between 1801 and 1831, for instance, Marx noted indignantly, 3,511,770 acres of common land were appropriated by parliament and presented "to the landlords by the landlords" and not a farthing was paid in compensation to peasants who no longer had use of the land. Political economists, he said, view this shameless violation of the "sacred rights of property" with "stoical peace of mind." Adam Smith noted that "Civil government, so far as it is instituted for the security of property, is in reality instituted for the defence of the rich against the poor, or of those who have some property against those who have none at all" (*Wealth of Nations,* Bk V, chap. 1, pt. 2).

24. Hegel, *Philosophy of Right,* trans. Knox, Oxford 1967, p. 42.

25. The root of Marx's theory of alienation is Hegel's move from this position to the view that property into which I have put my will is inalienable. Inalienable property belongs above all to the class of civil servants, "whose basis is family life," and whose livelihood is the possession of land (*Philosophy of Right,* sections 305-7).

26. Marx and Engels, *Collected Works,* vol. 5, p. 229.

27. Marx, *Grundrisse,* ed McClellan, Harmondsworth, Penguin 1973, p. 491.

28. Marx, *Capital,* p. 715.

29. L. Johnson, *Sharing Possessions,* London, SCM 1981. Johnson acknowledges no explicit debt to Hegel.

30. Ibid p. 37.

31. Ibid pp. 39-40.

32. D. Jenkins, *The Contradiction of Christianity,* London 1976, p. 102.

33. Johnson, *Sharing Possessions,* p. 69.

34. Chrysostom, in *Inscriptionem Altaris et in Principium Actorum,* cited in Avila, p. 88.

35. Meeks, p. 117.

36. Ambrose, Exposition of Psalm 118, cited in Avila, p. 74.

37. Augustine, Sermon 50, cited in Avila, p. 115.

38. Johnson, *Sharing Possessions,* p. 138.

39. C. B. Macpherson, "Human Rights as Property Rights," in *The Rise and Fall of Economic Justice,* Oxford 1986, p. 76ff.

40. Basil, *Homilies on Luke,* cited in Avila, p. 49.

41. Ambrose, *Hexaemeron* 5.26, cited in Avila, p. 72; Augustine, *Sermon 85,* cited in Avila, p. 113.

42. Meeks, p. 109.

10. The Spoil of the Poor

1. *The State of the World's Children,* Oxford University Press 1989.

2. Griffiths, pp. 135-36.

3. I follow G. d'Souza, *British Rule*, Bangalore, CSA 1979.

4. P. Griffiths, *The British Impact on India*, London, Macdonald 1952, pp. 374-75, 402-3. These profits were often obtained in the most barbarous way. British taxes far exceeded those imposed by local rulers and were extorted regardless of conditions. During the great famine of 1769-70 Warren Hastings reported:

> Notwithstanding the loss of at least one-third of the inhabitants of the province and the consequent decrease of the cultivation, the net collections of the year 1771 exceeded even those of 1768. . . . It was naturally to be expected that the diminution of the revenue should have kept pace with the other consequences of so great a calamity. That it did not was owing to its being violently kept up to its former standard (cited in R. C. Dutt, *The Economic History of India*, London 1902, p. 109).

5. L. H. Jenks, *Migration of British Capital up to 1875,* New York, Borzoi 1927, p. 230.

6. Food exports rose from £858,000 in 1849 to £19.3 million in 1914.

7. Dutt, vol. 2, pp. 349, 530.

8. H. H. Wilson, *History of British India, London 1845-8,* vol. 1, p. 385. Cf. also D. Naoroji, *Poverty and UnBritish Rule in India*, London 1902; and P. J. Marshall *Bengal: The British Bridgehead*, Cambridge University Press 1987.

9. Both cited in S. George, *How the Other Half Dies*, Harmondsworth, Penguin 1986, pp. 70, 78. Henceforth cited as HOHD.

10. G. and V. Curzon, cited in Singer and Ansari, *Rich and Poor Countries*, 4th ed, London, Unwin Hyman 1988, p. 74.

11. S. George, *A Fate Worse than Debt*, Harmondsworth, Penguin 1988, p. 66. Henceforth cited as FWD.

12. In 1983 11 percent of imports from third-world countries to the EC were beneficiaries of GSP; in the United States, 12 percent. B. Coote, *The Trade Trap*, Oxfam 1992.

13. Coote, p. 120.

14. C. Elliott, *Comfortable Compassion*, London 1987, referring to work by R. Prebisch and H. Singer.

15. OCF, pp. 71-72.

16. Cited in George, FWD, p. 99.

17. Coote, p. 153.

18. *The Economist,* 26 December 1992. The issue carries an advertisement for a luxury car on its inside cover proclaiming, "You are what you drive." The morality of the advertisement and of the editorial are more or less equivalent.

19. Shiva, p. 11. She cites the African book *Poverty: The Wealth of the People* as the source of this argument but does not name the author.

20. Singer and Ansari, p. 251.

21. F. Gaffikin and A. Nickson, *Jobs Crisis and the Multinationals*, Birmingham Trade Union Group, no date. Gaffikin and Nickson show that transnational response to industrial unrest and the lure of cheaper labour elsewhere have played a big part in the deindustrialization, and hence rise in unemployment, in the West Midlands of Britain.

22. The CAFOD report, "Free Trade Zones, in People and Work," 1982, notes:

"Almost one million people are now employed in Free Trade Zones around the world (70% of them in Asia) and the great majority are girls or young women between the ages of 15 and 25. Prized for their nimble fingers, supposed tolerance of boring yet strenuous work, their docility and lower expectations of worker's rights, they comprise at least 85 percent of the workforce in such countries as Malaysia, the Philippines, Taiwan and Mexico." A brochure produced in Malaysia proclaims: "The manual dexterity of the oriental female is famous the world over. Her hands are small and she works fast with extreme care. Who, therefore, could better qualify by nature and inheritance to contribute to the efficiency of a bench-assembly production line than the oriental girl?" (quoted in *Feminist Review,* Spring 1981). Cf. the following advertisement by the Central Bank of Philippines which appeared in the Financial Times on 7 November 1980:

The Philippines
Consider its huge potential
Highly Literate
English-Speaking Manpower
Cheap Labour Rate

23. Gaffikin and Nickson, p. 49.
24. R. J. Barnet, *The Lean Years,* London, Abacus 1981, p. 171.
25. OCF, pp. 73-74.
26. The collapse of commodity prices was partly due to IMF and World Bank policies, because they have insisted on all debtor countries exporting a limited range of raw materials and semi-finished or finished products.
27. Mellor, p. 173.
28. FWD, p. 53.
29. Ibid p. 55.
30. Körner, Maass, Siebold, Tetzlaff, *The IMF and the Debt Crisis*, London, Zed Books 1986, p. 63.
31. FWD, p. 263.
32. *Poverty, World Development Report 1990*, Oxford 1990, p. 20.
33. Singer and Ansari, p. 26.
34. FWD, p. 259. Brian Griffiths is evidently more than terminally myopic.
35. An Amnesty Report in September 1990 speaks of death squads killing children who roam the streets in the big cities of Brazil as a way of "cleaning the place up." Naturally this has nothing to do with Brazil's economic policies.
36. Cited in FWD, p. 234.
37. I have used this phrase rather than the "New International Economic Order" of the Brandt report because the proposals outlined there were widely seen to be cosmetic.
38. *Pacem in Terris* 137, April 1963, Denzinger 3955ss.
39. U. Duchrow, *Global Economy: A Confessional Issue for the Churches?*, Geneva, WCC 1987, p. 125.

11. The Longing of Creation

1. D. and D. Meadows, J. Randers, *Beyond the Limits*, London, Earthscan 1992, p. 152.

2. It is estimated, for instance, that six million Amazonian Indians have been killed in the process of ranch clearances (E. N. Ikanan, "The Myth of Amazonian Development," *Green Line* 82, pp. 12-13.

3. R. W. Southern, *Western Society and the Church in the Middle Ages,* Harmondsworth, Penguin 1970, p. 305.

4. L. White, "The Historical Roots of Our Ecologic Crisis," in *Ecology and Religion in History*, ed D. and E. Spring, New York, Harper & Row 1974.

5. C. Merchant, *The Death of Nature*, New York, Harper & Row 1980; also in J. Rothschild, ed, *Machina ex Dea*, Oxford, Pergamon 1983.

6. For what follows cf. *Global Warming, The Greenpeace Report*, Oxford University Press 1990.

7. Meadows et al, p. 96.

8. I am drawing on S. Postel, *The Last Oasis*, London, Earthscan 1992.

9. Quoted in S. Postel, *The Last Oasis*, London, Earthscan 1992, p. 36, from whom the information in this paragraph is taken.

10. I am drawing on C. Sargent and S. Bass, "The Future Shape of Forests," in *Policies for a Small Planet,* ed J. Holmberg, London, Earthscan 1992.

11. G. Porter and J. Welsh Brown, *Global Environmental Politics*, Colorado, Westview Press 1991, p. 97ff.

12. Porter and Brown, p. 81.

13. Meadows and Randers, p. 90.

14. G. Hardin and J. Baden, *Managing the Commons*, San Francisco, Freeman 1977.

15. J. Fletcher, cited in HOHD, p. 210.

16. Elliott and Lawrence, p. 231. This is said in regard to misleading informants in market research.

17. C. Manes, *Green Rage,* Boston 1990.

18. Thomas R. Malthus, *An Essay on the Principle of Population as It Affects the Future Improvement of Society*, Ann Arbor, Mich., 1959.

19. Cited in Holmberg, p. 329.

20. Ibid p. 27.

21. Holmberg, p. 323, citing articles by Pradervand and Paul Harrison, *Living Dangerously*.

22. A. T. Durning, *How Much Is Enough?* London, Earthscan 1992, p. 52.

23. Quoted in Durning, p. 71.

24. Brown, Flavin, and Postel, *Saving the Planet,* London, Earthscan 1992, p. 22.

25. As argued by W. F. Haug, *Critique of Commodity Aesthetics,* Cambridge, Polity 1986.

26. See, for example, her *Metaphysics as a Guide to Morals,* London, Chatto & Windus 1992.

27. This is why many people who went through the hardships of the Second World War found it the high point of their lives. Not because of the excitement of battle, which was understood only too soberly, but because of the experience of shared *communitas*, of a shared common project, which broke through gender and class boundaries in a way hitherto unimagined.

28. Margaret Thatcher, *Womans Own*, 31 October 1987. "There are individuals, and there are families. There is no such thing as society."

29. See the discussion in *On the Soul*, passim.

30. *Nicomachean Ethics*, Bk III, 1119b.

12. Two Ways

1. Cited in Duchrow, p. 163ff.

2. Griffiths refers to Stalinism (which he calls communism) as a "devilish religion and ideology," but if what is devilish is measured by what a system does to people, then this applies equally to the free market.

3. Anthony, p. 162.

4. Friedman and Friedman, p. 136. Paying high taxes to support the weak, however, the Friedmans find "immoral and improper."

5. Ms. Friedman apparently acquiesces in this example.

6. HOHD, p. 46.

7. Hayek, *The Road to Serfdom,* p. 11. We inherited this individualism, Hayek tells us, from Pericles, Thucydides, Cicero, Tacitus, and Erasmus.

8. F. Hayek, *Individualism and the Economic Order*, London, RKP 1949, p. 32.

9. I am following F. Hinkelammert, *The Ideological Weapons of Death: A Theological Critique of Capitalism*, Maryknoll, New York, Orbis Books 1986, p. 179.

10. Meeks, p. 48. Cf. Jeremy Seabrook, who notes that in the financial press markets are endowed with superhuman characteristics and that any denunciation of the market is met with the kind of denunciation traditionally attracted by blasphemy, an attack upon the sacred.

11. M. Novak, *The Spirit of Democratic Capitalism*, New York, Simon & Schuster 1983, pp. 53-55.

12. Bonhoeffer, p. 85.

13. General Humberto Gordon, *Mercurio*, Santiago, 4 December 1983. The general insists he is a Christian.

14. Edward and Eleanor Marx-Aveling, *Shelley's Socialism*, cited in E. P. Thompson, *William Morris,* New York, Pantheon 1976, p. 332.

15. *Rerum Novarum*.

16. Green and Sutcliffe, *The Profit System*, Harmondsworth, Penguin 1987, p. 373.

17. Cf. the alternative economic proposals of R. Steppacher outlined in Duchrow, p. 158ff.

18. Robertson, *Future Wealth*, p. 14.

19. Though for this to work, the flow of wealth from South to North would have to be reversed rather than just halted.

20. The fanatical opposition to planning by writers like Hayek overlooks the fact that private enterprises (like transnationals, for example) could not exist for a single day without the most sophisticated planning. The publishing firm McGraw-Hill thought so highly of one econometric consulting firm that it paid $103 million for its programme in 1979 (Galbraith, *History of Economics,* p. 262).

21. Green and Sutcliffe, p. 369.

22. M. Kennedy, *Interest and Inflation Free Money*, Steyerberg, Permaculture Institute Publications 1988, cited in Robertson, *Future Wealth*, p. 130. Kennedy's research showed that, dividing all households into ten groups of 2.5 million in order of household wealth, the effect of interest payments was the transfer of wealth to the two richest groups. In an earlier chapter we saw that this happens on an international level.

23. Robertson, *Future Wealth*, p. 131.

24. Cf. Robertson, *Future Wealth*, p. 116.

25. Green and Sutcliffe, p. 370.

26. Robertson, *The Sane Alternative*, p. 36.

27. S. Verney, *Into the New Age*, London, Fontana 1976, cited by Robertson, *The Sane Alternative*, 2nd edition, p. 100.

28. Green and Sutcliffe, p. 365.

29. Green and Sutcliffe, p. 364.

30. Robertson, *Future Wealth*, p. 10.

31. For the church as an International, cf. the famous words of the Epistle to Diognetus: "Christians are not distinguished from the rest of mankind by country or language or customs. ... While they live in cities both Greek and oriental, as falls to the lot of each, and follow the customs of the country in dress, food, and general manner of life, they display the remarkable and confessedly surprising status of their citizenship. They live in countries of their own, but as sojourners. ... Every foreign land is their native land, every native place is foreign." Cf. also Augustine, *De Moribus Ecclesiae Catholicae*, 1.30.63: "You (the church) link citizen to citizen, nation to nation, indeed, you bind all men together in remembrance of their first parents."

32. The British churches have named the 1990s the decade of evangelism, but if this decade does not lead every congregation to study documents like the World Commission's report and to find ways to act upon it, this will be a vacuous farce.

Index